Force.com Development Blueprints

Design and develop real-world, cutting-edge
cloud applications using the powerful Force.com
development framework

Stephen Moss

BIRMINGHAM - MUMBAI

Force.com Development Blueprints

First Published: May 2014

Production reference: 1140514

Published by Packt Publishing Ltd.
Livery Place
35 Livery Street
Birmingham B3 2PB, UK.

ISBN 978-1-78217-245-1

www.packtpub.com

Cover Image by Tony Shi (shihe99@hotmail.com)

Credits

Author
Stephen Moss

Reviewers
Naveen Gabrani

Srikanth Goati

Aruna A Lambat

Caleb Poitevien

Karanraj Sankaranarayanan

Michael Edward Vargas Jr.

Commissioning Editor
Akram Hussain

Acquisition Editor
Owen Roberts

Content Development Editor
Govindan K

Technical Editors
Mrunal Chavan

Gaurav Thingalaya

Copy Editors
Sarag Chari

Mradula Hegde

Adithi Shetty

Project Coordinator
Venitha Cutinho

Proofreaders
Simran Bhogal

Amy Johnson

Samantha Lyon

Indexer
Mariammal Chettiyar

Graphics
Sheetal Aute

Production Coordinator
Saiprasad Kadam

Cover Work
Saiprasad Kadam

About the Author

Stephen Moss is a Salesforce.com-certified administrator and Force.com developer.

After his first brush with computing on Apple II, he was hooked to it and started programming on a Commodore 64 computer, back in the 1980s, to automate his math homework.

He has over 20 years' experience in the IT industry in a multitude of roles, ranging across application domains as diverse as CRM, GIS, manufacturing, broadcast engineering, billing, field services, IVR speech recognition, and call center management systems.

In addition to cloud computing, he also has a keen interest in the SOA/BPM systems (he is an Oracle BPM Suite Certified Implementation Specialist) and mobile device development (he even has an original PalmPilot in his attic somewhere!).

He is currently consulting with a range of clients, helping them embrace cloud computing and digitizing their businesses for the 21st century.

I dedicate this book to my mother and father, whose love and understanding made me into the person I am today (they also bought me my Commodore 64). I only wish they were here today to share this achievement with me. Wherever you are, this book is for you.

Also, I want to thank my wife and children for their understanding and patience in having a husband/father who worked during the day and lived in his study for the months it took to write this book. Finally, I want to thank my two sisters, their partners, and my nieces and nephews, who also had to put up with an "invisible" brother and uncle. Thank you all from the bottom of my heart.

About the Reviewers

Naveen Gabrani is a Force.com architect and the founder/CEO of a Salesforce consulting company, Astrea IT Services. Astrea is a leader in providing Salesforce.com services. Astrea has seven apps on AppExchange, such as Smart vCard, Astrea Clone, Smart Calendar, Print It, Format Me, Chatrules, and Object Hierarchy that were envisioned by Naveen. He has 20 years' experience in the IT Industry in various technical and management positions. Naveen is passionate about providing high-quality software deliveries that exceed customers' expectations, and building teams of motivated and happy members.

Srikanth Goati is a Salesforce-certified professional and the cofounder of Salesforce Hyderabad User Group. Currently, he is working as a Salesforce Administrator with Birlasoft India Pvt. Ltd., Bangalore, India. He is an MCA graduate from Hyderabad and has certificates in DEV401 and ADM201. Overall, he has four years' experience in developing and administering Salesforce.com. Birlasoft is a global IT services provider and part of the 150 year old, multibillion dollar CK Birla Group. With a global workforce of over 4,000 employees, Birlasoft has global footprints and best-in-class delivery centers in China and India.

Srikanth has reviewed *Force.com Tips and Tricks*, *Packt Publishing*. He can be contacted via e-mail at `srikanth.sfa@gmail.com` and followed on Twitter at `@srikanthsfdc`. He can be searched on LinkedIn using the name `Srikanth Goati` and on Facebook with `/srikanth.goti`.

I wish to thank my parents and all my family members, friends, and colleagues for all the joy they bring into my life. Thanks to my Salesforce community friends. Thanks to the folks at Packt Publishing, the author of this book, and many others who have provided help and inspiration along the way.

Aruna A Lambat is an enthusiastic architect working on Salesforce.com technology with a profound understanding of software design and development. She is passionate about building better products and providing excellent services, thereby leading to healthier customer satisfaction. She has been working on the Salesforce.com platform since 2008. She entered IT acquaintance as a student in 2004. She has completed her master's degree in Computer Applications from Maharashtra, India. She is associated with the IT industry since 2007. Having started her career as a Java developer, she has shifted her focus to cloud computing, specifically in Salesforce.com.

She is a Salesforce-certified developer (DEV401), administrator (ADM201), and advanced administrator (ADM301/211) along with her regular contribution to the Salesforce developer community. Also, she is certified in Java as a Sun Certificated Java Programmer (SCJP) and Sun Certified Web Component Developer (SCWCD).

Before contributing to this book as a reviewer, she worked as a technical reviewer for *Force.com Tips and Tricks*, *Visualforce Development Cookbook*, *Visualforce Developer's Guide*, and *Salesforce CRM: The Definitive Admin Handbook*. All these books were published by Packt Publishing. She has also contributed for a technical example cited in *Force.com Developer Certification Handbook (DEV401)*, *Packt Publishing*.

Aruna works with a reputed India-based IT MNC; it is primarily engaged in providing a range of outsourcing services, business process outsourcing, and infrastructure services. She works as a project manager on Salesforce.com technology-based customer services. She can be contacted via e-mail at `Aruna.Lambat@gmail.com` and on LinkedIn using the name `Aruna Lambat`. She can be contacted via Twitter at `@arunalambat` and on Facebook with `/aruna.lambat`.

Special thanks to my parents, Mrs. and Mr. Anandrao Lambat, for always being there with me, their immense help and support, and guiding me through each and every step of making the book reviewing process enlightened.

Caleb Poitevien is an analytic philosopher with a deep passion for continual improvement. He has grown due to diverse experiences ranging from eight years in financial operations to over 12 years in IT in enterprise application development based on Java and Salesforce. He has been consulting for XM Satellite Radio, Motorola, Level3 Communications, Quick Loans, MTS, NBTY, Apple, and currently Tata Consultancy Services. Caleb lives by Colin Powell's quote:

> *Excellence is not an exception, it is a prevailing attitude.*

Karanraj Sankaranarayanan, who likes to go by Karan, is a certified Salesforce.com developer and works as a Salesforce consultant at HCL Technologies. Karan holds a bachelor's degree in Engineering from Anna University with a specialization in Computer Science. He has more than three years' experience in the Salesforce platform and IT industry. He is passionate about the Salesforce platform and is an active member/contributor of the Salesforce customer community/developer forum. He writes technical blogs too.

He is also the leader of Chennai Salesforce Platform Developer User Group based in Chennai, India. He is one of the reviewers of *Force.com Tips and Tricks* and *Visualforce Development Cookbook*, both by Packt Publishing. He can be reached via Twitter (@karanrajs) and through the Salesforce community at https://success.salesforce.com/profile?u=00530000004fXkCAAU.

Michael Edward Vargas Jr. is an American software engineer and entrepreneur who is best known for his ongoing involvement in the development of federal and private enterprise application systems using the best of breed technologies. He is currently a member of the Java User Group in Miami. In addition, he is a huge fan of Douglas Crockford and John Resig for their involvement with the JavaScript community. On his mornings, nights, and sometimes weekends, he is passionately devoted to the discipline of software engineering. Originally, he started out in the field working at Motorola and has gone on to contribute to organizations such as ADT Security Services, Interval International, and Engility Corporation.

I'd like to acknowledge all of the publishers, editors, authors, colleagues, friends, and family for the development of this book. I would particularly like to thank Teo Montoya, Russell Reynolds, and Michelle Reagin for all they have taught me along the way. Also, many thanks to my beautiful wife and gorgeous daughter, who inspire and motivate me to achieve great things.

www.PacktPub.com

Support files, eBooks, discount offers, and more

You might want to visit www.PacktPub.com for support files and downloads related to your book.

Did you know that Packt offers eBook versions of every book published, with PDF and ePub files available? You can upgrade to the eBook version at www.PacktPub.com and as a print book customer, you are entitled to a discount on the eBook copy. Get in touch with us at service@packtpub.com for more details.

At www.PacktPub.com, you can also read a collection of free technical articles, sign up for a range of free newsletters and receive exclusive discounts and offers on Packt books and eBooks.

http://PacktLib.PacktPub.com

Do you need instant solutions to your IT questions? PacktLib is Packt's online digital book library. Here, you can access, read and search across Packt's entire library of books.

Why subscribe?

- Fully searchable across every book published by Packt
- Copy and paste, print and bookmark content
- On demand and accessible via web browser

Free access for Packt account holders

If you have an account with Packt at www.PacktPub.com, you can use this to access PacktLib today and view nine entirely free books. Simply use your login credentials for immediate access.

Instant updates on new Packt books

Get notified! Find out when new books are published by following @PacktEnterprise on Twitter, or the *Packt Enterprise* Facebook page.

Table of Contents

Preface

Welcome to *Force.com Development Blueprints*.

Since its unveiling in 2008, the Force.com platform has been used by developers all over the world to build a multitude of business applications running on Salesforce-powered cloud computing infrastructure.

The true strength of the Force.com platform is the ease with which developers can quickly acquire the application development skills required for today's modern cloud-based development, without the burden of configuring and managing infrastructure such as operating systems, application servers, and databases.

To their credit, Salesforce has invested heavily in the platform to ensure that it remains state of the art. Force.com provides out-of-the-box support for modern web browsers, mobile devices, and importantly, integration standards such as REST and SOAP. This ensures that Force.com applications can be easily integrated with other cloud-based and enterprise applications.

Throughout this book, we will see how the versatility of the Force.com platform can be leveraged to develop a range of cloud-based solutions across various application domains. I sincerely hope that by the time you have read this book, you will be confident enough to apply your Force.com development skills to build virtually any business application.

What this book covers

Chapter 1, Building and Customizing Your Own Sites, demonstrates how to build a Salesforce community using Site.com. We will also access the data of Force.com in the site and provide the ability to users to log in to the community.

Chapter 2, The E-commerce Framework, shows how to build an e-commerce application on Heroku, powered by data from Force.com. We will also be building a Force.com fulfillment application using Visualforce.

Chapter 3, Building a Full CRM System, covers how to build a traditional Salesforce CRM application to manage student admissions for a university, which features a custom Apex workflow engine to automatically route the course applications to a faculty.

Chapter 4, Building a Reporting System, provides guidance on how to build a custom reporting dashboard using Visualforce, Apex, and Visualforce charting.

Chapter 5, The Force.com Mobile SDK Application, leverages the Salesforce mobile SDK to build a mobile application to display the opportunity data of Salesforce. The technologies used with the mobile SDK in this chapter include HTML5, Heroku, AngularJS, Twitter Bootstrap, and Google Maps.

Chapter 6, Cloud-connected Applications, combines multiple techniques used throughout the previous chapters to build a Visualforce page that can send push notifications of Windows Azure Notification Hubs to an Android application that is running.

Appendix A, Importing Data with the Apex Data Loader, shows you how to import data with the Apex Data Loader.

Appendix B, Installing Ruby on Rails on Ubuntu, provides guidance on installing a Ruby on Rails development environment on the Ubuntu distribution of Linux.

What you need for this book

To build the applications in this book, you will need an Enterprise, Unlimited, or Developer (recommended) edition of Salesforce and system administrator access. You will also need a modern web browser such as the latest version of Google Chrome, Mozilla Firefox, Safari 5 or 6, or Internet Explorer 9 or 10.

The downloading and installation instructions for other technologies used throughout the book will be presented in the relevant chapters.

Who this book is for

This book is intended for intermediate Visualforce developers, who are familiar with the basics of Force.com, Visualforce, and Apex development. An understanding of HTML5, CSS, and JavaScript is also useful for some of the more advanced chapters.

Conventions

In this book, you will find a number of styles of text that distinguish between different kinds of information. Here are some examples of these styles, and an explanation of their meaning.

Code words in text are shown as follows: "The first step in creating a custom application is to create a custom object tab for the `VolunteerEvent` custom object."

A block of code is set as follows:

```
// results from the Order search
public List<Order__c> orderSearchResults {get; set;}

// textbox for search parameters
public string orderNumber {get; set;}
```

When we wish to draw your attention to a particular part of a code block, the relevant lines or items are set in bold:

```
<apex:column style="width:15%" headerValue="Actions"
  rendered="{!line.id == editOrderLineId}">
  <apex:commandButton action="{!saveOrderLine}"
    rerender="OrderInformation, OrderLines, messages"
    value="Save" />
  <apex:commandButton action="{!cancelEditOrderLine}"
    rerender="OrderInformation, OrderLines, messages"
    value="Cancel" />
</apex:column>
```

Any command-line input or output is written as follows:

```
$ cd ~/rails_projects/ecommerce_app
$ git status
# On branch master
nothing to commit (working directory clean)
```

New terms and **important words** are shown in bold. Words that you see on the screen, in menus or dialog boxes for example, appear in the text like this: "Click on the **Edit** link in the **Action** column for the **Force Volunteers Community** option."

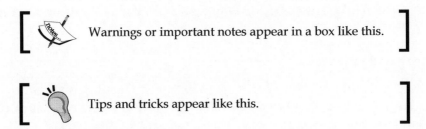

> Warnings or important notes appear in a box like this.

> Tips and tricks appear like this.

Reader feedback

Feedback from our readers is always welcome. Let us know what you think about this book—what you liked or may have disliked. Reader feedback is important for us to develop titles that you really get the most out of.

To send us general feedback, simply send an e-mail to feedback@packtpub.com, and mention the book title via the subject of your message.

If there is a topic that you have expertise in and you are interested in either writing or contributing to a book, see our author guide on www.packtpub.com/authors.

Customer support

Now that you are the proud owner of a Packt book, we have a number of things to help you to get the most from your purchase.

Downloading the example code

You can download the example code files for all Packt books you have purchased from your account at http://www.packtpub.com. If you purchased this book elsewhere, you can visit http://www.packtpub.com/support and register to have the files e-mailed directly to you.

Errata

Although we have taken every care to ensure the accuracy of our content, mistakes do happen. If you find a mistake in one of our books—maybe a mistake in the text or the code—we would be grateful if you would report this to us. By doing so, you can save other readers from frustration and help us improve subsequent versions of this book. If you find any errata, please report them by visiting http://www.packtpub.com/submit-errata, selecting your book, clicking on the **errata submission form** link, and entering the details of your errata. Once your errata are verified, your submission will be accepted and the errata will be uploaded on our website, or added to any list of existing errata, under the Errata section of that title. Any existing errata can be viewed by selecting your title from http://www.packtpub.com/support.

Piracy

Piracy of copyright material on the Internet is an ongoing problem across all media. At Packt, we take the protection of our copyright and licenses very seriously. If you come across any illegal copies of our works, in any form, on the Internet, please provide us with the location address or website name immediately so that we can pursue a remedy.

Please contact us at copyright@packtpub.com with a link to the suspected pirated material.

We appreciate your help in protecting our authors, and our ability to bring you valuable content.

Questions

You can contact us at questions@packtpub.com if you are having a problem with any aspect of the book, and we will do our best to address it.

1
Building and Customizing Your Own Sites

Communities were made generally available in the Salesforce Summer '13 release and are available in Performance, Unlimited, Developer, and Enterprise editions of Salesforce. The purpose of communities is to share information and support collaboration between companies, their customers, and their partners. A Salesforce organization can have multiple communities, each serving a distinct purpose or segment of customers/partners.

A community can be implemented using a Force.com site augmented by Visualforce where required, or by a more traditional HTML/CSS-based site using Site.com.

Communities share a lot in common with the customer and partner portals, which have been a mainstay to connect your Salesforce organization to external customers and partners. Although they are still available, and still supported by Salesforce, it is clear that the future direction of Salesforce is to use (or migrate to) communities in lieu of these portals.

In this chapter, we will be building a Volunteer Community for Force volunteers, a volunteer organization dedicated to providing support services for youth as they reach adolescence and approach adulthood. They already use Force.com to track sponsors, volunteer teams, and volunteer events, but would like to implement a community to connect to their growing network of volunteers.

 I strongly encourage that you work through each chapter and build the examples. Feel free to use them as a springboard for your own Force.com application development projects.

Determining the community requirements

Some key points to keep in mind when determining the requirements for a Salesforce community are as follows:

- Who is my target audience?
- What business processes am I trying to add value to?
- What Salesforce information do I need to expose to my community?
- What changes will be required to my organization's security model?
- Will the standard Salesforce styling and appearance suffice, or do I need the HTML/CSS capabilities of Site.com?
- Will I need to use Visualforce? In this case, you will probably need to use Force.com sites for your community.
- Do I need to purchase more Salesforce licenses for my community members?

Building a community

The community we are building will be provided by a Site.com site. Site.com is a cloud-based content management system of Salesforce used to build websites and social pages. The community that we are building will provide the following pages:

Community page	Description
Home	This is the welcome page for the community.
Services	This is the description of the support services offered by the Force volunteers.
Who We Are	This is the information about the Force volunteers' organization.
Events	This is the display of current events being volunteered.
Contact Us	This is the contact information and an online form to send a message to Force volunteers. This form will populate a custom object in Force.com.
Volunteers Online	This is an online area for volunteers to collaborate with the volunteer Force employees using Salesforce Chatter.

An overview of the steps that we will follow to build a community is as follows:

1. Enable the communities.
2. Create a community.
3. Configure the custom objects and user profiles for the community.
4. Add members to the community.
5. Brand the community.
6. Create a public community site.
7. Publish the community.

 This chapter assumes that you have enabled the improved setup user interface in Salesforce by going to **Customize | User Interface** and selecting the **Enable Improved Setup User Interface** checkbox.

Enabling communities

To use communities in Salesforce, we need to enable them first. To enable communities in Salesforce, log in to your Salesforce Developer edition and complete the following steps:

1. Go to **Setup | Customize | Communities | Settings**.

 As a shortcut, you can use the **Quick Find** feature in **Setup** to search for communities.

2. Select **Enable communities**.
3. At this point, you will be asked for a domain prefix to use for your communities. Enter a domain name prefix that will uniquely identify your communities on Force.com, and click on the **Check Availability** button. If the domain prefix is already used, enter a different domain prefix and try again.

It is worth noting at this stage the URL naming conventions that Force.com uses for Developer, Sandbox, and Production instances of Force.com sites. Your unique subdomain is listed first, followed by the edition or environment type, then the instance name, and a Force.com suffix. Sandbox organizations also use the sandbox name as an extra identifier to distinguish them even further. In the following examples, the unique subdomain prefix is `volunteerforce`, and the sandbox name is `vfsandbox`. The instance name is `na1`, and the sandbox instance name is `cs1`. The URLs for different type of organizations are summarized as follows:

Type of organization	URL
Developer edition	`https://volunteerforce-developer-edition.na1.force.com`
Sandbox	`https://vfsandbox-volunteerforce.cs1.force.com`
Production	`https://volunteerforce.secure.force.com`

4. Once your domain prefix has been accepted, your screen should resemble the following screenshot (except for the domain prefix):

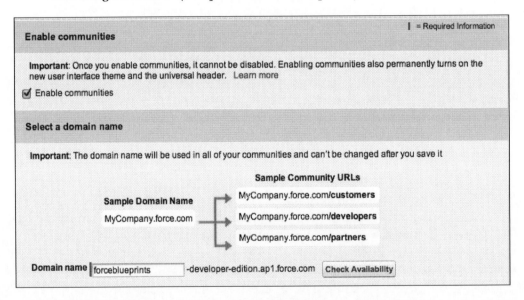

5. Click on **Save** and then click on **OK** in the dialog window that will give you a warning that the changes cannot be undone.

You will also notice a new item titled **Manage Communities** in the **Customize | Communities** section of the **Setup** menu.

Creating the community

To create the Volunteer Community, complete the following steps:

1. Go to **Setup | Customize | Communities | Manage Communities**.
2. Click on the **New Community** button.
3. Enter Force Volunteers for the community name.
4. Enter A Community to connect Force Volunteers with their growing network of volunteers for the **Description** field to describe the purpose of the community.
5. The next step is to enter a URL for the community. This will equate to a subdirectory name underneath the domain prefix entered by you, when you enabled the communities and the Salesforce instance that you are running on. For this example, enter volunteers.
6. Your screen should resemble the following screenshot:

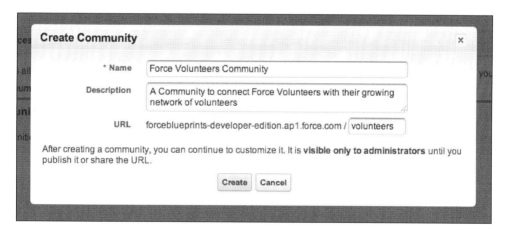

7. Click on the **Create** button to create the community.
8. Click on **Close**. You will configure the community later.

Configuring custom objects and user profiles

Now that we have created a community, there is some configuration required to ensure that the users can access your community and view data from your Salesforce organization.

The objects that we will be configuring and the relationships between them are depicted in the following diagram:

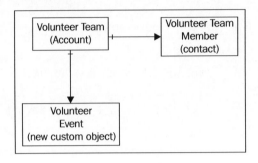

Customizing the Account object

The Account object will be used to represent a team of volunteers. Each volunteer within a team will be stored as a contact on the volunteer team account.

To configure the Account object, complete the following steps:

1. Navigate to **Setup | Customize | Accounts | Fields**.
2. In the **Account Custom Fields and Relationships** section, click on the **New** button.
3. For the **Data Type** section, select **Lookup Relationship** and click on **Next**.
4. Select **User** as the related object in the **Related To** drop-down list and then click on **Next**.
5. Enter Team Leader for the **Field Label** field.
6. Press *Tab* to automatically generate **Field Name** as Team_Leader.
7. Enter A Volunteer Force Team Leader in the **Description** field and click on **Next**.
8. Accept the default values of the **Field-Level Security for Profile** section and click on **Next**.
9. Add the field to the **Account Layout** option only and click on **Save**, as shown in the following screenshot:

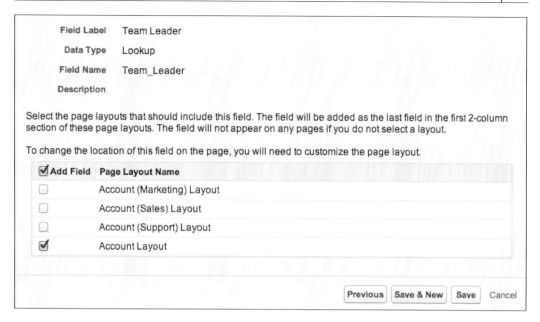

Creating a volunteering event custom object

Your community will require a custom object to display the volunteering events for the community users and volunteers. The steps to create a custom object to display the volunteering events are as follows:

1. Navigate to **Setup | Create | Objects**.

2. Press the **New Custom Object** button.

3. Enter `VolunteerEvent` for the object's **Label** field.

4. Enter `VolunteerEvents` for the **Plural Label** field.

5. Enter `Events for Volunteers to attend` for the **Description** field to describe the purpose of the custom object.

6. Enter `Event_Name` for the **Record Name** field and leave the **Data Type** drop-down menu as **Text**.

7. Select the following checkboxes:

   ◦ **Allow Reports** (optional)

   ◦ **Allow Activities** (optional)

   ◦ **Track Field History**

   ◦ **Add Notes and Attachments related list to default page layout**

8. Assuming that you are using a development environment, ensure that the **Deployment Status** section is set to **Deployed**.

9. Click on the **Save** button to create the custom object.

Creating volunteering event custom fields

You will now need to configure some custom fields for the VolunteerEvent object. The following steps will create the custom fields:

1. Navigate to **Setup | Create | Objects**.

2. Click on the **VolunteerEvent** label hyperlink.

3. Click on the **New** button in the **Custom Fields & Relationships** section.

4. For the **Data Type** section, select **Date/Time** and click on **Next**.

5. Enter Start/Date Time for the **Field Label** field.

6. Enter The date/time that the volunteering event starts for the **Description** field and click on **Next**.

7. Accept the defaults for the **Field-Level Security for Profile** section and click on **Next**.

8. Accept the defaults for the **Page Layouts** section and select **Save & New**.

9. Repeat the steps to create the remaining fields as described in the following table:

Field type	Field label description	Description
Date/Time	End Date/Time	The date/time that the volunteering event ends
Text Area	Location	The location of the volunteering event
Text Area	Description	A description of the volunteering event
Text Area	Special Skills	Any special skills required for the volunteering event; for example, driver's license and first aid

Connecting the Account and VolunteerEvent objects

The final step in configuring our data model is to connect the `Account` and `VolunteerEvent` objects together. This will be a simple lookup relationship from the `VolunteerEvent` object to the `Account` object to record which team of volunteers will be the primary point of contact for the `Volunteer` event.

1. Navigate to **Setup | Create | Objects**.
2. Click on the **VolunteerEvent** label hyperlink.
3. Click on the **New** button in the **Custom Fields & Relationships** section.
4. For the **Data Type** section, select **Lookup Relationship** and click on **Next**.
5. Select **Account** as the related object in the **Related To** drop-down list and click on **Next**.
6. Enter `Volunteer Team` for the **Field Label** field.
7. Enter `The Volunteer Team attending the event` for the **Description** field and click on **Next**.
8. Accept the defaults for the **Field-Level Security for Profile** section and click on **Next**.
9. Accept the defaults for the **Page Layouts** section of `VolunteerEvent` (there should only be one page layout) and click on **Next**.
10. Add the custom-related list only to the **Account Layout** option, as per the following screenshot:

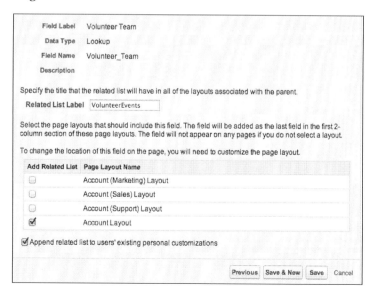

11. Click on **Save**. We will now need to add one more custom field to **VolunteerEvent** to display the volunteer team leader, using the following steps:

    1. Navigate to **Setup | Create | Objects | VolunteerEvent**.

    2. Click on the **New** button in the **Custom Fields & Relationships** section.

    3. For the **Data Type** section, select **Formula** and click on **Next**.

    4. Enter `Team Leader` for the **Field Label** field.

    5. Select **Text** for the **Formula Return Type** section and click on **Next**.

    6. Click on the **Advanced Formula** tab in the formula editor.

    7. Click on the **Insert Field** button; the **Insert Field** dialog will be displayed.

    8. Navigate to **Volunteer Event > | Volunteer Team > | Team Leader > | First Name** and then click on **Insert**, as shown in the following screenshot:

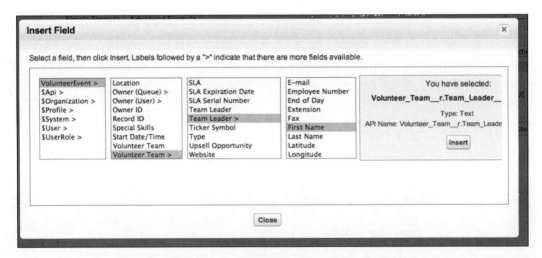

    9. From the **Insert Operator** drop-down menu in the formula editor, select the **& Concatenate** operator. Enter a space between two quotes: **" "**. Then, select another concatenation operator. Your formula should resemble the following screenshot:

```
Volunteer_Team__r.Team_Leader__r.FirstName  &  " "  &
```

10. Click on the **Insert Field** button; the **Insert Field** dialog will be displayed.

11. Select **Volunteer Event >** | **Volunteer Team >** | **Team Leader >** | **Last Name** and click on **Insert**.

12. Your formula editor should now resemble the following screenshot:

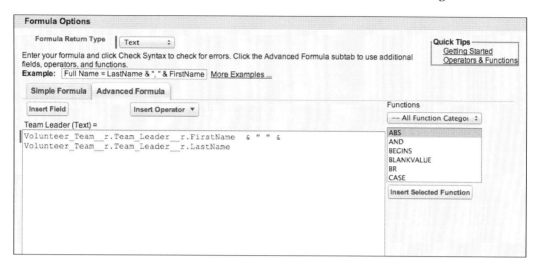

13. Enter Team Leader of Volunteer Team in the **Description** field and click on **Next**.

14. Accept the default settings for the **Field-Level Security for Profile** section and click on **Next**.

15. Accept the default values for the **Page Layouts** section of VolunteerEvent and click on **Next**.

16. Your `VolunteerEvent` custom fields should now resemble the following screenshot:

Custom Fields & Relationships			New	Field Dependencies
Action	**Field Label**	**API Name**	**Data Type**	
Edit | Del	Description	Description__c	Text Area(255)	
Edit | Del	End Date/Time	End_Date_Time__c	Date/Time	
Edit | Del	Location	Location__c	Text Area(255)	
Edit | Del	Special Skills	Special_Skills__c	Text Area(255)	
Edit | Del	Start Date/Time	Start_Date_Time__c	Date/Time	
Edit | Del	Team Leader	Team_Leader__c	Formula (Text) ℒₒ	
Edit | Del	Volunteer Team	Volunteer_Team__c	Lookup(Account)	

Configuring the community public user profile

When you create a community, a public user profile is automatically created for any guest (unauthenticated) users who access the community. This profile is cloned from the default guest user profile, but can be customized for your needs. The profile does not exist in the standard user profile maintenance screen, so to configure the profile you will need to complete the following steps:

1. Navigate to **Setup | Customize | Communities | Manage Communities**.

2. Click on the **Force.com** hyperlink to access the underlying Force.com site for the community.

3. Click on the **Public Access Settings** button to access the Force Volunteers Community profile, as shown in the following screenshot:

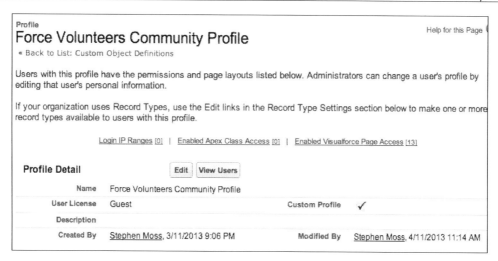

4. Click on the **Edit** button.

5. Scroll down to the **Standard Object Permissions** section.

6. Select the **Read permission** option for the **Account** standard object.

7. Scroll down to the **Custom Object Permissions** section.

8. Select the **Read permission** option for the **VolunteerEvent** custom object.

9. Click on **Save**.

10. Scroll to the **Custom Field-Level Security** section.

11. Click on the **View** hyperlink next to **VolunteerEvent**.

12. Click on the **Edit** button.

13. Make sure that the **Description, End Date/Time, Location,** and **Start Date/Time** fields are selected as **Visible**. There will be system-level fields selected as well and they can't be changed.

14. Click on the **Save** button.

15. Click on the **Back to Profile** button.

This ensures that any guest users accessing the community can see a list of the volunteering events that we will be constructing later in the chapter.

Creating authenticated community user profiles

To allow volunteers to log into your community, they will need a Salesforce user account and an associated profile. When you enabled the communities in your Salesforce organization, a default set of communities-related profiles was created, as shown in the following screenshot:

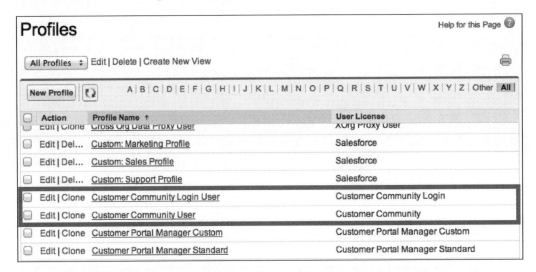

Although you can use these default profiles and assign them to the users, it is recommended to clone one of the default profiles and customize it for your needs. This is the approach that we will be taking for the Volunteer Community.

To clone and customize a default community profile, complete the following steps:

1. Navigate to **Setup** | **Manage Users** | **Profiles**.
2. Select the **Clone** link for the **Customer Community User** profile.
3. Enter `Volunteer Community User` for the **Profile Name** field.
4. Click on **Save**. We will now need to configure the **Volunteer Community User** profile to restrict access to only the objects that volunteers will need, using the following steps:

   1. Navigate to **Setup** | **Manage Users** | **Profiles**.
   2. Select the **Edit** link for the **Volunteer Community User** profile.
   3. Scroll down to the **Standard Object Permissions** section of the **Volunteer Community User** profile page and ensure that the profile has only a **Read** access to **Accounts** and **Contacts** (deselect all permissions for any other objects).

4. In the **Custom Object Permissions** section, ensure that the profile has only a **Read** access to the **VolunteerEvents** custom object.

5. Your object permissions for the profile should resemble the following screenshot:

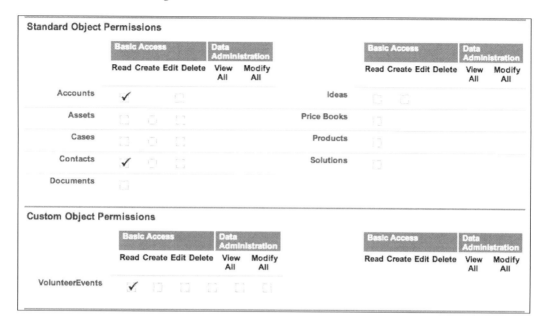

6. Click on **Save**.

7. Scroll to the custom **Field-Level Security** section.

8. Click on the **View** hyperlink next to **VolunteerEvent**.

9. Click on the **Edit** button.

10. Make sure that **Description**, **End Date/Time**, **Location**, **Special Skills**, **Start Date/Time**, **Team Leader**, and **Volunteer Team** are selected as **Visible**. There will also be system-level fields selected, which can't be changed.

11. Click on the **Save** button.

12. Click on the **Back to Profile** button.

Configuring Force volunteers Salesforce user profiles

The final profile that we will need to configure is for the Force volunteers Salesforce users. For these users, you can clone almost any standard Salesforce user profile. However, to make the most efficient use of the limited number of licenses available in a development organization, we will use **Force.com - App Subscription User** as the base license (for full details of the licenses supplied with a Developer edition, refer to `https://wiki.developerforce.com/page/Developer_Edition`). This profile can be cloned and configured to give sufficient access without using one of the very limited full Salesforce licenses available in a development organization. To configuring Force volunteers Salesforce user profiles, perform the following steps:

1. Navigate to **Setup | Manage Users | Profiles**.

2. Select the **Clone** link for the **Force.com – App Subscription User** profile.

3. Enter `Volunteer Force User` for the **Profile Name** field.

4. Click on **Save**.

5. Assuming that you are at the **Volunteer Force User** profile screen after saving, click on **Edit**.

6. Scroll down to the **Standard Object Permissions** section and ensure that the profile has the **Read**, **Create**, **Edit**, and **Delete** access to **Accounts** and **Contacts** only (deselect all permissions for any other objects).

7. In the **Custom Object Permissions** section, ensure that the profile has the **Read**, **Create**, **Edit**, and **Delete** access to the **VolunteerEvents** custom object.

8. Your object permissions for the profile should resemble the following screenshot:

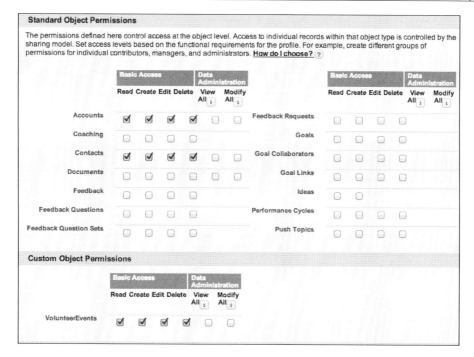

9. Click on **Save**.

Configuring Chatter

Volunteer Force has decided to use Salesforce Chatter as a key component of their Volunteer Community. It is envisaged that the collaborative features of Chatter will form a natural fit with those volunteers who are naturally inclined to form self-organizing teams for volunteering events.

It is assumed in this section that you have already activated Chatter for your Salesforce organization. Note that Chatter is automatically enabled when a developer organization is created.

Enabling Chatter feeds for VolunteerEvent

To enable community users to subscribe to a volunteer event and to collaborate and receive notifications, we will need to activate Chatter feed tracking for the `VolunteerEvent` object.

1. Navigate to **Setup | Customize | Chatter | Feed Tracking**.
2. In the list of objects being tracked, select **VolunteerEvent**.

3. Select the **Enable Feed Tracking** checkbox.

4. In the list of fields available to be tracked, select **Description**, **Event Name**, **Start Date/Time**, **End Date/Time**, **Location**, and **Special Skills**.

5. Click on **Save**.

6. Your Chatter feed tracking for VolunteerEvent should now resemble the following screenshot:

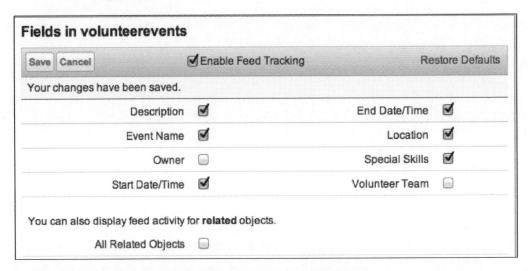

Creating a volunteer Force.com application

The final step to perform before working on the Volunteer Community site is to create a Force.com custom application to tie all of the components of the community together into a cohesive unit. This will provide a consistent interface and a set of Salesforce tabs for volunteer Force employees.

Creating the VolunteerEvent custom object tab

The first step in creating a custom application is to create a custom object tab for the VolunteerEvent custom object. The steps to do this are as follows:

1. Navigate to **Setup | Create | Tabs**.

2. Select the **New** button in the **Custom Object Tabs** section.

3. In the **Object** drop-down menu, select **Volunteer Event**.

4. Select the **Tab Style** lookup icon and select a style from the **Tab Style** dialog (if it is unused, a good match is the tab titled **People**).

5. Enter `Events for Volunteers to attend` in the **Description** field to describe the purpose of the tab and click on **Next**.

6. Accept the default value to add the tab to the user profiles and click on **Next**.

7. Deselect all of the checkboxes (a shortcut is to use the **Include Tab** checkbox, which will deselect all checkboxes) in the next screen, so that the tab will not be included in any application, and click on **Save**.

Creating a custom application

Now that `VolunteerEvent` has a custom object tab, we can go ahead and create the custom application by performing the following steps:

1. Navigate to **Setup | Create | Apps**.

2. Select the **New** button to create a new application.

3. Ensure that **Custom app** is selected for the application type and click on **Next**.

4. Enter `Volunteers` for the **App Label** field.

5. Enter `Collaborative Community for Volunteer Force Members` in the **Description** field to describe the purpose of the community and click on **Next**.

6. Accept the default application logo and click on **Next**.

7. Move **Chatter**, **Accounts**, and **VolunteerEvents** from the **Available Tabs** list to the **Selected Tabs** list by highlighting the relevant tab and clicking on the **Add** button. Leave the option for **Home** as **Default Landing Tab** and click on **Next**.

8. Assign the application as **Visible** and **Default** for the **Volunteer Community User** and **Volunteer Force User** profiles, and **Visible** for the **System Administrator** profile. All other profiles should not have access to the application.

9. Click on **Save**.

Progress check – what have we achieved so far?

If you want to keep progressing with building the community, feel free to skip this section and continue to the *Adding community members* section.

You might be questioning what you have been doing up to this point. Aren't we supposed to be working with communities? It is worth remembering that a community is really an extension of a Force.com application. You have actually successfully built a Force.com application that can now serve as the basis for your Volunteer Community.

To see your application in action, create and activate a user account with the **Volunteer Force User** profile.

When you log in as a volunteer Force user, you can see the application you have built, as shown in the following screenshot:

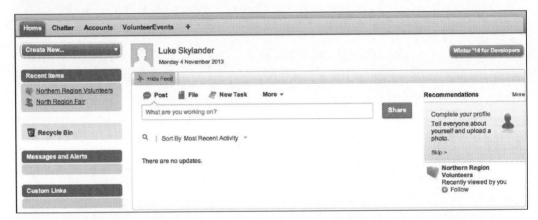

It is now possible to perform the following functions from within the application:

- Record the volunteer teams using the `Accounts` object
- Associate a team leader (via the `User` object) with a volunteer team
- Record the volunteers against a volunteer team (as **Contacts**)
- Record a volunteer event using the `VolunteerEvent` custom object
- Associate a volunteer event with a volunteer team

Congratulations! You are now in a position to build out the rest of the Volunteer Community.

Adding community members

Now, we will add members to the Volunteer Community. This can be a set of profiles or permission sets. Adding members will enable them to log into the community and collaborate on the volunteer events together. The following steps will guide you to add members to the Volunteer Community:

1. Navigate to **Setup** | **Customize** | **Communities** | **Manage Communities**.

2. Click on the **Edit** link in the **Action** column for the **Force Volunteers Community** option.

3. The **Community Settings** dialog is displayed, as shown in the following screenshot:

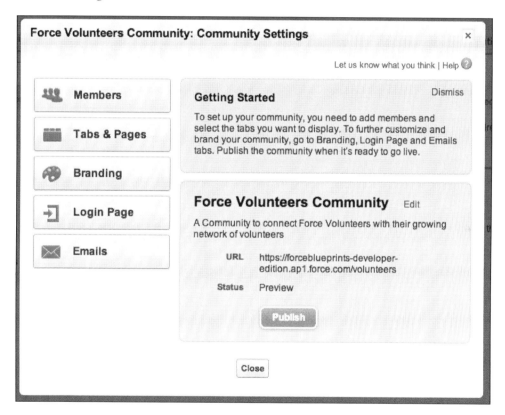

4. Click on the **Members** button.

5. In the **Select Profiles** section of the window, select **Internal** in the **Search** drop-down list.

6. Move the **Volunteer Force User** profile from the **Available Profiles** list to the **Selected Profiles** list by highlighting it and clicking on the **Add** button, as shown in the following screenshot:

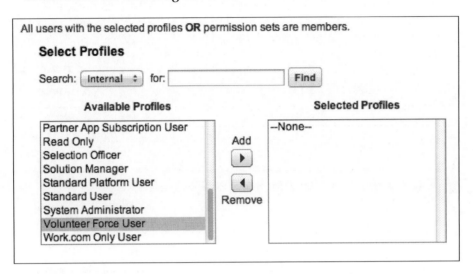

7. In the **Select Profiles** section of the window, select **Portal** in the **Search** drop-down list.

8. Move the **Volunteer Community User** profile from the **Available Profiles** list to the **Selected Profiles** list by highlighting it and clicking on the **Add** button.

9. The community members list should now resemble the following screenshot:

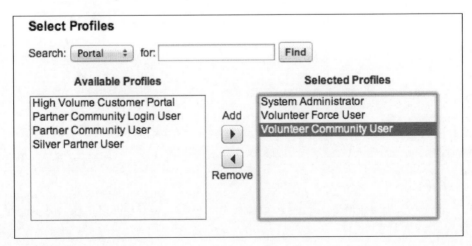

10. Click on **Save**.

The addition of members to a community runs as a background process. You will receive an e-mail notification entitled **Force Volunteers: Processing Complete** when the processing is complete.

Branding the community

Communities provide a declarative interface to define the following elements:

Branding element	Description
Header	This specifies a default header for the pages in your community. For best results, it is recommended that the header be a publicly-accessible HTML document stored using the **Documents** tab.
Footer	This specifies a default footer for the pages in your community. For best results, it is recommended that the footer be a publicly-accessible HTML document stored using the **Documents** tab.
Color scheme	This selects a default color scheme for your community. This can be a predefined color palette from the **Select color scheme** drop-down list, or a custom color palette defined using HTML color notation for each color, for example, #FFFFFF for white color.

For the Volunteer Community, we do not need to specify a default header and footer as we will be building the community pages with Site.com. Make the following minor adjustments to the community branding:

1. Navigate to **Setup | Customize | Communities | Manage Communities**.

2. Click on the **Edit** link in the **Action** column for the Force Volunteers Community.

3. The **Community Settings** dialog is displayed.

4. Click on the **Branding** button to display the **Branding Settings** for the community.

5. Set the background for each page to white by entering #FFFFFF into the **Page Background** field.

6. Assuming that you are using the default color palette, the **Colors** section of the dialog should resemble the following screenshot:

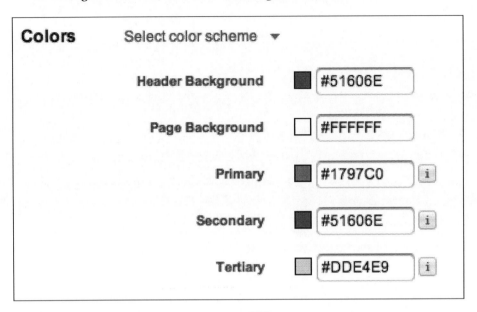

7. Click on **Save**.

 Any changes that you make to the community branding declaratively are automatically propagated to Site.com in the community site template and style sheet.

Specifying Site.com for the community

Force.com sites are a feature of Salesforce that allow you to create public websites and applications that are directly integrated with a Salesforce organization. As mentioned earlier, Site.com is designed as a content management system and provides more fine-grained control over the HTML and CSS of your site.

Force.com sites are available in Developer, Enterprise, Performance, and Unlimited editions of Salesforce. Visualforce is available in Contact Manager, Group, Professional, Enterprise, Unlimited, Performance, and Developer editions of Salesforce. However, if you wish to use Apex, you will need the Performance, Unlimited, Developer, or Enterprise edition of Salesforce (Apex is also available on Database.com).

Site.com is purchased as a separate license for Enterprise, Performance, and Unlimited Salesforce editions (a limited Site.com license for use only with communities is available in a Developer edition).

For more information about Site.com and links to resources and recommended learning path, refer to https://wiki. developerforce.com/page/Site.com.

By default, Salesforce will use a standard Force.com site for the community. This allows the website to be configured in a declarative fashion by specifying the Salesforce tabs that will be made available to the community users. This can then be customized or extended as required by using Visualforce and Apex.

The second option to define a community website is to use Site.com. This is better suited to build a more customized interface using HTML and CSS as the key components, with a limited set of data access functionality.

For the Volunteer Community, we will be using Site.com to provide a more customized interface for the community website. Our data access requirements can also be supported by Site.com out of the box, without the need to use Visualforce or Apex.

To define a Site.com website for the Volunteer Community, the following steps will need to be completed:

1. Navigate to **Setup | Customize | Communities | Manage Communities**.
2. Click on the **Edit** link in the **Action** column for the Force Volunteers Community.
3. The **Community Settings** dialog is displayed.
4. Click on the **Tabs & Pages** button.
5. The drop-down list at the top of the **Tabs & Pages** dialog will be set to **Use Salesforce.com tabs**, by default.
6. Select **Use Site.com to create custom community pages** from the drop-down list to specify that you will be using Site.com.
7. The **Tabs & Pages** dialog should now resemble the following screenshot:

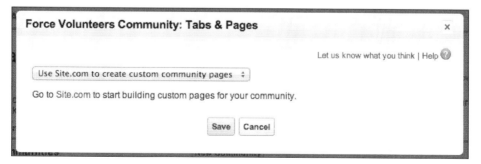

8. Click on **Save** and then on **Close** to dismiss the **Community Settings** dialog.

Creating a public community site

Now, we get to the fun part! We are going to use Site.com to build the custom user interface for the Volunteer Community.

A quick tour of the Site.com community

When you selected Site.com to build the pages for the community, Salesforce automatically created a skeleton website with minimal content.

To open your Site.com community website, complete the following steps:

1. Navigate to **Setup** | **Customize** | **Communities** | **Manage Communities**.

2. Click on the **Site.com** link in the **Custom Pages** column for the **Force Volunteers Community** option.

3. If this is the first time you are using Site.com, you will be presented with the **Getting Started with Site.com Studio** introduction window. Select the **Don't show this again** checkbox, and click on the **x** icon in the top-right corner of the window.

4. You will now be presented with the Site.com landing page for your community, as shown in the following screenshot:

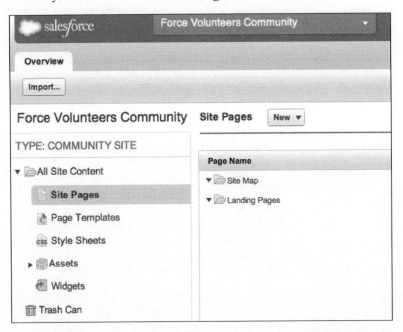

As seen in the screenshot, the **Site Pages** section displays the pages for your site. Currently, this is empty as you haven't created any pages yet.

Clicking on the **Page Templates** section will display the current list of templates that can be used for the pages on your site. Your screen should look like the following screenshot:

Salesforce has automatically generated the **Community Template** page for you, based on your selections when branding the community.

Clicking on the **Style Sheets** section will display the current list of style sheets associated with your site. Your screen should look like the following screenshot:

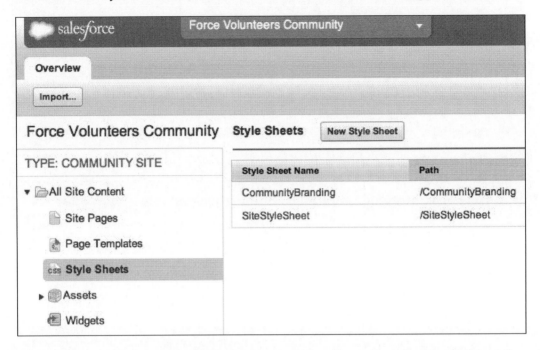

Salesforce has automatically generated the **CommunityBranding** style sheet for you, again based on your selections when branding the community. The default **SiteStyleSheet** is also generated by Salesforce, and supplies a base level of styling for site elements, such as menus, tables, and forms.

The **Assets** section is where you upload any images, scripts, videos, or documents that will be used by your site. Currently, this is empty as we haven't uploaded anything yet.

Clicking on the **Widgets** section will display the current list of reusable components that can be used for the pages on your site. Your screen should look like the following screenshot:

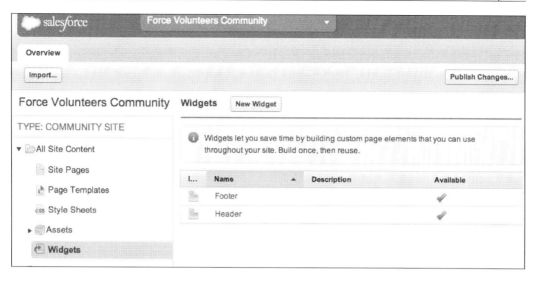

Salesforce has automatically generated the **Header** and **Footer** widgets for you, also based on your selections when branding the community.

Customizing the site header and footer

The initial items that we will need to customize for the community site are the header and footer.

Customizing the header

The following sections detail the steps required to customize the community header.

Importing the community logo

The steps to import the community logo are as follows:

1. Navigate to **Setup** | **Customize** | **Communities** | **Manage Communities**.
2. Click on the **Site.com** link in the **Custom Pages** column for the **Force Volunteers Community** option.
3. On the **Overview** tab, hover over **Assets** and click on **Import**.
4. In the **Import an Asset** dialog, click on the **Browse...** button.
5. In the file picker dialog, locate the image **Force Volunteers Logo.png** from the code download for this chapter and click on **Open**.
6. Leave the **Overwrite existing files** checkbox selected and click on **Import**.

7. Once the file has been uploaded, you will see a success message. At this point, you can click on **Browse...** again to import another asset if required. We don't have any more assets to upload at this point, so click on the **x** sign in the top-right corner of the window to close the dialog.

8. The `ForceVolunteersLogo.png` file will now appear in the **Assets** list for the site.

Adding the community logo to the header

The steps to add the community logo to the header are as follows:

1. On the **Overview** tab, click on **Widgets**.

2. In the list of widgets, click on **Header**.

3. Ensure that the **Page Structure** tab is selected, as shown in the following screenshot:

4. In the **Page Structure** tab, there will be a page element of type **Custom Code** underneath the **Widget** section. This contains any header information that has been saved as part of the community branding. You can leave this page element as it is since you didn't enter any header information when branding the community.

> If you subsequently enter any header information into the community branding, it will appear in the **Custom Code** element. You may wish to delete the **Custom Code** page element to prevent this from happening. To restore the default header at a later stage, you will need to readd a **Custom Code** page element with the following code:
>
> `{!Network.header}`

5. Select **Widget**, click on the gear icon, and select **Add Page Elements**. From the list of page elements, select **Image**.

6. In the **Add an Image** dialog, select **ForceVolunteersLogo.png**. A preview of the logo will be displayed. Click on **Apply**.

Adding the site navigation menu

To add the site navigation menu, perform the following steps:

1. Select **Widget**, click on the gear icon, and select **Add Page Elements**. From the list of page elements, select **Panel**. Close the dialog.

2. Using the **Properties** pane on the right of the screen, type navigation in the **Class Name** field, and press *Enter*.

3. Select the **div.navigation** panel, click on the gear icon, and select **Add Page Elements**, as shown in the following screenshot. From the list of page elements, select **Menu**. Close the dialog.

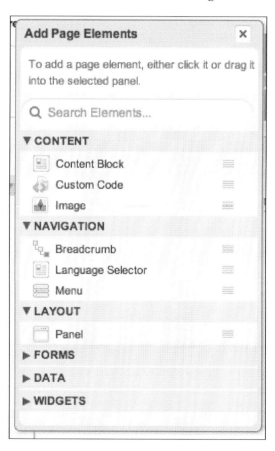

4. From the **Properties** pane, expand the **THEME** section and select **Default** for the menu **Theme Name**.

 At this point the menu is blank. The menu will be built automatically from the pages in the site.

5. Your **Header** widget should now resemble the following screenshot:

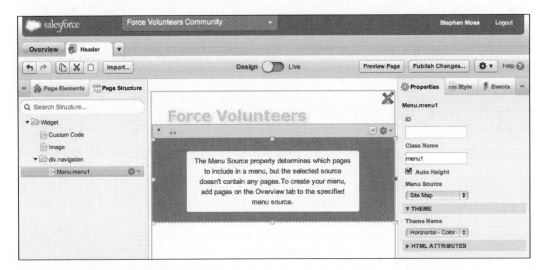

6. Close the **Header** tab.

Customizing the footer

To customize the footer, perform the following steps:

1. Assuming that you are still in Site.com, in the list of widgets, click on **Footer**.

2. Ensure that the **Page Structure** tab is selected.

3. In the **Page Structure** window, there will be a page element of type **Custom Code** underneath the **Widget** section. This contains any footer information that has been saved as part of the community branding. You can leave this page element as it is since you didn't enter any footer information when branding the community.

> If you subsequently enter any footer information into the community branding, it will appear in the **Custom Code** element. You may wish to delete the **Custom Code** page element to prevent this from happening. To restore the default footer at a later stage, you will need to readd a **Custom Code** page element with the following code:
>
> ```
> {!Network.footer}
> ```

4. Select **Widget**, click on the gear icon, and select **Add Page Elements**. From the list of page elements, select **Content Block**.

5. Select the content block, click on the gear icon, and select **Edit**.

6. Delete the existing text.

7. From the **Insert Symbol** drop-down menu (the drop-down menu on the right-hand side of the **Add or Edit Media** drop-down list in the top toolbar), select the copyright symbol.

8. In the content block, type `Copyright 2014 Volunteer Force. All rights reserved.` and click on **Save**, as shown in the following screenshot:

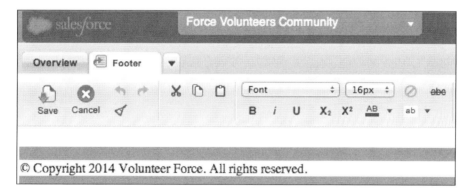

9. Close the **Footer** tab.

Adding some style to the community site

Currently, your community site is using a base collection of styling information determined by the **CommunityBranding** style sheet and the default **SiteStyleSheet**. You will now upload an additional style sheet to add some more CSS styling information using the following steps:

1. Navigate to **Setup | Build | Customize | Communities | Manage Communities**.

2. Click on the **Site.com** link in the **Custom Pages** column for the **Force Volunteers Community** option.

3. Click on **Style Sheets** to display the list of style sheets currently available.

4. Click on the **Import...** button at the top of the page, underneath the **Overview** tab.

5. In the **Import an Asset** dialog, click on the **Browse...** button.

6. In the file picker dialog, locate the **force.css** style sheet from the code download for this chapter and click on **Open**.

7. Leave the **Overwrite existing files** and **Convert CSS files into style sheets** checkboxes selected and click on **Import**.

8. Once the file has been uploaded, you will see a success message. At this point, you can click on **Browse...** again to import another asset if required. We don't have any more assets to upload at this point, so click on the **x** in the top-right corner of the window to close the dialog.

9. Click on **Page Templates** to display the list of templates for community pages.

10. In the list of page templates, select **Community Template**, click on the gear icon, and select **Edit**.

11. In the **Properties** pane, expand the **STYLE SHEETS** section, as shown in the following screenshot:

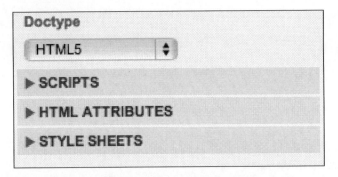

12. Click on the **+** button underneath the **Style Sheets** list.

13. A drop-down list containing the style sheets loaded into the community is displayed. Select **/force.css** and click on the **+** button next to the drop-down list (the highlighted button in the following screenshot):

14. The styles from **force.css** will now be applied to the **Community Template**.

15. Close the **Community Template** tab.

Creating the static site pages

The building of the site infrastructure for the community is now complete. We are now in a position to build the pages of the site itself. The following steps are to be completed to create the static site pages:

1. Navigate to **Setup | Customize | Communities | Manage Communities**.

2. Click on the **Site.com** link in the **Custom Pages** column for the **Force Volunteers Community** option.

3. Click on **Site Pages** to display the list of pages for the community. At this stage, it should be blank.

4. Click on the **New** drop-down button at the top of the list and select **Site Page**.

5. In the **Create a Site Page** dialog, enter **Page name** as Home.

6. Ensure that **Community Template** is selected in the **Page templates** list.

7. Click on **Create**.

8. The **Home** page will be created and displayed in the Site.com editor.

9. Close the **Home** page.

10. Repeat steps 4 to 9 to create the following pages:
    ○ **Services**
    ○ **Who We Are**
    ○ **Events**
    ○ **Contact Us**
    ○ **Volunteers**

Adding text to static pages

To add text to static pages, perform the following steps:

1. Click on **Site Pages** to display the list of pages for the community.

2. Hover over **Home**, click on the gear icon, and select **Edit**.

3. Select the **div#content.brandPrimaryBrd** page element, click on the gear icon, and select **Override Parent Content**. Click on **OK** to confirm your wish to override inherited content.

4. Select the **div#content.brandPrimaryBrd** page element, click on the gear icon, and select **Add Page Elements**.

5. Click on **Panel** in the **Add Page Elements** dialog and close it.

6. Select the **div** page element you have just created, click on the gear icon, and select **Add Page Elements**.

7. Click on **Content Block** in the **Add Page Elements** dialog and close it.

8. Select the content block you have just created, click on the gear icon, and select **Edit**.

9. Delete the existing text.

10. Currently, **Paragraph** is the selected style for the text. Click on the style drop-down menu where **Paragraph** is selected and select **Heading 1**.

11. Type `Welcome to Force Volunteers!` and press *Enter*.

12. Click on the **Style** drop-down menu and select **Paragraph**.

13. Type `We are an organization dedicated to supporting young people and helping them make positive life choices.`

14. Click on **Save**.

15. Click on **Preview Page** and admire your home page, as shown in the following screenshot:

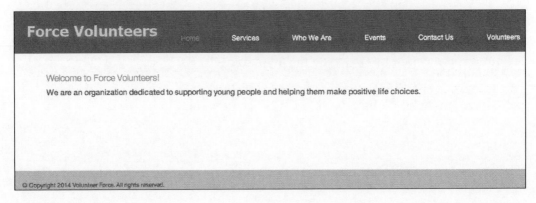

16. Repeat steps 1 to 15 and add static text to the following pages as per the following table:

Page	Heading	Paragraph text
Services	`Services We Offer`	`We offer a range of support services encompassing Schools, Universities, Festivals and Events.`
Who We Are	`Who We Are`	`Our founders recognized the need for an organization to support young people at a very vulnerable stage of their lives. We now offer a comprehensive range of programs aimed at helping young people make positive life choices.`
Events	`Events`	`A list of volunteer events we will be involved in.`
Contact Us	`Contact Us`	`For any enquiries, contact us at volunteers@forcevolunteers.com.`
Volunteers	`Volunteers Online`	`Welcome to our Volunteers Online Page.`

The e-mail address link for the **Contact Us** page will be automatically generated by Site.com.

Creating a data access page

Before creating the volunteer events' data access page, take some time to create some sample volunteer teams, volunteers, and volunteer events in your Salesforce development organization.

It will be beneficial to display a list of volunteer events on the **Events** page. This will require us to utilize the Salesforce data access functionality built into Site.com. Fortunately, for us, Salesforce has gone to great lengths to make the process as painless as possible.

To add a list of events to the **Events** page, complete the following steps:

1. Click on **Site Pages** to display the list of pages for the community.

2. Hover over **Events**, click on the gear icon, and select **Edit**.

3. Select the **div#content.brandPrimaryBrd** page element, click on the gear icon, and select **Add Page Elements**.

4. Click on **Panel** in the **Add Page Elements** dialog and close it.

5. In the **Properties** pane, give the **div** page element an ID of EventList.

6. Click on the **div#EventList** element, click on the gear icon, and select **Add Page Elements**.

7. From the **DATA** section of page elements, select **Data Table**. The **Create Data Table** wizard will open.

8. In the **Choose a Salesforce object** drop-down menu, choose **VolunteerEvent**. You will notice that the **Connection Preview** section is populated with data from **VolunteerEvent**.

9. We don't want to display events from the past, so we will need to filter the data to display events with a date on or after the current date. Expand the **FILTERS** section.

10. From the **Field** drop-down list, select **Start Date/Time**.

11. From the **Operator** drop-down list, select **Greater than or equal to**.

12. From the **Source** drop-down list, select **Global Property**.

13. From the **Value** drop-down list, select **Current date**.

14. We will be sorting the events by **Start/Date Time** in an ascending order. Expand the **SORTING** section.

15. In the **Field** drop-down list, select **Start Date/Time**.

16. In the **Sort Order** drop-down list, select **Ascending**.

17. Your filtering and sorting criteria should resemble the following screenshot:

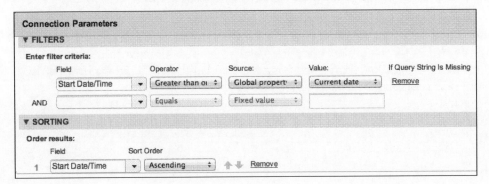

18. Click on **Next**.

19. You will now need to select the data fields to be displayed in the table. From the **Available Fields** list, select **Start Date/Time** and move it across to the **Selected Fields** list by clicking on the **>** button.

20. Move the **End Date/Time**, **Event Name**, **Description**, and **Location** fields across to the **Selected Fields** list by pressing the **>** button.

21. Click on the **Reload Preview** button to see a preview of your table.

22. When you are satisfied with the results, click on **Save**.

23. The events list will now appear on your **Events** page. At this point, you can select **Preview Page** to see your events list in action.

Customizing the events list

Congratulations! You now have a list of events on your site.

However, there are a few improvements that we can make to the events list, which are listed as follows:

- Fix the styling and placement of the events list to match the rest of the site
- Format the **Start Date/Time** and **End Date/Time** columns to display the dates and times correctly
- Add paging support to limit the number of events listed on a page and provide a mechanism to scroll through them

Styling the events list

To correct the styling and placement of the events list, complete the following steps:

1. Open the **Events** page from the **Site Pages** list.

2. Select the **div#EventsList** page element.

3. Select the **Style** pane (next to the **Properties** pane).

4. Expand the **DIMENSIONS** section.

5. Scroll down to the **Padding** section and enter 15 for the **Top** padding value.

6. From the drop-down menu, next to the **Top** textbox, select **pixels**.

7. Click on the **Overview** tab and select **Style Sheets**.

8. Click on **SiteStyleSheet** to open it.

9. From the list of CSS styles on the left-hand side, find the **.Tabletheme thead th** style and select it.

10. In the CSS code box to the right-hand side of the style, add the following line of CSS code, as shown in the following screenshot:

```
font-size:12px;
```

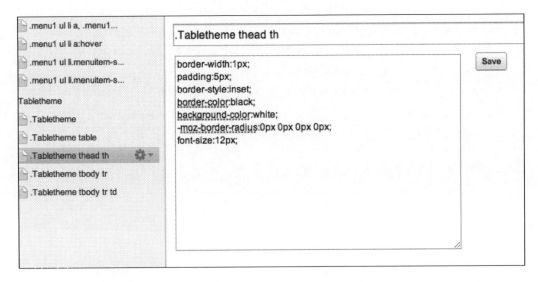

11. Click on **Save**.

12. From the list of CSS styles, find the **.Tabletheme tbody tr td** style and select it.

13. In the CSS code box to the right-hand side of the style, change the **border-color** entry to `black`, so the line reads the following code:

```
border-color:black;
```

14. Finally, add the following line of CSS code, as shown in the following screenshot:

```
font-size:12px;
```

15. Click on **Save** and close **SiteStyleSheet**.

Fixing the Date/Time columns

Now, we need to fix the formatting of the **Start Date/Time** and **End Date/Time** columns in the events list. To reformat the columns, complete the following steps:

1. Open the **Events** page from the **Site Pages** list.
2. Double-click on the **Start_Date_Time__c** table cell. The **Edit Column** dialog will be displayed.
3. From the **Display the field value as:** drop-down list, select **Formatted Text**.
4. From the **Format** drop-down list, select **Short date and time**.
5. Click on **Save**.
6. Perform the same steps for the **End_Date_Time__c** table cell.

Add paging support to the events list

The final step in customizing the events list is to add paging support to the table. This will allow a user to step through the list of events. To add paging support, complete the following steps:

1. Select the **Default View** option of the **Data Table.Tabletheme** page element, click on the gear icon and select **Edit**, as shown in the following screenshot:

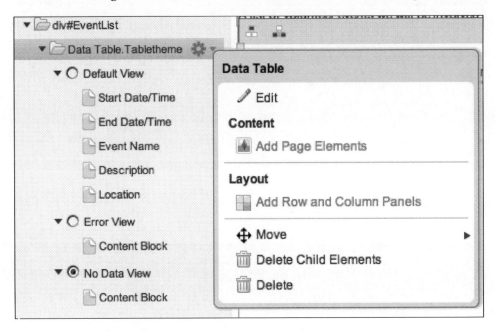

2. Expand the **LIMITS** section and enter 5 for the **Results per page** field.

3. Click on **Next** and then on **Save**.

4. Select the **div#EventsList** page element from the **Page Structure** tab, click on the gear icon, and select **Add Page Elements**.

5. Select **Panel**. In the **Properties** pane, give the panel an ID of ButtonRow.

6. Select the **Style** pane (next to the **Properties** pane).

7. Expand the **DIMENSIONS** section.

8. Scroll down to the **Padding** section and enter 15 for the **Top** padding value.

9. From the drop-down menu next to the **Top** textbox, select **pixels**.

Adding the paging buttons

The steps to add the paging buttons are as follows:

1. Select the **div#ButtonRow** page element, click on the gear icon, select **Add Row and Column Panels**, and then select **Add Row and Column Panels** from the **Inside the panel...** section.

2. Select a **1 x 2** grid (two columns in the first row).

3. Select the first **div** page element underneath **div#ButtonRow** and give it an ID of PrevButton in the **Properties** pane.

4. In the **Style** pane, expand the **DIMENSIONS** section, and set the **Width** field to 100 pixels.

5. Select the second **div** page element underneath **div#ButtonRow** and give it an ID of **NextButton** in the **Properties** pane.

6. In the **Style** pane, expand the **DIMENSIONS** section, and set the **Width** field to 100 pixels.

7. Select the **div#PrevButton** page element, click on the gear icon, select **Add Page Elements**, and then select **Button**. Close the dialog.

8. In the **Properties** pane, change the name to Previous Page.

9. In the **Events** pane, select the **click** event.

10. Click on the **+** button underneath the **Actions** list.

11. In the **Select an Action** drop-down list, select **Previous Page**.

12. In the **Target Element** drop-down list, ensure that **VolunteerEvent__c Data Table** is selected (it should be the only element in the list).

13. Click on **Save**.

14. Select the **div#NextButton** page element, click on the gear icon, select **Add Page Elements**, and then select **Button**. Close the dialog.

15. In the **Properties** pane, change the name to Next Page.

16. In the **Events** pane, select the **click** event.

17. Click on the **+** button underneath the **Actions** list.

18. In the **Select an Action** drop-down list, select **Next Page**.

19. In the **Target Element** drop-down list, ensure that **VolunteerEvent__c Data Table** is selected (it should be the only element in the list).

20. Click on **Save**.

Catering for the end of the event list

To cater for the end of the event list, perform the following steps:

1. Select the **Content Block** option underneath the **No Data View** page element of **Data Table.Tabletheme**, click on the gear icon, and then select **Edit**.

2. Replace the text **No Data Found** with `No More Events....`

3. Replace the text **There is no data to display for this query** with `There are no more Events to display at this time. Please check back later.`, as shown in the following screenshot:

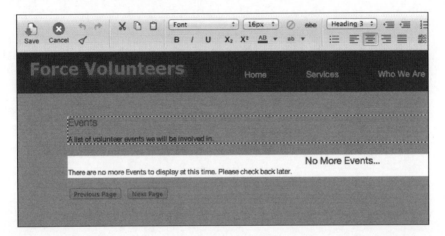

4. Click on **Save**.

5. Your **Events** page should now resemble the following screenshot:

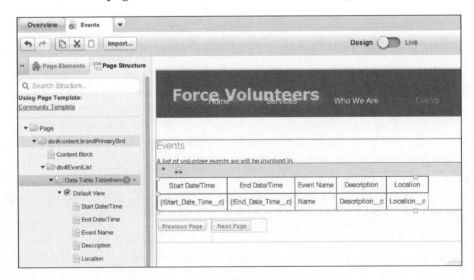

Securing the volunteers page

The build of the Volunteer Community is nearly complete. Our last task is to secure the volunteers page. This is achieved by activating **Authorization** for the site.

There are three options available when activating authorization in Site.com, as shown in the following screenshot:

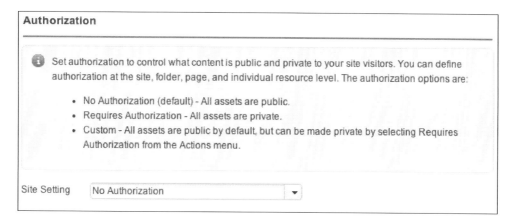

We want all pages to be available for public access, except the volunteers page. In this case, the custom authorization setting suits our purpose.

Complete the following steps to activate authorization for the community site:

1. On the **Overview** tab of the site, expand the **Site Configuration** section, and select **Authorization**.

2. The default setting is **No Authorization**. To change this, select **Custom** from the **Site Setting** drop-down list.

By default, all site pages are still publicly available when enabling the **Custom** authorization. We will need to manually configure the authorization for the volunteers page by completing the following steps:

1. On the **Overview** tab of the site, select **Site Pages**.

2. Select the **Volunteers** page, click on the gear icon, and select the **Requires Authorization** checkbox.

3. A padlock icon will now appear next to the **Volunteers** page name indicating that it is now secured. This is illustrated in the following screenshot:

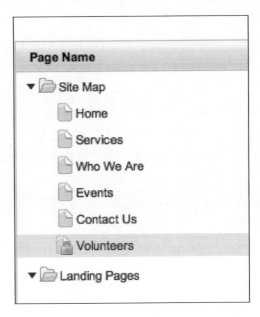

To personalize the **Volunteers** page, we will now add a Chatter feed for the logged in user:

1. Double-click on the **Volunteers** page to open it for editing.

2. Select the **div#content.brandPrimaryBrd** page element, click on the gear icon, and then select **Add Page Elements**.

3. Click on **Panel** in the **Add Page Elements** dialog and close it.

4. In the **Properties** pane, give the **div** page element an ID of VolunteerChatter.

5. Select the **Style** pane (next to the **Properties** pane).

6. Expand the **DIMENSIONS** section.

7. Scroll down to the **Padding** section and enter 15 for the **Top** padding value.

8. From the drop-down list, next to the **Top** textbox, select **pixels**.

9. Click on the **div#VolunteerChatter** element, then on the gear icon, and select **Add Page Elements**.

10. From the **WIDGETS** section of the dialog, select the **News Feed** widget.

11. Click on **x** to close the **Add Page Elements** dialog.

12. Click on **Preview Page** to see your Volunteers page with a personalized Chatter feed for the currently logged in user, as illustrated in the following screenshot:

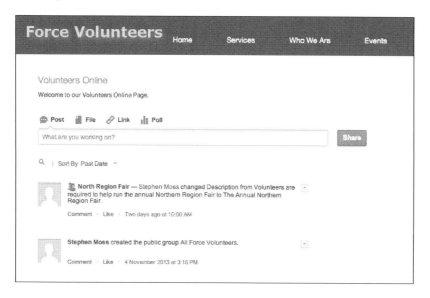

 The first time you display the Volunteers page after it has been secured, you may be prompted to log in. If so, make sure that you select the link to log in as **Member Of your Salesforce Organization**.

Congratulations! The build of the community is now complete!

Creating the Volunteer users

To create community users, they must first be added as contacts against a Salesforce account. To add a community user, complete the following steps:

1. Open the contact record for the community user in Salesforce.
2. Click on **Manage External User** and select **Enable Customer User**.
3. The **New User** screen will now be displayed.
4. Complete the user details for the user (you can use any data you like) and be sure that you select **Volunteer Community User** for the profile (assuming the profile has been created previously and is active).
5. Ensure that **Customer Community** is selected for the **User License** section.
6. Click on **Save**.

In order to create community users, the logged in user must be assigned to any role, or else the **Portal Account Owner Has No Role** error will be displayed. Also, the community user will not receive an activation e-mail until the community is live.

Going live

Now, we are ready to publish the community on Salesforce. Once the community has been published, it will be available to all users with the correct access privileges. In our case, this will be public (anonymous) users, and users with a profile of **Volunteer Force User** or **Volunteer Community User**.

To publish the Volunteer Force community, complete the following steps:

1. Navigate to **Setup | Customize | Communities | Manage Communities**.
2. Click on the **Edit** link in the **Action** column for the **Force Volunteers Community** option.
3. Click on the green button labeled **Publish**.
4. A dialog box will be displayed informing you that publishing the community will make it available to all members, and that all members will be sent a welcome e-mail. Click on **OK**.
5. A success message will be displayed and the community status will change to **Published**, as shown in the following screenshot:

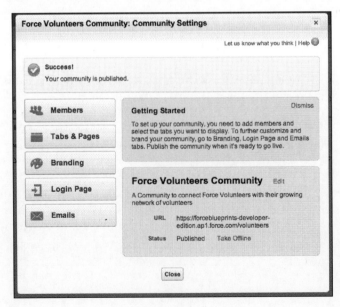

6. The community users will also receive a welcome e-mail, as shown in the following screenshot:

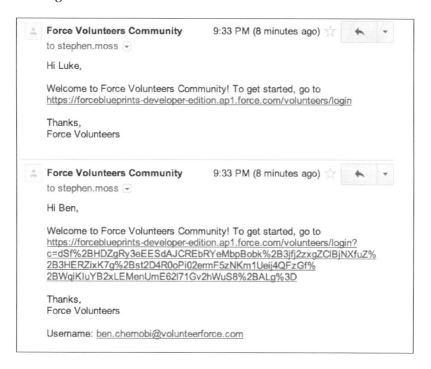

Congratulations! Your community is now live!

To view the licensing options for Salesforce communities, visit
`https://help.salesforce.com/HTViewHelpDoc?id=users_`
`license_types_communities.htm&language=en_US`.

Summary

In this chapter, we built a fully functional Salesforce community that is powered by Site.com.

First, we enabled Salesforce communities for our development organization. We then proceeded to create a new community. From there, we configured the Force.com objects and user profiles required for the community, before adding some community members. With the building blocks in place, we branded the community and built the public-facing site with Site.com. Finally, we integrated the community site to our Force.com data, secured the community, and published it.

Some possible enhancements that you could make to the community are as follows:

- Add a **status** field to the **VolunteerEvent** object, with statuses such as **Draft** and **Published**. Use the data filtering capabilities of Site.com to only display the published events.

- Publish a form for prospective volunteers to register their interest and capture this as a lead in Salesforce.

- Customize the community login page that is displayed when a volunteer logs in.

The E-Commerce Framework

2

E-commerce was a major driving force behind the Internet in the late 1990s and early 2000s and continues to be a major driver of Internet innovation and growth to this current day.

The ability to order goods and services via the Internet revolutionized how companies interacted with customers, and the addition of Web 2.0 technologies and the social media has allowed the development of some very sophisticated and personalized online shopping experiences. The ongoing success of companies such as Amazon, eBay, and PayPal has ensured that e-commerce will continue to be a major Internet force in the future.

In this chapter, we will be building an e-commerce solution for the fictional Force E-Commerce company. They specialize in the development and sales of high-performance and racing car engines for motoring enthusiasts and racing teams.

The company has decided to increase their digital footprint by offering online ordering of their high performance engines on the Internet. We have been engaged by them to develop a Force.com powered e-commerce solution to achieve this requirement.

In this chapter we will be:

- Building a Heroku-powered Ruby on Rails e-commerce application that will allow Force E-Commerce customers to sign up and place orders. Heroku has been chosen, because it is Salesforce's **Platform as a Service (PaaS)** offering, which makes integrating to Force.com extremely simple.

- Building a Visualforce Force.com fulfillment application to allow Force E-Commerce employees to manage and fulfill orders placed in the e-commerce application.

- Using the new Salesforce1 `force.rb` Ruby gem to integrate the Heroku e-commerce application to Force.com to allow it to query and update Force.com data.

We have a lot to get through in this chapter, so let's get started!

Building a basic Force.com fulfillment application

The first step in building our e-commerce application is to develop a basic fulfillment application in Force.com. This will give us the base configuration and custom objects we need to allow us to integrate the e-commerce site on Heroku and ensure that the integration is working correctly.

You may be tempted at this stage to develop a full-blown fulfillment application in Force.com using Visualforce and Apex. Patience is a virtue! Experience has taught me (the hard way) that when integrating one or more applications, it is better in the early stages to have the bare minimum of application functionality required to prove that the integration(s) work. If integration issues do occur (and they will), it is a lot easier to debug a basic Force.com application with standard functionality rather than having to potentially wade through Visualforce pages, Apex, and, if you are particularly unlucky, Ajax and JavaScript as well.

Defining the data model

The first step in building the base fulfillment application is to define the **Order**, **Order Line**, and **Order Line Item** custom objects and the relationships between them.

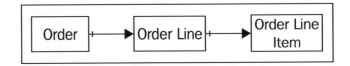

Defining the Order object

Your application will require a custom object to store the orders placed on the e-commerce site:

1. Navigate to **Setup | Create | Objects**.
2. Click on the **New Custom Object** button.
3. Enter Order for **Label**.
4. Enter Orders for the **Plural Label**.

5. Enter `An Order Placed by a Customer` for **Description** to describe the purpose of the custom object.

6. Enter `Order No` for the **Record Name** and change the **Data Type** to **Auto Number**.

7. Enter `Order-{00000}` in the **Display Format** field.

8. Enter `1` in the **Starting Number** field.

9. Select the following checkboxes:

    ○ **Allow Reports** (optional feature)

    ○ **Allow Activities** (optional feature)

    ○ **Track Field History** (optional feature)

    ○ **Add Notes and Attachments related list to default page layout** (object creation option)

10. Ensure that the **Deployment Status** is set to **Deployed**.

11. Press the **Save** button to create the custom object.

You will now need to configure the custom fields for the **Order** object:

1. Navigate to **Setup | Create | Objects**.

2. Click on the **Order** hyperlink.

3. Click on the **New** button in the **Custom Fields & Relationships** section.

4. For the **Data Type,** select **Picklist** and click on **Next**.

5. Enter `Channel` for the **Field Label**.

6. Ensure that the **Field Name** equals `Channel`.

7. In the picklist values field enter `Internal` and `External`.

8. Select the checkbox titled **Use first value as default value**.

9. If desired, enter a **Description** and **Help Text**. Your field definition should look similar to the following screenshot:

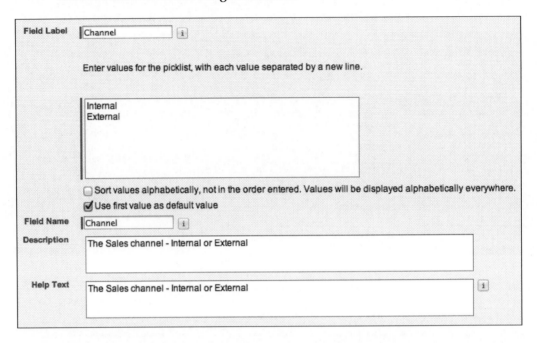

10. Click on **Next**.

11. Accept the defaults for field-level security and click on **Next**.

12. Accept the defaults for the **Page Layout Name** and click on **Save & New**.

13. Create the remaining fields described in the following table:

Field Type	Field Label	Field Name	Description
Text Area	Comments	Comments	Comments entered against the order on the e-commerce site.
Text Area	Customer Address	Customer_ Address	The delivery address of the customer placing the order. Ensure that the **Required** checkbox is selected.

Field Type	Field Label	Field Name	Description
Email	Customer Email	Customer_ Email	The e-mail address of the customer placing the order. Ensure that the **Required** checkbox is selected.
Number	Customer ID	Customer_ ID	The unique identifier for the customer from the e-commerce site. Ensure that the **External ID** checkbox is selected.
Text	Customer Name	Customer_ Name	The name of the customer placing the order. Ensure that the **Required** checkbox is selected and the maximum length is 255 characters.
Checkbox	Delivered	Delivered	Flag to indicate whether the order has been delivered to the customer.
Percent	Discount	Discount	A discretionary discount that can be applied to an order. Ensure that the **Length** is set to 3, and the **Decimal Places** are set to 2.
Date	Planned Delivery Date	Planned_ Delivery_ Date	The planned delivery date for the order.

 It is imperative that the **Field Type** and **Field Name** for each field in this table is an exact match to your custom object to ensure that the e-commerce site will integrate correctly.

Defining the Order Line Item object

Your application will require a custom object to store the **Order Line Item** objects that represent products in the product catalog on the e-commerce site. Perform the following steps to define the **Order Line Item** object:

1. Navigate to **Setup | Create | Objects**.
2. Click on the **New Custom Object** button.
3. Enter Order Line Item for **Label**.
4. Enter Order Line Items for the **Plural Label**.
5. Enter A product item ordered on an Order Line for **Description** to describe the purpose of the custom object.
6. Enter Order Item Number for the **Record Name**, and change the **Data Type** to **Auto Number**.
7. Enter OLI-{00000} in the **Display Format** field.
8. Enter 1 in the **Starting Number** field.
9. Select the following checkboxes:
    - **Allow Reports** (optional feature)
    - **Allow Activities** (optional feature)
    - **Track Field History** (optional feature)
    - **Add Notes and Attachments related list to default page layout** (object creation options)
10. Ensure that the **Deployment Status** is set to **Deployed**.
11. Press the **Save** button to create the Custom Object.

You will now need to configure the custom fields for the **Order** object:

1. Navigate to **Setup | Create | Objects**.
2. Click on the **Order Line Item** hyperlink.
3. Click on the **New** button in the **Custom Fields & Relationships** section.
4. Create the fields described in the following table:

Field Type	Field Label	Field Name	Description
Number	Capacity	Capacity	The capacity of the engine in cubic inches

Field Type	Field Label	Field Name	Description
Picklist	`Induction`	`Induction`	The induction method of the engine. Picklist values are `Naturally Aspirated`, `Supercharged`, and `Turbocharged`. Select the checkbox titled **Use first value as default value**.
Text	`Item Name`	`Item_Name`	The name of the `item`. The maximum length is `255` characters. Ensure that the **Required** checkbox is selected.
Number	`Power Output`	`Power_ Output`	The power output of the engine in horsepower.
Number	`Torque`	`Torque`	The pulling power of the engine in ft lb.
Currency	`Unit Price`	`Unit_Price`	The price of the engine. Ensure that the **Required** checkbox is selected.

 It is imperative that the **Field Type** and **Field Name** for each field in this table is an exact match to your custom object to ensure that the e-commerce site will integrate correctly.

Defining the Order Line object

Your application will require a custom object to store the **Order Line** objects that represent products purchased in an order on the e-commerce site. Perform the following steps to do so:

1. Navigate to **Setup | Create | Objects**.
2. Click on the **New Custom Object** button.
3. Enter `Order Line` for **Label**.
4. Enter `Order Lines` for **Plural Label**.

5. Enter `An Order Line Item for an ordered item` for the **Description** to describe the purpose of the custom object.

6. Enter `Order Line No` for the **Record Name**, and change the **Data Type** to **Auto Number**.

7. Enter `OL-{00000}` in the **Display Format** field.

8. Enter `1` in the **Starting Number** field.

9. Select the following checkboxes:
    - **Allow Reports** (optional feature)
    - **Allow Activities** (optional feature)
    - **Track Field History** (optional feature)
    - **Add Notes and Attachments related list to default page layout** (object creation option)

10. Ensure that the **Deployment Status** is set to **Deployed**.

11. Press the **Save** button to create the Custom Object.

You will now need to configure the **Custom Fields** for the **Order** object:

1. Navigate to **Setup | Create | Objects**.

2. Click on the **Order Line** hyperlink.

3. Click on the **New** button in the **Custom Fields & Relationships** section.

4. Create the fields described in the following table:

Field Type	Field Label	Field Name	Comments
Currency	Line Item Price	Line_Item_Price	The price of the item in the order. Set the default value to 0.
Number	Quantity	Quantity	The quantity of the item ordered. Ensure that this field is a **Required** field.

 It is imperative that the **Field Type** and **Field Name** for each field in this table is an exact match to your custom object to ensure that the e-commerce site will integrate correctly.

Defining the Order Line relationships

To complete our data model, we will need to establish the following relationships:

- A master-detail relationship from the **Order** object to the **Order Line** object.
- A lookup relationship from the **Order Line** object to the **Order Line Item** object

First, we will configure the **lookup relationship** for the **Order Line Item** object:

1. Navigate to **Setup | Create | Objects**.
2. Click on the **Order Line** hyperlink.
3. Click on the **New** button in the **Custom Fields & Relationships** section.
4. For the **Data Type**, select a **Lookup Relationship**. Click on **Next**.
5. In the **Related To** picklist, select **Order Line Item**. Click on **Next**.
6. For the **Field Label**, accept the default **Order Line Item**.
7. Ensure that the **Field Name** defaults to **Order_Line_Item**.
8. Accept the default **Child Relationship Name** of **Order_Lines**.
9. Ensure that the **Required** checkbox is selected.
10. Ensure that the **Don't allow deletion of the lookup record that's part of a lookup relationship** option is selected to preserve the referential integrity of orders. Click on **Next**.
11. Accept the defaults for field-level security and click on **Next**.
12. Accept the defaults to add the lookup field to the **Order Line** standard page layout. Click on **Next**.
13. Accept the defaults for the related lists and click on **Save**.

Finally, we will configure the master-detail relationship for the **Order** object:

1. Navigate to **Setup | Create | Objects**.
2. Click on the **Order Line** hyperlink.
3. Click on the **New** button in the **Custom Fields & Relationships** section.
4. For the **Data Type**, select a **Master-Detail Relationship**. Click on **Next**.
5. In the **Related To** picklist, select **Order**. Click on **Next**.
6. For the **Field Label**, accept the default of **Order**.
7. Ensure that the **Field Name** defaults to **Order**.
8. Accept the default **Child Relationship Name** of **Order_Lines**.

9. Ensure that the **Sharing Settings** are set to **Read/Write: Allows users with at least Read/Write access to the Master record to create, edit, or delete related Detail records**. Click on **Next**.

10. Accept the defaults for the field-level security page and click on **Next**.

11. Accept the defaults to add the **Order** field to the **Order Line** page layout. Click on **Next**.

12. Accept the defaults to add the **Order Lines** related list to the **Order** page layout. Click on **Save**.

Finishing the data model

Now that the objects and relationships for the data model are complete, we can finish it off by adding the following fields:

- Add **Order Line Total** and **Grand Total** formula fields to the **Order** object to support discounting and displaying the overall amount of an order

- Adding a formula field to the **Order Line** object to lookup the **Item Name** for an **Order Line**

- Adding a formula field to the **Order Line** object to calculate the total amount for the **Order Line**

We will start by configuring the fields for the **Order Line** object:

1. Navigate to **Setup | Create | Objects**.

2. Click on the **Order Line** hyperlink.

3. Click on the **New** button in the **Custom Fields & Relationships** section.

4. For the **Data Type**, select **Formula**. Click on **Next**.

5. For the **Field Label**, enter Line Item Total.

6. Ensure that the **Field Name** defaults to **Line_Item_Total**.

7. Select **Currency** for the **Formula Return Type**. Click on **Next**.

8. Select **List Item Price** from the **Insert Field** drop-down list, **Multiply** from the **Insert Operator** drop-down list, and then **Quantity** from the **Insert Field** drop-down list. The Formula Editor looks as follows: Line_Item_Price__c * Quantity__c. At the beginning, we created a formulae field on **Order Line** in the Formula Editor. Click on **Next**.

9. Accept the defaults for the field-level security page. Click on **Next**.

10. Accept the defaults to add the field to the **Order Line** page layout. Click on **Save & New**.

11. For the **Data Type**, select **Formula**. Click on **Next**.

12. For the **Field Label**, enter Item Name.

13. Ensure that the **Field Name** defaults to **Item_Name**.

14. Select **Text** for the **Formula Return Type**. Click on **Next**.

15. Enter Order_Line_Item__r.Item_Name__c in the Formula Editor. Click on **Next**.

16. Accept the defaults for the field-level security page. Click on **Next**.

17. Accept the defaults to add the field to the **Order Line** page layout. Click on **Save**.

Finally, we will configure the fields for the **Order** object:

1. Navigate to **Setup | Create | Objects**.

2. Click on the **Order** hyperlink.

3. Click on the **New** button in the **Custom Fields & Relationships** section.

4. For the **Data Type**, select a **Roll-Up Summary**. Click on **Next**.

5. For the **Field Label**, enter Order Lines Total.

6. Ensure that the **Field Name** defaults to **Order_Lines_Total**. Click on **Next**.

7. Select **Order Lines** in the **Summarized Object** drop-down list.

8. Select **SUM** for the **Roll Up Type**.

9. In the **Field to Aggregate** drop-down list, select **Line Item Total**. Click on **Next**.

10. Accept the defaults for the field-level security page. Click on **Next**.

11. Accept the defaults to add the **Line Item Total** to the **Order** page layout. Click on **Save & New**.

12. For the **Data Type**, select **Formula**. Click on **Next**.

13. For the **Field Label**, enter Grand Total.

14. Ensure that the **Field Name** defaults to **Grand_Total**.

15. Select **Currency** for the **Formula Return Type**. Click on **Next**.

16. Enter Order_Lines_Total__c - (Order_Lines_Total__c * Discount__c) in the Formula Editor. Click on **Next**.

17. Accept the defaults for the field-level security page. Click on **Next**.

18. Accept the defaults to add the field to the **Order** page layout. Click on **Save**.

Congratulations! The data model for the application is now complete.

Defining application tabs and page layouts

Our next task is to define the tabs required for the **Orders** application and make some minor adjustments to some page layouts generated by Force.com.

To define the application tabs, perform the following steps:

1. Navigate to **Setup | Create | Tabs**.
2. Click on **New** in the **Custom Object Tabs** section.
3. In the **Object** dropdown list select **Order**.
4. Select the Lookup icon to set a **Tab Style** (a suggestion is **Stack of Cash**). Click on **Next**.
5. Accept the defaults for the **Add to Profiles** page and click on **Next**.
6. Deselect all applications to ensure this tab is not added. Click on **Save**.
7. Click on **New** in the **Custom Object Tabs** section.
8. In the **Object** drop-down list, select **Order Line Item**.
9. Select the Lookup icon to set a **Tab Style** (a suggestion is **Treasure Chest**). Click on **Next**.
10. Accept the defaults for the **Add to Profiles** page and click on **Next**.
11. Deselect all applications to ensure this tab is not added. Click on **Save**.

 We don't add a tab for **Order Line** as they will only ever be displayed as a related list on the **Order** tab in our application.

To adjust the dialog lookup for **Order Line Item** objects, perform the following steps:

1. Navigate to **Setup | Create | Objects**.
2. Click on the **Order Line Item** hyperlink.
3. Scroll down to the **Search Layouts** section and select the **Edit** link next to **Lookup Dialogs**.
4. Add **Item Name** and **Unit price** to the **Selected Fields** list.
5. Click on **Save**.
6. Finally, we will adjust the **Order Lines** related list on the **Orders** page layout:
7. Navigate to **Setup | Create | Objects**.
8. Click on the **Order** hyperlink.

9. Scroll down to the **Page Layouts** section, and select the **Edit** link next to **Order Layout**.

10. Scroll down to the **Order Lines** related list and select the wrench icon to adjust the list properties.

11. Add the **Order Line No**, **Item Name**, **Quantity**, **Line Item Price**, and **Line Item Total** to the **Selected Fields** list.

12. Select **Order Line No** in the **Sort By** drop-down list. Ensure that **Ascending** is selected for the sort order:

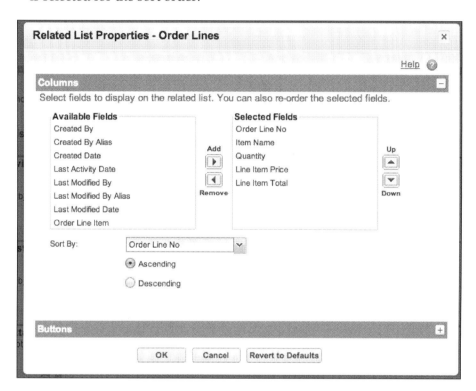

13. Click on **OK** and then on **Save** in the page layout header to complete the changes.

Creating the application

To define the **Orders** application, perform the following steps:

1. Navigate to **Setup | Create | Apps**.

2. Click on the **New** button.

3. Select **Custom app** as the type of app to create. Click on **Next**.

4. For the **App Label**, enter `Orders`. The **App Name** should also be defaulted to **Orders**. Click on **Next**.

5. Click on **Next** to accept the default logo.

6. Move **Orders** and **Order Line Items** to the **Selected Tabs** list.

7. Leave **Home** as the **Default Landing Tab**. Click on **Next**.

8. Make the application visible to **System Administrator** and click on **Save**.

A dash of workflow

The next step in our base application is to configure a workflow rule to populate the **Line Item Price** of an **Order Line** when it is created. The price will be sourced from the **Order Line Item** object.

The workflow will check if the **Line Item Price** on an **Order Line** is blank at the time of creation, and if true, copy the price from the linked **Order Line Item** into the **Line Item Price** field of the **Order Line**. In our sample application, this will be true for orders created through the Salesforce interface. The e-commerce site will automatically populate the **Unit Price** on an **Order Line**.

> In the sample application, we are using a workflow to populate the **Order Line** price to shield against a price change in the underlying **Order Line Item** object. If licensing allows it in a production application, it is recommended to use the standard products and price book functionality instead.

To configure the workflow, perform the following steps:

1. Navigate to **Setup | Create | Workflow & Approvals | Workflow Rules**.

2. If an **Understanding Workflow** page is displayed, click on **Continue**.

3. Click on the **New Rule** button to create a new workflow rule.

4. Select the **Order Line** as the object to apply this workflow rule to. Click on **Next**.

5. For the **Rule Name**, enter `Order Line Created`.

6. In the **Evaluation Criteria**, select the **Evaluate the rule when a record is created** option.

7. In the Rule Criteria, select the drop-down list option to **Run this rule if the following formula evaluates to true**.

8. In the Formula Editor, enter `Line_Item_Price__c = 0`. Click on **Save & Next**

9. In the **Specify Workflow Actions** screen, click on the **Add Workflow Action** dropdown, and select **New Field Update**.

10. Enter `Insert Order Line Price` for the **Name** of the action. The **Unique Name** should default to **Insert_Order_Line_Price**.

11. In the **Fields to Update**, select **Order Line** and **Line Item Price**.

12. In the **Specify New Field Value** section, select **Use a formula to set the new value**.

13. For the **Formula Value**, enter `Order_Line_Item__r.Unit_Price__c`. Click on **Save**. Your workflow rule should resemble the following screenshot:

14. Your workflow action should resemble the following screenshot:

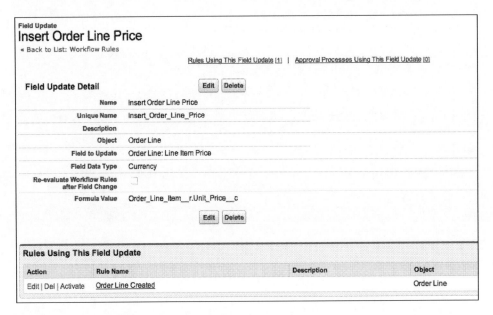

Loading in Order Line Items

In the code download for this chapter, you will find a file called `Order Line Item. csv` in the `sample_data` directory. This file contains some sample **Order Line Items** to get you started. You can use the import wizard or apex data loader to load the sample data into your development organization.

Importing with the Custom Object Import Wizard

1. Navigate to **Setup | Data Management | Import Custom Objects**.

2. In the **Custom Object Import Wizard** introduction screen, select **Start Import Wizard!**:

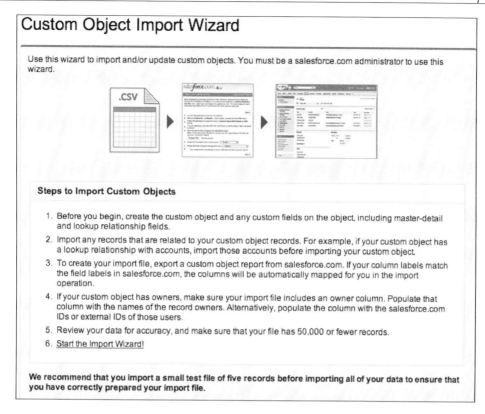

Custom Object Import Wizard

Use this wizard to import and/or update custom objects. You must be a salesforce.com administrator to use this wizard.

Steps to Import Custom Objects

1. Before you begin, create the custom object and any custom fields on the object, including master-detail and lookup relationship fields.

2. Import any records that are related to your custom object records. For example, if your custom object has a lookup relationship with accounts, import those accounts before importing your custom object.

3. To create your import file, export a custom object report from salesforce.com. If your column labels match the field labels in salesforce.com, the columns will be automatically mapped for you in the import operation.

4. If your custom object has owners, make sure your import file includes an owner column. Populate that column with the names of the record owners. Alternatively, populate the column with the salesforce.com IDs or external IDs of those users.

5. Review your data for accuracy, and make sure that your file has 50,000 or fewer records.

6. Start the Import Wizard!

We recommend that you import a small test file of five records before importing all of your data to ensure that you have correctly prepared your import file.

3. In **Step 1** of the import wizard, choose to import **Order Line Item** objects and click on **Next**:

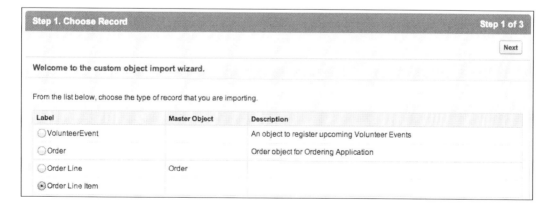

4. In **Step 2** of the import wizard, select **No – insert all records in my import file** and click on **Next**:

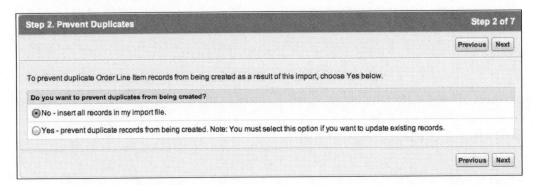

5. In **Step 3** of the import wizard, select **None** so that no fields from the file are used to specify the record owner for the imported objects. The import process will then use your login ID as the record owner. Click on **Next**:

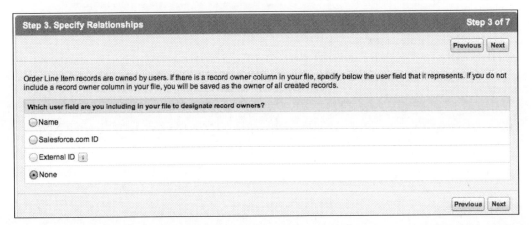

6. In **Step 4** of the import wizard, select the `Order Line Item.csv` file from the code download for the chapter and click on **Next**:

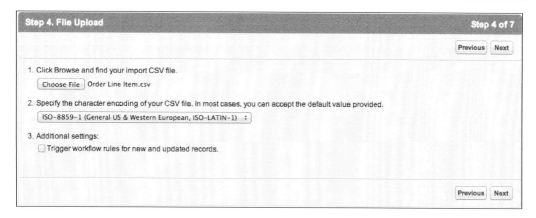

7. In **Step 5** of the import wizard, set the **Field Mapping** as per the following screenshot and click on **Next**:

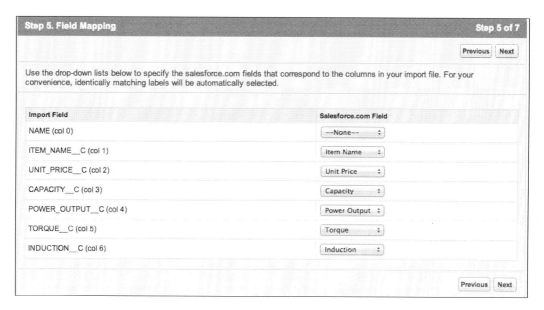

8. Click on **OK** in the warning dialog that is displayed:

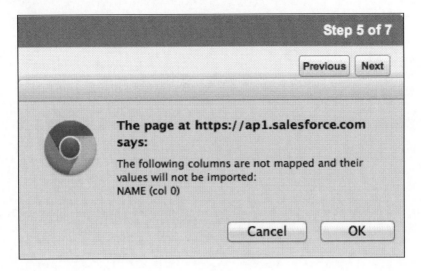

9. In **Step 6** of the import wizard, click on **Import Now!** to submit the import request:

10. Click on **Finish** in **Step 7** of the import wizard:

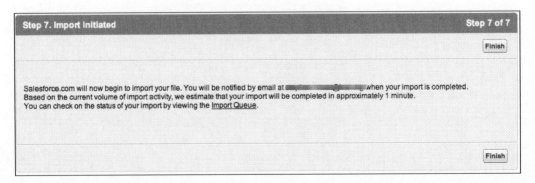

11. When the import has completed, you will receive a confirmation e-mail:

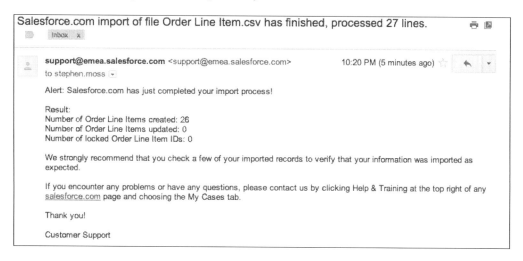

Building the e-commerce application

We are now ready to build the e-commerce application. It will be written in Ruby on Rails and hosted on the Heroku platform (`http://www.heroku.com`).

> In this chapter, we will be configuring and deploying a prebuilt Ruby on Rails e-commerce application to Heroku. We will only be examining in detail the aspects of the application that integrate to Force.com. If you are familiar with Ruby on Rails, I encourage you to explore the source code included in the code download for the chapter to understand the mechanics of the application. If you are unfamiliar with Ruby on Rails, a great place to start learning is `http://rubyonrails.org` before starting to familiarize yourself with the source code.

Heroku is a PaaS acquired by Salesforce in 2010 to provide a state-of-the-art cloud development platform to help organizations accelerate their adoption of cloud computing. Heroku is a polyglot platform and provides excellent support for Ruby on Rails applications as well as applications written in multiple languages, including the following:

- Java
- Node.js
- Python

A book could easily be written about the Heroku platform in its own right. In this chapter, we will concentrate on the steps required to get our e-commerce application running on the platform. To find out more information about Heroku, refer to the following websites: `http://developer.salesforce.com/` and `http://www.heroku.com`.

> As part of the **Salesforce1** development platform announcement, Heroku was rebranded as **Heroku1**, and a number of new features and APIs were announced (including the `force.rb` Ruby gem we will be using in this chapter). For the purposes of this chapter, the terms are interchangeable. Whenever we refer to Heroku, we are also referring to Heroku1.

Setting up the development environment

To configure a local development environment, you will need to install and configure the following software on your local machine:

- Ruby on Rails
- Git
- Heroku toolbelt

> If you have any or all of these already installed, feel free to skip through the relevant section(s).

Ruby on Rails

Ruby is an object-oriented language released in 1995 by Yukihiro "Matz" Matsumoto. The language blended parts of Perl, Smalltalk, Eiffel, Ada, and Lisp to form a new language. The intent of Ruby is to strike a balance between functional programming and imperative programming styles.

Ruby has grown into a full-fledged programming language backed by a very active community of developers. However, it was the arrival of the Rails framework in 2003 that fueled a massive amount of interest and growth in Ruby. Rails was developed by David Heinemeier Hansson as a better way of building web applications. Two standout features of Rails are its native support for both the **model-view-controller (MVC)** paradigm and the REST routing style.

The installation of Ruby on Rails can be challenging, especially for Windows users where Ruby 2.0.0 support is still evolving. To ensure a consistent experience, I recommend that you use the instructions contained in *Appendix B*, *Installing Ruby on Rails on Ubuntu*, to install Ruby on Rails on an Ubuntu-based Linux system.

> For Windows and Mac users, I recommend that you set up an Ubuntu virtual machine using applications such as VirtualBox (https://www.virtualbox.org/) and install Ubuntu (http://www.wikihow.com/Install-Ubuntu-on-VirtualBox). Be sure to download and use Ubuntu Desktop version 14.04 LTS as a minimum.

Once you have Ruby on Rails installed on your system, use a command window and issue the following command to check the version of Ruby you are running:

```
$ ruby -v
```

If Ruby 2.0.0 is installed correctly, you will see a response similar to the following (the version may differ):

```
ruby 2.0.0p247 (2013-06-27 revision 41674)
```

Issue the following command to check your Rails installation:

```
$ rails -v
```

If Rails is installed correctly, you will see a response similar to the following (again, the version may differ):

```
Rails 4.0.0
```

Note that a minimum of Rails 4.0.0 is required for the e-commerce application. If you have installed Ruby 2.0.0, Rails 4.0.0 will be installed by default.

If you have successfully run the previous commands and received the correct responses, Ruby on Rails is successfully installed on your system.

> On some systems, particularly if there is an existing Ruby installation, there may be a conflict when attempting to check the Ruby 2.0.0 installation. In this case, it will be necessary to run the following commands to explicitly use the Ruby 2.0.0 and Rails 4.0.0 environment installed with rvm:
>
> ```
> $ rvm 2.0.0 do ruby -v
> $ rvm 2.0.0 exec bundle install --without production
> $ rvm 2.0.0 rails -v
> ```

Git

Git is a source code control system developed by Linus Torvalds in 2005 to manage builds of the Linux kernel. It was released in December 2005 and now enjoys a wide level of support among software developers. Online code repositories such as GitHub (`https://github.com/`) provide an extensive level of support for Git and host some of the most popular open source projects on the Internet (Twitter Bootstrap, Node.js, jQuery, and Ruby on Rails to name just a few).

If you are running on a Mac, and you have installed the Xcode 4 or Xcode 5 command-line tooling, you should already have Git installed on your system.

If you don't have Git installed, go to `http://git-scm.com/` to download and install it on to your system.

Once you have Git installed on your system (or to verify that it is already installed), open a command window and issue the following command:

```
$ git --version
```

If Git is installed correctly, you will see a response similar to the following (the version may differ):

```
git version 1.7.12.4
```

If you have successfully run the previous command and received the correct response, it means that Git has been successfully installed on your system.

Heroku

To begin working with Heroku, you will first need to sign up at `https://www.heroku.com/`. This is an easy process, and fortunately Heroku provides enough free processing capacity for us to develop and run the e-commerce application.

After you have established your Heroku account, you will need to install the **Heroku toolbelt** on your system. This is a command line utility that will allow you to deploy applications to Heroku and interact with the Heroku environment. To install the Heroku toolbelt for your system, go to `https://toolbelt.heroku.com/`.

Once the Heroku toolbelt is installed, you can log in to your Heroku account by issuing the following command:

```
$ heroku login
```

You will then be asked to enter your user credentials to log in to your account.

The first time you log in to your Heroku account from the command line, you will be asked to generate a public key. This key is required to be able to deploy applications to Heroku. Windows users will be unable to generate a public key using the Windows command shell. A workaround is to login in to Heroku using the bash shell that is installed with Git.

Congratulations! You have now successfully configured your development environment.

Configuring the e-commerce application

The download for the chapter contains the source code for the Ruby on Rails e-commerce application. The download also comes with a preconfigured Git repository.

From the chapter download, copy the `ecommerce_app` folder to a working directory. From a command prompt, navigate to the working directory and check the status of the Git repository. For example, if you copy the application to a `rails_projects` subdirectory in your home directory, the commands and results would be as follows:

```
$ cd ~/rails_projects/ecommerce_app

$ git status

# On branch master

nothing to commit (working directory clean)
```

Downloading the example code

You can download the example code files for all Packt books you have purchased from your account at http://www.packtpub.com. If you purchased this book elsewhere, you can visit http://www.packtpub.com/support and register to have the files e-mailed directly to you.

All of the remaining commands in this section assume you are using the application root directory.

The next step is to install the required Ruby gems contained in the application `Gemfile`. Issue the following command:

```
$ bundle install --without production
```

The `--without production` flag ensures that gems that are specific to Heroku are not installed in our local environment.

The following commands will create a local development database and populate it with some sample data:

```
$ rake db:migrate
$ rake db:populate
```

You will now see a file named `development.sqlite3` in the `db` subdirectory. The **Rails console** can be used to check that the database has been populated correctly:

```
$ rails console
```

The Rails console will start, and you will be presented with the console prompt. Issue the following command to check how many sample users have been loaded into the database:

```
2.0.0p247 :001 > User.count
```

The response should be similar to the following, indicating that there are 100 sample users in the database:

```
  (1.3ms)  SELECT COUNT(*) FROM "users"
 => 100
```

To check the details of the first user in the database, issue the following command:

```
2.0.0p247 :001 > User.first
```

The response should be similar to the following displaying the details of the first user in the database:

```
  User Load (0.9ms)  SELECT "users".* FROM "users" ORDER BY "users"."id"
ASC LIMIT 1
 => #<User id: 1, name: "Example User", email: "example@
forceblueprints.com", address: nil, created_at: "2013-12-03 10:42:17",
updated_at: "2013-12-03 10:42:17", password_digest: "$2a$10$yHa/
zgmLzZS5W1VGIo7.GO0wnVm2NUsaMCbYGwnSeG3....", remember_token:
"225f81230d98caef6074b145b25023e33833f70d", admin: true>
```

A sample Rails console session is illustrated in the following screenshot:

```
xwing:ecommerce_app stephenmoss$ rails console
Loading development environment (Rails 4.0.0)
2.0.0p247 :001 > User.count
   (1.4ms)  SELECT COUNT(*) FROM "users"
 => 100
2.0.0p247 :002 > User.first
  User Load (0.9ms)  SELECT "users".* FROM "users" ORDER BY "users"."id" ASC LIM
IT 1
 => #<User id: 1, name: "Example User", email: "example@forceblueprints.com", ad
dress: nil, created_at: "2013-12-03 10:42:17", updated_at: "2013-12-03 10:42:17"
, password_digest: "$2a$10$yHa/zgmLzZS5W1VGIo7.GO0wnVm2NUsaMCbYGwnSeG3....", rem
ember_token: "225f81230d98caef6074b145b25023e33833f70d", admin: true>
2.0.0p247 :003 > 
```

Type exit or press *Ctrl + D* to exit the Rails console.

Finally, we will create a target Heroku application. Assuming you have previously issued the heroku login command and are currently logged into your Heroku account, issue the following command:

```
$ heroku create
```

Heroku will create a new application against your account, and you should get a response similar to the following (the application name will differ):

```
Creating polar-cliffs-8870... done, stack is cedar
```

```
http://polar-cliffs-8870.herokuapp.com/ | git@heroku.com:
polar-cliffs-8870.git
```

```
Git remote heroku added
```

There is quite a bit happening behind the scenes when issuing the heroku create command, so let's examine it in a bit more detail:

- Heroku creates a blank application against your account and gives it a default name, in this case, polar-cliffs-8870.

- Heroku assigns an **application stack** to your new application. In Heroku parlance, an application stack is a deployment environment that includes the operating system, language runtime, and associated libraries. In our case, we have been assigned the cedar application stack.

- Heroku assigns a default URL to your application. In our case, the default URL is http://polar-cliffs-8870.herokuapp.com/.

- Heroku creates a remote Git repository for our application. In our case, the remote repository is named git@heroku.com:polar-cliffs-8870.git.

- Finally, our local Git repository is updated to add the remote repository created by Heroku.

To confirm that the Heroku remote Git repository has been added, issue the following command:

```
$ git remote
```

The response should list `heroku` and any other remote repositories that have been configured. (A local Git repository can be linked to more than one remote repository, which is very useful if you wish to also store your code at a repository such as GitHub.)

If you log in to your Heroku dashboard at www.heroku.com, you will also see that your new application has been added:

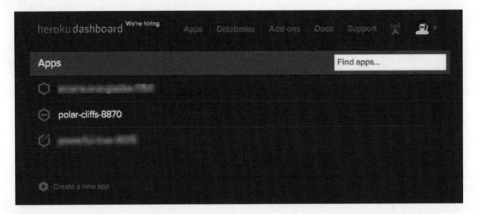

At this point, we now have a local development environment configured, our development database populated with some sample data, and a target application created on the Heroku platform. Our final task before deploying the application to Heroku is to configure the Force.com remote access connection that will allow us to view and modify the Force.com data.

Configuring a Force.com remote access application

To be able to access Force.com data from our Heroku e-commerce application, we need to configure a remote-access application in Force.com. This will give us the authentication and authorization information we need to be able to configure our e-commerce application. To configure a remote-access application, perform the following steps:

1. Navigate to **Setup | Create | Apps**.
2. Scroll down to the **Connected Apps** section and click on **New**.

3. Enter `Heroku E_Commerce App` for the **Connected App Name**.

4. The **API Name** will be autopopulated.

5. Enter your e-mail address in the **Contact Email** field.

6. Enter `Test E-Commerce Heroku app to access Salesforce.com data` for the **Description**. Your screen should now resemble the following screenshot:

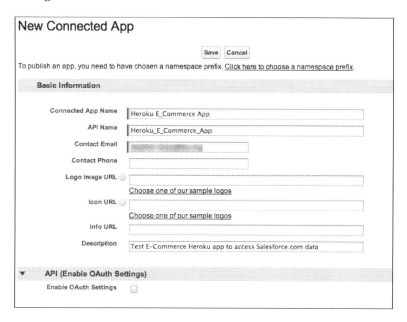

7. Select the **Enable OAuth Settings** checkbox. A new set of fields will be displayed.

8. Enter `https://<<your app name>>.herokuapp.com/_auth` for the **Callback URL**. For example, using the application created in the previous section, the callback URL would be `http://polar-cliffs-8870.herokuapp.com/_auth`.

9. From the **Available OAuth Scopes** list, move the **Provide access to your data via the Web (web)** option to the **Selected OAuth Scopes** list.

10. Under **Web App Settings** enter `https://<<your app name>>.herokuapp.com/` for the **Start URL**. For example, using the application created in the previous section, the **Start URL** would be `http://polar-cliffs-8870.herokuapp.com/`. Your screen should now resemble the following screenshot:

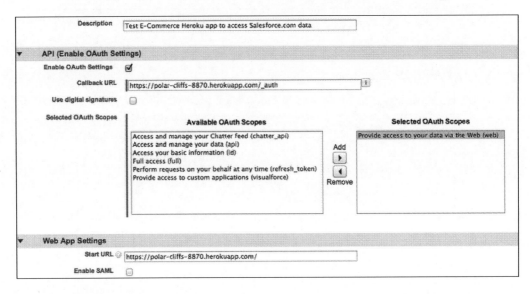

11. Click on **Save**.

Force.com will now configure the remote-access application and present you with a screen similar to the following:

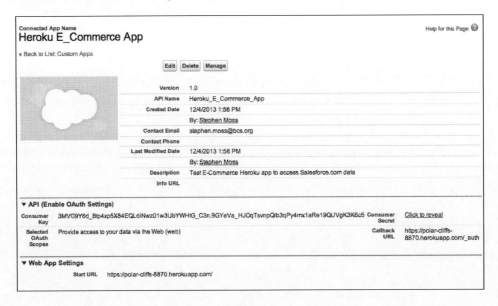

The key information that you will need from this screen to connect the Heroku e-commerce to Force.com consists of the consumer key and consumer secret. You will need them when we configure the e-commerce application in the next task.

The e-commerce application uses the `force.rb` Ruby gem to connect to Force.com. The gem provides a nice wrapper around the Force.com REST API and relieves us of writing a lot of boilerplate to make the REST API calls. More information on the `force.rb` gem is available at the project homepage hosted at GitHub: `https://github.com/heroku/force.rb`.

To configure local development environment access for the e-commerce application, we need to set some operating system environment variables with our Force.com OAuth credentials. To do this, perform the following steps (Windows users can use the Git bash shell):

1. Open a command prompt. Issue the following command and substitute `<<username>>` with your Force.com username:

   ```
   $ export SALESFORCE_USERNAME="<<username>>"
   ```

2. Issue the following command and substitute `<<password>>` with your Force.com password:

   ```
   $ export SALESFORCE_PASSWORD="<<password>>"
   ```

3. Issue the following command and substitute `<<security token>>` with your Force.com security token:

   ```
   $ export SALESFORCE_SECURITY_TOKEN="<<security token>>"
   ```

4. Issue the following command and substitute `<<client id>>` with your Force.com remote application consumer key:

   ```
   $ export SALESFORCE_CLIENT_ID="<<client id>>"
   ```

5. Issue the following command and substitute `<<client secret>>` with your Force.com remote application consumer secret:

   ```
   $ export SALESFORCE_CLIENT_SECRET="<<client secret>>"
   ```

With the environment variables in place, you can now run the application on your local workstation. At the command prompt in the application root directory, issue the following command:

```
$ rails server
```

On some systems, particularly if there is an existing Ruby installation, there may be a conflict when attempting to run the application. In this case, it will be necessary to run the following commands to explicitly use the Ruby 2.0.0 and Rails 4.0.0 environment installed with rvm:

```
$ rvm 2.0.0 exec bundle install --without production
$ rvm 2.0.0 rails server
```

When the application has booted up, you will see the following, which indicates that it is now ready to be accessed locally:

```
=> Booting WEBrick
=> Rails 4.0.0 application starting in development on http://0.0.0.0:3000
=> Run `rails server -h` for more startup options
=> Ctrl-C to shutdown server
[2013-12-04 14:44:33] INFO  WEBrick 1.3.1
[2013-12-04 14:44:33] INFO  ruby 2.0.0 (2013-06-27) [x86_64-darwin11.4.2]
[2013-12-04 14:44:33] INFO  WEBrick::HTTPServer#start: pid=3178 port=3000
```

If you navigate to `http://localhost:3000/products` with your web browser, you will see the product catalog populated with data from Force.com:

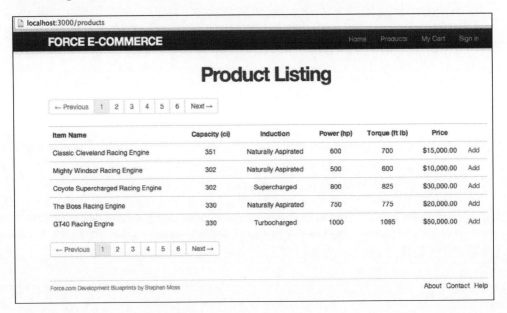

An extremely useful source of information about your running application is the log files in the `log` subdirectory. When running locally in the development mode, the log file will be named `development.log`.

Congratulations! We have now finished the configuration of the e-commerce application and can run it locally. The next step is to deploy the application to Heroku.

Deploying to Heroku

After all of the configuration so far, it might seem a bit of an anticlimax when you see how easy it is to deploy the e-commerce application to Heroku. For this, we can thank the folks at Heroku who have really turned this into a simple operation.

Assuming you are in the `ecommerce_app` application root directory and are logged in to your Heroku account, issue the following command:

```
$ git push heroku master
```

Similar to the `heroku create` command, there is quite a bit happening behind the scenes here, so let's examine it in a bit more detail:

1. The current contents of the `master` branch in your local Git repository are uploaded to the remote Git repository that was automatically created when you issued the `heroku create` command earlier.

2. Heroku detects that you are installing a Ruby on Rails application and starts compiling it into an executable format for the Heroku environment.

3. Heroku examines the `Gemfile` shipped with your application and links it to existing gems and installs any missing gems.

4. The database configuration is rewritten to point to a Heroku Postgres instance.

5. The Heroku compilation is completed, and the compiled application (a **slug** in Heroku parlance) is installed and accessible at your application URL; in the case of the example in this chapter, the URL is `http://polar-cliffs-8870.herokuapp.com`.

If you are having issues deploying to Heroku, check that your Git repository is configured correctly by referring to the following blog at github.com: https://gist.github.com/bhousman/8713170. If you are having permission issues with the remote Git repository, refer to https://devcenter.heroku.com/articles/keys for information on generating and managing the SSH keys required to deploy to Heroku. Finally, if you are behind a corporate firewall, you might need to check with your network administrator to confirm that you are able to access Heroku from the command line.

Now that our application has been deployed to Heroku, our next task is to initialize the application database and populate it with some sample data. To initialize the application database, issue the following command:

```
$ heroku run rake db:migrate
```

This will initialize the database and set up the table structure for the objects defined in the e-commerce application.

To populate the database with some sample users, issue the following command:

```
$ heroku run rake db:populate
```

In some corporate environments, you may have some problems using the heroku run command, because it can't connect to a terminal instance on Heroku. In this instance, you can use the heroku run:detached command. For example, heroku run:detached rake db:migrate will initialize the database. You can the check the result of the initialization using the heroku logs command.

Finally, we need to set up some Heroku configuration variables to hold our Force.com OAuth credentials:

1. Issue the following command and substitute <<username>> with your Force.com username:

   ```
   $ heroku config:set SALESFORCE_USERNAME="<<username>>"
   ```

2. Issue the following command and substitute <<password>> with your Force.com password:

   ```
   $ heroku config:set SALESFORCE_PASSWORD="<<password>>"
   ```

3. Issue the following command and substitute <<security token>> with your Force.com security token:

   ```
   $ heroku config:set SALESFORCE_SECURITY_TOKEN="<<security token>>"
   ```

4. Issue the following command and substitute `<<client id>>` with your Force.com remote application consumer key:

   ```
   $ heroku config:set SALESFORCE_CLIENT_ID="<<client id>>"
   ```

5. Issue the following command and substitute `<<client secret>>` with your Force.com remote application consumer secret:

   ```
   $ heroku config:set SALESFORCE_CLIENT_SECRET="<<client secret>>"
   ```

> You only need to set the Heroku configuration variables once. They are retained by Heroku for all subsequent runs of your application even if it is shutdown and restarted. For more information, refer to `http://docs.developer.salesforce.com/docs/atlas.en-us.186.0.salesforce1api.meta/salesforce1api/heroku_best_practices.htm`.

At this stage, you can check the status of you application by checking the application log on your Heroku instance:

```
$ heroku logs
```

To see your application in action, issue the following command:

```
$ heroku open
```

You will now see your application running live on Heroku, similar to the following screenshot:

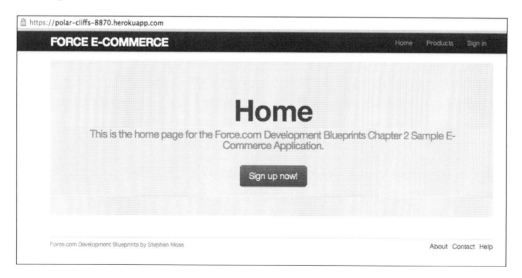

From here, you can also select the **Products** link to see the product catalog populated with data from your Salesforce development organization.

You can also select the **Sign in** link to log in as a preconfigured user. To log in as an administrator, use the following credentials:

- **Username**: example@forceblueprints.com
- **Password**: foobar

To log in as a regular user, use the following credentials:

- **Username**: example-1@forceblueprints.com
- **Password**: password

 You can use any regular user login ranging from example-1@ forceblueprints.com to example-99@forceblueprints.com.

Placing an order

Now that our Heroku site is up and running, we test that our integration is working by placing an order and verifying that it flows through to Force.com.

The e-commerce application supports orders being placed by anonymous or logged in users. For this example, we will use a logged in user and perform the following steps:

1. If you haven't already logged in, log in as an example user with the credentials specified in the previous section.
2. Select the **Products** link to display the product catalog.
3. For any product, select the **Add** link to add it to your cart.
4. When a product has been added successfully, you will see a success message displayed, which is similar to the following screenshot:

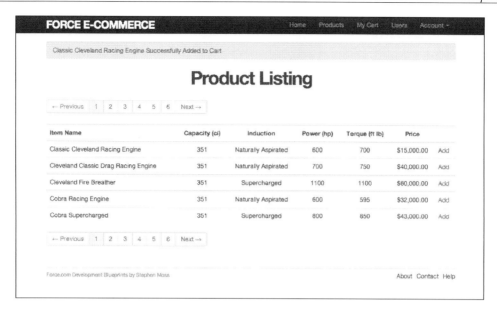

5. You can add additional products to the cart by pressing their **Add** links.

6. When you have finished adding products, select the **My Cart** link to display your shopping cart. Your screen should look similar to the following screenshot (your products may differ):

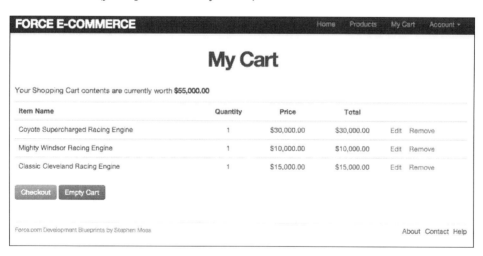

7. Click on the **Checkout** button to navigate to the checkout screen.

8. Enter an **Address** to ship the order to and any order **Comments** you might want to add. If you scroll to the bottom of the screen, you will also see a summary of the items in your order:

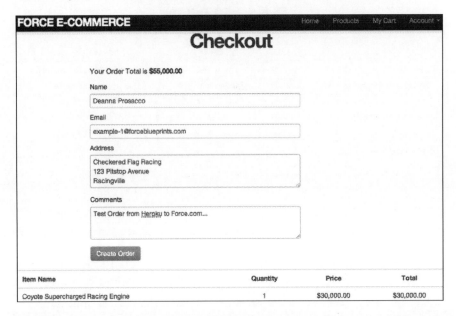

9. Click on the **Create Order** button to create the order in Force.com. You will then be directed to the **Account Profile** page, where you will see a success message and a summary of your orders:

10. We can now verify that the order exists in Force.com. Leave the **Account Profile** page open in your browser, open a new tab / browser window, and log in to your development organization. Select the **Orders** tab, and the newly created order should appear in your **Recent Orders** list:

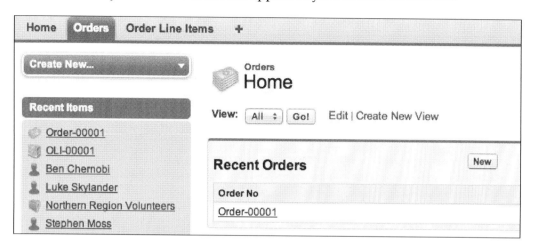

11. Click on the order name's link to display it in more detail:

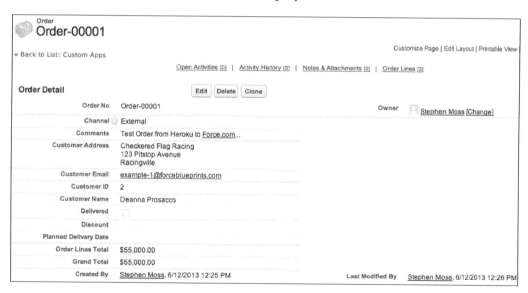

12. If you scroll down further to the related lists, you will also see the **Order Lines** for the order:

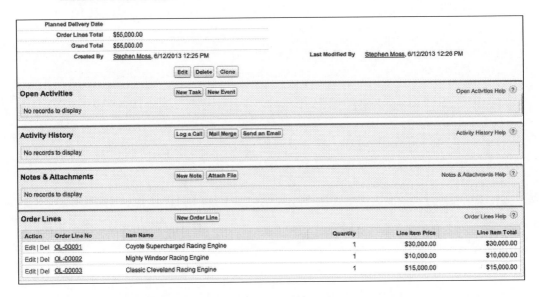

13. We can now edit the order in Force.com and see the update instantly in the e-commerce application. In the Force.com **Order Detail** screen, double-click on the **Planned Delivery Date** to edit it. Select a date and click on **Save**.

14. Navigate back to the **Account Profile** screen in the e-commerce application and refresh the browser window. You will now see the **Planned Delivery Date** populated in your **Order Summary**:

Congratulations! You now have a working e-commerce application deployed to Heroku and have successfully integrated it with Force.com.

Building the final Force.com Fulfillment application

At this point, we have a working Force.com Fulfillment application that can receive and update orders from the Heroku-powered e-commerce application. Admittedly, it is very basic, but it has provided us with enough confidence to trust that the integration between the e-commerce site and Force.com is working correctly. We are now in a position to enhance it with Visualforce and Apex to provide a much more advanced interface.

We will be modifying the **Orders** tab to provide a Visualforce interface, where users will be able to choose to create a new order or search for a specific order by the order reference number and display matching orders.

A new Visualforce page will also be developed to create and maintain orders.

 The steps in the following section can be performed using the Force. com declarative interface or the Force.com IDE. I have chosen to show the steps using the declarative interface due to the fact that I will be using prebuilt code contained within the code download for the chapter. When developing your own code from scratch, I recommend that you use the Force.com IDE.

Building the Order Search custom controller

Our first task is to create the order search custom controller. This controller will be responsible for searching the **Orders** object for records that match criteria entered by the user and returning the results of the search.

To create the order search custom controller, perform the following steps:

1. Navigate to **Setup** | **Develop** | **Apex Classes**.
2. All of the apex classes for your organization will be displayed. Click on **New**.
3. In the code download for the chapter, locate the `OrderSearchController.cls` file in the `force_com` folder.
4. Copy and paste the contents of `OrderSearchController.cls` into the **Apex Code Editor** in your **Force.com** window.
5. Click on **Save**.

The working of the Order Search custom controller

We start by declaring two controller properties:

```
// results from the Order search
public List<Order__c> orderSearchResults {get; set;}

// textbox for search parameters
public string orderNumber {get; set;}
```

The `orderSearchResults` property will contain a list of orders that match the search criteria entered by the user. The `orderNumber` property is used to store the criteria that will be used for the search.

Next, we implement the constructor for the custom controller:

```
public OrderSearchController() {
  // initialize Order No string
  orderNumber = 'Order-';
}
```

This constructor simply sets some initial text to aid the user in entering an order reference number provided on the e-commerce site.

Finally, we implement the controller method that performs the actual search and returns the results:

```
public PageReference searchOrders() {

  // initialize or clear order Search results
  if (orderSearchResults == null) {
    orderSearchResults = new List<Order__c>();
  } else {
    orderSearchResults.clear();
  }

  // Execute SOQL query
  orderSearchResults = [SELECT Id, Name, Customer_Name__c,
    Customer_Email__c, Planned_Delivery_Date__c, Delivered__c,
    Grand_Total__c FROM Order__c

      WHERE Name LIKE
      :String.escapeSingleQuotes(orderNumber)
      + '%'
      ORDER BY Name
      LIMIT 100];

  return null;
}
```

Initially, we check if we have an existing results list for an order search. If not, we create and initialize a new list of orders to hold the search results. If we do have an existing results list, we clear it out.

Next, we execute an SOQL query to search Force.com for any order(s) that match the search criteria. The key here is the WHERE clause, which uses the LIKE operator, substitutes the orderNumber controller property into the SOQL query, and appends the % character to perform a wildcard search (we escape the string to guard against SOQL injection attacks). The results of the search are then stored in the orderSearchResults controller property so that they can be accessed by the calling Visualforce page.

Finally, we return a null page reference to the calling Visualforce page to redisplay the order search page with the search results.

Building the Order Search Visualforce page

Now our custom controller for the order search is in place, we can build the Visualforce page that will be responsible for:

- Obtaining the order search criteria from the user
- Executing the search and passing the search criteria to the controller
- Receiving the results of the order search and presenting them to the user
- Allowing the user to select an existing order to edit it
- Allowing the user to create a new order if required

The **Order Search** page can be seen in the following screenshot:

To create the **Order Search** page, perform the following steps:

1. Navigate to **Setup | Develop | Pages**.
2. All of the Visualforce pages for your organization will be displayed. Click on **New**.

3. In the **Page Information** section, enter Order Search Page in the **Label** field.

4. Enter OrderSearchPage in the **Name** field.

5. In the code download for the chapter, locate the OrderSearchPage. page file in the force_com folder.

6. Clear the default markup in the **Visualforce Page Editor**.

7. Copy and paste the contents of OrderSearchPage.page into the **Visualforce Page Editor** in your **Force.com** window.

8. Click on **Save**.

The working of the Order Search page

The first line of the Visualforce page instructs it to use our custom OrderSearchController class, sets the tabStyle property to use the Order__c custom object tab, and finally hides the default Force.com sidebar to maximize the display area and to add a more customized feel to the interface:

```
<apex:page controller="OrderSearchController" tabStyle="Order__c"
  sidebar="false" >
```

The next item of interest is the PageBlockSection control that provides the interface to enter search criteria, execute the search, or create a new order:

```
<apex:pageBlockSection columns="1" >
  <apex:pageBlockSectionItem >
    <apex:outputLabel for="orderNumber"
      value="Order Number" />
    <apex:panelGroup >
      <apex:inputText id="orderNumber"
        value="{!orderNumber}" />
      <apex:commandButton value="Search Orders"
        action="{!searchOrders}"
        rerender="orderSearchResults,
          messages" />
    </apex:panelGroup>
  </apex:pageBlockSectionItem>
  <apex:outputLink value="/apex/OrdersPage">
    <apex:outputLabel value="Create New Order" />
  </apex:outputLink>
</apex:pageBlockSection>
```

The `apex:outputLabel` and `apex:panelGroup` controls provide the search criteria entry and execution interface. The `apex:inputText` control within the `panelGroup` control is linked to the `orderNumber` property on the controller through the `value` attribute. Thus, when the search is executed, the controller is automatically aware of the search criteria entered by the user.

The `apex:commandButton` control executes the search. The `action` attribute links the button to the `searchOrders` method on the controller. Recall that this method executes the SOQL query to find matching orders and returns the results to the Visualforce page.

The `apex:outputLink` control provides a link to the Visualforce `OrdersPage.page` file to allow the user to add a new order. We will be building this page shortly.

The next `PageBlockSection` control is responsible for displaying the results of an order search to the user:

```
<apex:pageBlockSection id="orderSearchResults" columns="1">
  <apex:pageBlockTable value="{!orderSearchResults}"
    var="order"
    rendered="{!NOT(ISNULL(orderSearchResults))}">
    <apex:column headerValue="Order No"
      style="text-align: center"
      headerClass="centerHeader">
      <apex:outputLink
      value="/apex/OrdersPage">
      <apex:param name="id"
        value="{!order.Id}" />
        <apex:outputLabel
        value="{!order.Name}" />
      </apex:outputLink>
    </apex:column>
    <apex:column headerValue="Customer Name" >
      <apex:outputLabel
        value="{!order.Customer_Name__c}" />
    </apex:column>

...more column definitions...

    <apex:column headerValue="Grand Total"
      style="text-align: center"
      headerClass="centerHeader">
      <apex:outputField
      value="{!order.Grand_Total__c}" />
    </apex:column>
  </apex:pageBlockTable>
</apex:pageBlockSection>
```

The apex:pageBlockTable control is used to present the list of orders found to the user. It is linked to the orderSearchResults property on the controller through the value attribute. The rendered attribute ensures that the pageBlockTable control is only displayed if matching orders have been found in Force.com.

The first apex:column control in the table is used to display the order number and provide a link to the Visualforce OrdersPage.page file to allow the order to be edited. This is achieved by embedding an apex:outputLink control inside the table column. Inside apex:outputLink, there is an apex:param control to supply the internal Force.com identifier to OrdersPage and an apex:outputField control to display the order number itself.

The final step is to configure the **Orders** tab in our Force.com application to use the custom **Order Search** page by default when it is clicked.

Configuring the Visualforce Orders tab

To finish the implementation of the custom order search functionality, we will now reconfigure the **Orders** tab in our Force.com application to use it when **Orders** is selected.

Your initial thought might be to override the List action in the buttons, links, and actions for the Order__c custom object. Unfortunately for us, this will not work because we are using a custom controller. You can only override the standard action(s) when your Visualforce page uses a standard controller or a standard controller with controller extensions.

The first step is to delete the existing custom object tab for Order__c:

1. Navigate to **Setup | Create | Tabs**.
2. In the **Custom Object Tabs** section, select the **Del** link in the **Actions** column for the **Orders** object.
3. Select **OK** in the confirmation dialog to delete the tab.

Next, we need to configure a new Visualforce tab to use the OrderSearchPage.page file we have just created:

1. Select **Setup | Create | Tabs**.
2. In the **Visualforce Tabs** section, click on **New**.
3. In the **Visualforce Page** drop-down list, select **Order Search Page**.
4. Enter Orders for the **Tab Label**.

5. Enter `VFOrders` for the **Tab Name**.

6. Choose **Stack of Cash** for the **Tab Style**.

7. Enter `Visualforce Order Search Page` for the **Description**. Your screen should resemble the following screenshot:

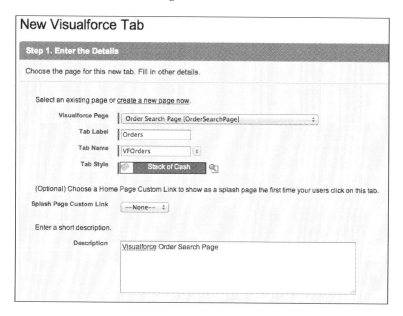

8. Click on **Next**. Accept the defaults for profile tab settings. Click on **Next** again.

9. Deselect the **Include Tab** checkbox.

10. Select the **Orders** checkbox in the **Include Tab** column.

11. Click on **Save**.

If you click on the **Orders** tab now, you will see the **Order Search** page displayed. However, if you look closely, you will see that there is a slight issue with the page. If you haven't spotted it already, you should now notice that the **Orders** tab is not highlighted when we clicked on it. Let's fix that now:

1. Select **Setup | Develop | Pages**.

2. Click on the **Edit** link in the **Action** column for the **Order Search Page**.

3. Modify the `apex:page` declaration at the top of the page so that it uses `VFOrders__tab` for the `tabStyle` property:

```
<apex:page controller="OrderSearchController"
    tabStyle="VFOrders__tab" sidebar="false" >
```

4. Click on **Save**.

If you click on the **Orders** tab now, you will see it highlighted and the custom **Order Search** page displayed:

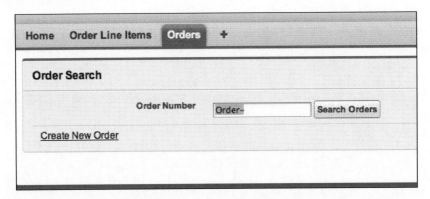

If you subsequently click on the **Search Orders** button, you will see a list of matching orders displayed (just don't click on any of the links yet!):

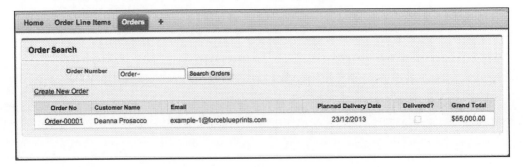

We are nearly finished with our e-commerce fulfillment application. Our next and final task is to build the Order Maintenance page.

Building the Orders custom controller

This controller will be responsible for the creation and maintenance of order records in our fulfillment application.

To create the Orders custom controller, perform the following steps:

1. Navigate to **Setup | Develop | Apex Classes**.
2. All of the Apex classes for your organization will be displayed. Click on **New**.
3. In the code download for the chapter, locate the `OrdersController.cls` file in the `force_com` folder.

4. Copy and paste the contents of `OrdersController.cls` into the **Apex Code Editor** in your **Force.com** window.

5. Click on **Save**.

The working of the Orders custom controller

We start by declaring the properties we need in the controller:

```
// Order for the current context
public Order__c CurrentOrder{get; set;}

// Order Lines for current Order
public List<Order_Line__c> OrderLines{get; set;}

// public property for inserting new Order Line record
public Order_Line__c NewOrderLine {get; set;}

// public property for the Order Line being edited
public Id editOrderLineId {get; set;}

// public property for the Order Line being removed
public Id removeOrderLineId {get; set;}

// flag whether to render Order Header only
public boolean renderOrderDetails {get; set;}

// flag whether any changes have been made to order
public boolean isOrderDirty {get; set;}
```

The code comments explain the purpose of each controller property. We will see them used throughout the code for the controller.

The first method in our controller is the constructor that is responsible for establishing the current context and initializing controller properties as required:

```
public OrdersController()
{
  // initialize CurrentOrder property
  CurrentOrder = new Order__c();

  // initialize property in case we want to add a new order
    line
  NewOrderLine = new Order_Line__c();

  // initialize editOrderLineId to null
  editOrderLineId = null;
```

```
      // get the Order Lines
    prepareFullOrder();

      // no changes to order at this point
    isOrderDirty = false;


}
```

The next method determines if we are editing an existing order. If so, it fetches the order and its linked order lines from the Force.com database:

```
public void prepareFullOrder()
{
  // get the Current Order using id page parameter
  String id =
    ApexPages.currentPage().getParameters().get('id');
  if (id <> null) {
    // attempt retrieve existing order
    try {
      // render all components by default
      renderOrderDetails = true;

      // attempt to retrieve order
      CurrentOrder = [select Id, Name,
        Delivered__c, Planned_Delivery_Date__c,
        Order_Lines_Total__c, Discount__c,
        Comments__c, Grand_Total__c,
        Customer_Name__c,
        Customer_Email__c,
        Channel__c,
        Customer_Address__c
        from Order__c
    where id = :id];

      // Get the Order Lines for the Order
      OrderLines = new List<Order_Line__c>();
      OrderLines = [Select Name, Order_Line_Item__c,
        Line_Item_Price__c, Line_Item_Total__c,
        Order_Line_Item__r.Item_Name__c,
        Order__c, Quantity__c
        FROM Order_Line__c
        WHERE Order__c = :this.CurrentOrder.Id
        ORDER BY Name ASC];
    } catch (QueryException ex) {
      ApexPages.Message myMsg = new ApexPages.Message(
        ApexPages.Severity.ERROR,
        'Order ID does not exist or is not unique!');
```

```
      ApexPages.addMessage(myMsg);
    } catch (Exception ex) {
      ApexPages.addMessages(ex);
    }
  } else {
    // we are adding a new Order
    renderOrderDetails = false;
  }
}
```

First, we check if an `id` parameter has been passed to the page as part of the HTTP request. If an `id` parameter is found, we substitute it into an SOQL query to retrieve the order from the Force.com database (refer to the highlighted code).

Once we have retrieved the order, we execute another SOQL query to retrieve the order lines associated with the order. It is important to note that we substitute the Force.com unique identifier for the order into the SOQL query in the highlighted code.

We then use two `catch` statements to handle any errors encountered during the data access operations. The first catch statement handles a `QueryException`, which will be thrown if we can't uniquely identify an order using the ID passed into the page. The second `catch` statements acts as a "catch all" to handle any other errors we might encounter. If an error is encountered, we write a message to the Visualforce page.

Finally, if an ID is not passed into the page as part of the HTTP request, we assume we are adding a new order and only render the order header information.

The next method in the controller saves the order header information to Force.com:

```
public PageReference saveOrderHeader() {
  PageReference pageRef = null;
  try {
    if (CurrentOrder.Id == null)
    {
      // add record and reset flags
      insert CurrentOrder;
      renderOrderDetails = true;
      // set up page reference to display newly
      // added order
      pageRef = ApexPages.currentPage();
      pageRef.getParameters().put('id', CurrentOrder.Id);
      pageRef.setRedirect(true);
    } else {
      // update the current order
      update CurrentOrder;
    }
```

```
      // reset flag and refresh order details in controller
      isOrderDirty = false;
      prepareFullOrder();
      successMessage('Order Successfully Saved!');
    } catch (DmlException ex) {
      ApexPages.addMessages(ex);
    }
    return pageRef;
}
```

We begin by entering a `try-catch` block and checking if the `CurrentOrder` controller property has a unique ID. If it doesn't, we are adding a new order to Force.com. We call the `insert` statement to create the new order. After the order is inserted, it will contain the unique Force.com identifier. We then use this unique identifier to set up a redirection to the Order Maintenance page for the newly created order and set the `renderOrderDetails` controller property to `true` to instruct the Visualforce page to display all order information.

If we do detect a unique identifier for the `CurrentOrder` property, we are updating an existing order. We call the `update` statement to save the order to Force.com.

Finally, we set the `isOrderDirty` controller property to `false` to indicate that there are no pending changes for the order and call the `prepareFullOrder` method to refresh the `CurrentOrder` and `OrderLines` controller properties with the latest information from the Force.com database.

The next controller method cancels an order, in effect deleting it, and its linked order lines, from the Force.com database:

```
public PageReference cancelOrder() {
  try {
    // Delete Order
    delete CurrentOrder;
  } catch (DmlException ex) {
    ApexPages.addMessages(ex);
    return null;
  }
  // re-direct back to Orders tab
  return closeOrder();
}
```

The method begins by calling the `delete` statement against the `CurrentOrder` controller property. If the deletion is successful, the user is redirected to the **Orders** tab. If the deletion is unsuccessful, a message is displayed and the order is not deleted.

The next set of methods maintains the order lines that are linked to an order. The following method adds a new order line to an order:

```
public PageReference insertOrderLine() {
  try {
    NewOrderLine.Order__c = this.CurrentOrder.Id;
    insert NewOrderLine;
    // re-display Order Line Items
    prepareFullOrder();
    // reset public property for new insert
    NewOrderLine = new Order_Line__c();
    successMessage('Order Line Successfully Added!');
  } catch (DmlException ex) {
    ApexPages.addMessages(ex);
  }
  return null;  // no page re-direct
}
```

The method begins by assigning the unique identifier from the `CurrentOrder` controller property to the new order line to establish the link between them. Next, the `insert` statement is called to create the order line in the Force.com database. The `CurrentOrder` controller property is refreshed by calling the `prepareFullOrder` method. Finally, the `NewOrderLine` controller property is reinitialized, ready to add another new order line.

Next, we add a method to delete an order line that is linked to an order:

```
public PageReference removeOrderLine() {
  try {
    Order_Line__c lineToDelete = [SELECT Id
        FROM Order_Line__c
        WHERE Id = :removeOrderLineId
        LIMIT 1];
    delete lineToDelete;
    prepareFullOrder();
    successMessage('Order Line Successfully Removed!');
    removeOrderLineId = null;
  } catch (DmlException ex) {
    ApexPages.addMessages(ex);
  }
  return null;
}
```

First, we execute an SOQL query to retrieve the order line to be deleted, based on the unique identifier in the `removeOrderLineId` controller property. When we have retrieved the order line, we remove it from the Force.com database using the `delete` statement. Finally, we refresh the `CurrentOrder` controller property by calling the `prepareFullOrder` method.

The next method updates the order lines that are linked to an order:

```
public PageReference saveOrderLine()
{
  try {
    update OrderLines;
    successMessage('Order Line Successfully Saved!');
  } catch (DmlException ex) {
    System.debug(TAG + methodName  + ex);
    ApexPages.addMessages(ex);
    return null;
  }
  return cancelEditOrderLine();
}
```

In this method, we simply pass the order lines held in the OrderLines controller property to the update statement that will save them to the Force.com database.

The next method resets the controller in case the editing of an order line is cancelled:

```
public PageReference cancelEditOrderLine()
{
  editOrderLineId = null;
  prepareFullOrder();
  return null;
}
```

In this method, we simply reset the editOrderLineId controller property to null to indicate that no order line is being edited and refresh the CurrentOrder controller property by calling the prepareFullOrder method.

The last two utility methods set up a page redirection back to the **Visualforce Orders** tab and set up the display of messages in the Visualforce page:

```
public PageReference closeOrder()
{
  // Note this may differ for your org
  return new PageReference('/apex/OrderSearchPage');
}

private void successMessage(string messageToDisplay) {
  ApexPages.Message myMsg = new
    ApexPages.Message(ApexPages.Severity.INFO,   messageToDisplay);
  ApexPages.addMessage(myMsg);
}
```

Building the Orders Visualforce page

The final piece of the fulfillment application is the Order Maintenance page.

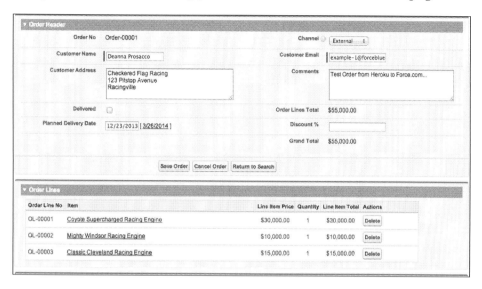

This page will be responsible for providing the following functionality to a user:

- Creating a new order
- Editing an existing order
- Adjusting the quantity of existing order lines on an order
- Deleting existing order lines from an order
- Adding new order lines to an order

To create the **Orders** page, perform the following steps:

1. Navigate to **Setup | Develop | Pages**.
2. All of the Visualforce pages for your organization will be displayed. Click on **New**.
3. In the **Page Information** section, enter Orders Page in the **Label** field.
4. Enter OrdersPage in the **Name** field.
5. In the code download for the chapter, locate the OrdersPage.page file in the force_com folder.
6. Clear the default markup in the **Visualforce Page Editor**.
7. Copy and paste the contents of OrdersPage.page onto the **Visualforce Page Editor** in your **Force.com** window.
8. Click on **Save**.

The working of the Orders page

The first line of the Visualforce page instructs it to use our custom `OrdersController` control, sets the `tabStyle` property to use the `VFOrder__tab` Visualforce tab, and finally hides the default Force.com sidebar to maximize the display area and to add a more customized feel to the interface:

```
<apex:page controller="OrdersController" tabStyle="VFOrders__tab"
  sidebar="false">
```

The top of the file defines a few small JavaScript functions to stop the planned delivery date control from grabbing the focus when the page is loaded and a utility function to display a confirmation message when the user is about to perform a destructive action:

```
<!-- this small script stops date picker from grabbing focus -->
  <script>
    function setFocusOnLoad() {}
  </script>
<!-- this script allows user to confirm a destructive action -->
  <script type="text/javascript">
    function confirmAction(confirmMessage) {
      return confirm(confirmMessage);
    }
  </script>
```

Next, we define two `apex:actionFunction` controls:

```
<apex:actionFunction name="editOrderLine" rerender="OrderLines">
  <apex:param name="editOrderLineId" value=""
    assignTo="{!editOrderLineId}" />
</apex:actionFunction>
<apex:actionFunction name="isOrderDirty"
    rerender="OrderInformation"
    immediate="true">
  <apex:param name="isOrderDirtyFlag" value=""
    assignTo="{!isOrderDirty}" />
</apex:actionFunction>
```

The `editOrderLine` action function is called when an order line is selected to be edited and sets the `editOrderLineId` controller property to the unique identifier of the order line. The `isOrderDirty` action function is called when the value of an `Order` field is changed. When this occurs, it sets the value of the `isOrderDirty` controller property to indicate that there are pending changes on the order.

The `apex:pageBlockButtons` control is defined next to provide a row of buttons for saving and canceling an order and returning to the order search page:

```
<apex:pageBlockButtons location="bottom">
  <apex:commandButton value="Save Order"
    action="{!saveOrderHeader}" />
  <apex:commandButton value="Cancel Order"
    onClick="if (!confirmAction('Are your sure?')) return false;"
    rendered="{!renderOrderDetails}"
    action="{!cancelOrder}" />
  <apex:commandButton value="Return to Search"
    onClick="if ({!isOrderDirty}) {if (!confirmAction('Abandon
      Unsaved Changes?')) return false;}"
    immediate="true"
    action="{!closeOrder}" />
</apex:pageBlockButtons>
```

When the **Save Order** button is pressed, the `saveOrderHeader` controller method will be invoked to save the current order header information to the Force.com database.

Pressing the **Cancel Order** button will first call the `confirmAction` JavaScript function, which will display a confirmation dialog with the message specified. If the user clicks on **OK** in the dialog, the `cancelOrder` controller method will be invoked and the order will be deleted. If the user clicks on **Cancel**, the deletion is aborted.

Clicking on the **Return to Search** button will first check if the `isOrderDirty` controller property is `true`. If so, it will call the `confirmAction` JavaScript function to confirm if the changes need to be saved. If the user confirms that they wish to abandon the changes by clicking on **OK** in the dialog, they will be redirected to the **Order Search** page and the changes will be lost. If they click on **Cancel** in the dialog, they will be returned to the **Orders** page where they can save their changes. If there are no pending changes on the order, the user will be instantly redirected back to the **Order Search** page.

The following `pageBlockButtons` is an `apex:pageBlockSection` control containing the order header information:

```
<apex:pageBlockSection title="Order Header" id="OrderHeader">
  <apex:outputField value="{!CurrentOrder.Name}" />
  <apex:inputField value="{!CurrentOrder.Channel__c}"
    onchange="isOrderDirty('true')" />
  <apex:inputField value="{!CurrentOrder.Customer_Name__c}"
    onchange="isOrderDirty('true')" />

  ...more control definitions for Order Header...

  <apex:outputField value="{!CurrentOrder.Grand_Total__c}" />
</apex:pageBlockSection>
```

The order header `apex:pageBlockSection` consists of the standard `apex:inputField` and `apex:outputField` control definitions. The only thing to note is the `onchange` attribute on fields that will invoke the `isOrderDirty` action function when the value in a field is changed. This will also set the `isOrderDirty` controller property to indicate that there are pending changes on the order.

An `apex:pageBlockSection` control containing the order lines is the next item of interest. There is quite a bit happening inside this `pageBlockSection` control, so we will examine it in small pieces.

Initially, `pageBlockSection` is declared with an `apex:pageBlockTable` control to render the order lines:

```
<apex:pageBlockSection title="Order Lines" columns="1"
  id="OrderLines">
<apex:pageBlockTable value="{!OrderLines}" var="line"
  style="width:90%">
```

The first `apex:column` control of interest in the table is the `Item` column. This displays the name of the order line item being ordered and provides a link to its detail page:

```
<apex:column headerValue="Item">
  <apex:outputLink value="/{!line.Order_Line_Item__c}"
    target="_blank">
  {!line.Order_Line_Item__r.Item_Name__c}
  </apex:outputLink>
</apex:column>
```

The quantity actually consists of two `apex:column` controls:

```
<!-- make Quantity editable if it is clicked on -->
<apex:column headerValue="Quantity"
    value="{!line.Quantity__c}"
    title="click to edit Quantity"
    onclick="editOrderLine('{!line.id}')"
    rendered="{!line.id != editOrderLineId}" />

<apex:column rendered="{!line.id == editOrderLineId}"
    headerValue="Quantity"
    style="text-align:center;width:5%" >
    <apex:inputField value="{!line.Quantity__c}"
    style="text-align:center;width:80%" />
</apex:column>
```

The actual column to be rendered depends on whether the order line being rendered is currently being edited.

When the current order line isn't being edited, the first `apex:column` control is used for `Quantity` because the `rendered` attribute expression evaluates to `true`.

When the `Quantity` Apex column for an order line is clicked on, the `editOrderLine` action function is invoked to set the `editOrderLine` controller property to the unique identifier for the order line that has been clicked on. The order lines are then rerendered, and if the unique identifier for the order line being rendered matches the `editOrderLine` controller property, the second `apex:column` control is rendered. This provides an `apex:inputField` control for the user to adjust the quantity of the item being ordered.

This provides a nice segue into the `apex:column` control, which provides a set of buttons for controlling the editing of an order line:

```
<apex:column style="width:15%" headerValue="Actions"
  rendered="{!line.id == editOrderLineId}">
  <apex:commandButton action="{!saveOrderLine}"
    rerender="OrderInformation, OrderLines, messages"
    value="Save" />
  <apex:commandButton action="{!cancelEditOrderLine}"
    rerender="OrderInformation, OrderLines, messages"
    value="Cancel" />
</apex:column>
```

The `rendered` attribute for the `apex:column` control also defines that it is rendered only when the current order line is being edited. When this is the case, two `apex:commandButton` controls are displayed: one to save the changes and another to cancel the edit.

When the **Save** button is pressed, the `saveOrderLine` controller method is invoked to save the order line being edited to the Force.com database. The order lines are then rerendered to display the most current information.

When the **Cancel** button is pressed, the `cancelEditOrderLine` controller method is invoked to abort the editing of the order line. The `editOrderLineId` controller property is cleared, and the `apex:inputField` control for the quantity will be dismissed.

The final `apex:column` control of interest in the order lines `pageBlockTable` is the button to delete an order line:

```
<apex:column style="width:15%" headerValue="Actions"
  rendered="{!line.id != editOrderLineId}">
<apex:commandButton onClick="if (!confirmAction()) return false;"
    action="{!removeOrderLine}"
    rerender="OrderInformation, OrderLines, messages"
```

```
        value="Delete">
        <apex:param name="removeOrderLineId"
        value="{!line.Id}"
        assignTo="{!removeOrderLineId}" />
    </apex:commandButton>
  </apex:column>
```

When the current order line isn't being edited, this `apex:column` control is rendered instead of the **Save** and **Cancel** buttons. When the **Delete** button is clicked on, the `confirmAction` JavaScript function is called to confirm if the user wishes to proceed. If so, an `apex:param` control is used to set the value of the `removeOrderLineId` controller property to the unique identifier of the order line where the **Delete** button was clicked. Then, the `removeOrderLine` controller action is invoked to delete the order line.

The final item of interest in the **Orders** page is an additional `apex:form` control to allow an order line to be added to the order:

```
<apex:form>
  <apex:pageBlock rendered="{!renderOrderDetails}">
    <apex:pageBlockSection title="Add New Order Line"
      columns="3">
    <apex:inputField
      value="{!NewOrderLine.Order_Line_Item__c}" />
    <apex:inputField
      value="{!NewOrderLine.Quantity__c}" />
    <apex:commandButton action="{!insertOrderLine}" value="Create
      Order Line" />
    </apex:pageBlockSection>
  </apex:pageBlock>
</apex:form>
```

This is a simple `apex:form` control that provides two `apex:inputField` controls to allow the order line item to be selected and a quantity entered. Clicking on the **Create Order Line** button invokes the `insertOrderLine` controller method to add a new order line to the order.

You might be wondering why we added an additional form to the page for the adding of order lines. If we didn't, the validation rules for the order line item and quantity fields will be evaluated whenever the page is posted to the server and will fail if both fields don't contain a value. This is especially inconvenient when performing operations such as saving the order header or editing an order line—they will never work. Encapsulating the adding of order lines in its own form ensures that these validation rules are only evaluated when adding an order line, which is the behavior we want. Another way to achieve this is through the use of `apex:actionRegion` controls, but due to the complexity of the page, an additional `apex:form` control was a much simpler and cleaner option.

Congratulations! You should now have a fully functional Order Maintenance page added to your Force.com Fulfillment application. Clicking on the link to an order in the **Order Search** page will now display it in the **Orders** page:

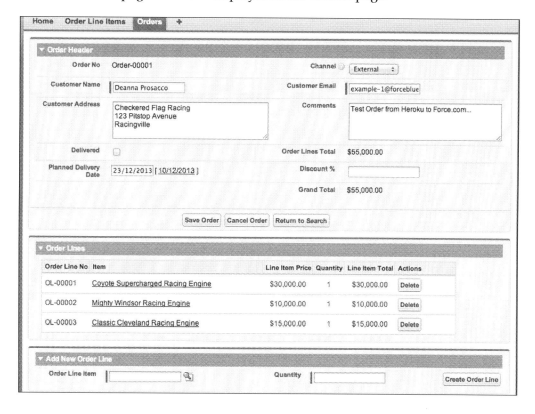

Clicking on the **Quantity** column of an order line will allow it to be edited:

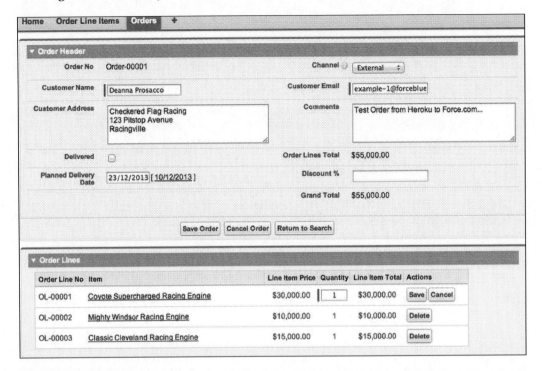

Summary

In this chapter, we built a fully functional Heroku powered e-commerce application and integrated it to our Force.com Fulfillment application.

We started by building a basic Force.com application and loading some sample data. We then built a Ruby on Rails / Heroku development environment and deployed a Ruby on Rails application to Heroku.

From there, we successfully integrated the Heroku e-commerce application to our Force.com application, which allowed us to display a product catalog and place orders. Users could also view their order status and order history in real time.

Finally, we implemented a full-blown Force.com application to handle order fulfillment using Visualforce and Apex custom controllers.

Some possible enhancements you could make are:

- Enhancing the product catalog in the Heroku e-commerce application to support the display of images from Force.com and display products in detail. (You will need to consult the `force.rb` gem documentation at `https://github.com/heroku/force.rb` to find out how to access attachments for a record.)

- Adding some Visualforce interface to the order line item detail page to add a more polished display.

- Adding some Ajax inline editing capabilities to the Heroku e-commerce application shopping cart. (Check out the bootstrap-editable-rails gem at `https://github.com/tkawa/bootstrap-editable-rails`.)

- Integrating the Salesforce product and price book functionality

Building a Full CRM System 3

In this chapter, we are going to build a more traditional CRM system to manage the student admissions process for the fictional **Force University**.

The student admissions system will allow the university staff to manage a catalog of courses, record the applicant details, and manage the course applications from applicants until a decision is made on whether the applicant is eligible or not.

In this process, we will be utilizing a great deal of the Force.com platform functionalities, which you will use to build your real-world applications, including the following:

- Custom data objects and relationships
- User profiles
- Organization-wide defaults and role hierarchy
- Chatter
- Custom object tabs
- Page layouts
- Lookup and search dialogs

We will also build a custom workflow to route the course applications to the relevant faculty within the university when they are created. The standard Force.com platform functionalities and workflows are not powerful enough for this, so we will construct a custom routing engine using queues, custom settings, and Apex.

Finally, we will implement a publisher action to allow a decision to be entered quickly against a course application.

Student admissions system requirements analysis

The first step in building a system is to analyze the business requirements that we intend to satisfy. The student admissions system will manage the overall process for admitting students into a university or higher education institution (for the rest of the chapter, I will be referring to a university).

The high-level business requirements of a system are as follows:

- The users of the system will be **course administrators**, the **admissions office staff**, and **faculty selection officers**

- The system will allow the course administrators to fully maintain the courses offered by the university

- The system will allow the admissions office staff to register applicants for a course and to register, manage, and allocate course applications to the faculty selection officers

- The system will allow the faculty selection officers to assess course applications and record their decisions

 I've highlighted the keywords that are crucial in helping us identify the functional, data, and security requirements, which are described in the following sections.

Functional requirements

A further analysis into business requirements yields the following functional requirements:

- The system will allow the course administrators to create, update, and delete courses that are offered by the university.

- The system will allow the admissions office staff to create, update, and delete applicants who wish to apply for a course.

- The system will allow the admissions office staff to create, update, and delete course applications.

- The system will allow the admissions office staff to assign a course application to the relevant faculty; for example, a business degree course application will be referred to the business faculty.

- Once a course application has been assigned to a faculty, the system will allow the faculty selection officers to assess it and record their decision.

- A successful course application will result in an admit, whereas an unsuccessful course application will result in denial.

Data requirements

Analyzing the business and functional requirements provides us with the following entities that we will need to record the information that we will be capturing in the system:

- The course entity will be used to record all of the individual courses offered by the university
- The applicant entity will be used to record the details of applicants who apply for a course
- The course application entity will be used to record an instance of an applicant applying for a course

The relationships between the entities are depicted in the following entity-relationship diagram:

The key cardinality rules for data requirements are as follows:

- An applicant may lodge one or more course applications
- A course application must have an applicant
- A course application must be linked to a course
- A course may have one or more course applications

 In Salesforce parlance, the course application is referred to as a junction object.

Security requirements

On Further analysis with business stakeholders, the following security requirements have been uncovered:

- Only the course administration staff can add, update, or delete courses. All other users will have read-only access.

- Only the admissions office staff can add, update, or delete applicants. The faculty selection officers will have read-only access.

- All the admissions office staff will have full access to all the course applications and their applicants.

- The faculty selection officers will only have access to the course applications they are assigned to within their faculty.

- The faculty management will have an access to all the course applications within their faculty.

Building the student admissions system

Now that we have captured all of the requirements for this version of the student admissions system (always assume there will be more requirements in the future!), we are in a position to build the system. Fortunately for us, the Force.com platform provides a rich base of functionalities we can leverage to build a comprehensive solution.

 You will find an unmanaged package that contains the application contents for this chapter at `https://login.salesforce.com/packaging/installPackage.apexp?p0=04t90000000ArFt`.

Defining the custom data objects

Our first task is to define the custom data objects we will require to capture information about the courses, applicants, and course applications.

Defining the Course object

Perform the following steps to configure the `Course` custom object:

1. Navigate to **Setup | Create | Objects**.

2. Click on the **New Custom Object** button.

3. Enter `Course` for the object's **Label** field.

4. Enter `Courses` for the **Plural Label** field.

5. Enter `A course offered by the University` for the **Description** field to describe the purpose of the custom object.

6. Enter `Course Code` for the **Record Name** field and change the **Data Type** drop-down menu to **Auto Number**.

7. Enter `Course-{00000}` in the **Display Format** field.
8. Enter `1` in the **Starting Number** field.
9. Select the following checkboxes:
    ◦ **Allow Reports** (an optional feature)
    ◦ **Allow Activities** (an optional feature)
    ◦ **Track Field History** (an optional feature)
    ◦ **Add Notes and Attachments related list to default page layout** (an object creation option)
10. Ensure that the **Deployment Status** section is set to **Deployed**.
11. Click on the **Save** button to create the custom object.

You will now need to configure the custom fields for the **Course** object.

1. If you aren't already on the **Course** object's detail page, navigate to **Setup Create | Objects**.
2. Click on the **Course** label hyperlink.
3. Click on the **New** button in the **Custom Fields & Relationships** section.
4. Create the fields described in the following table by accepting the Force.com default values for the field-level security and page layout assignments, unless otherwise specified, and clicking on **Save & New** after creating each field:

Field types	Field labels	Comments
Picklist	Faculty	This field indicates the faculty for the course. The **Picklist** values are `Business` and `Science`. Select the **Use first value as default value** checkbox.
Picklist	Faculty Course Area	This field indicates the courses offered by the faculty. The **Picklist** values are `Accounting`, `Management`, `Marketing`, `Chemistry`, `Physics`, and `Biotechnology`. Select both the **Sort values alphabetically not in the order entered. Values will be displayed alphabetically everywhere** and **Use first value as default value** checkboxes.

Field types	Field labels	Comments
Picklist	Achievement	This field indicates the academic achievement earned from the course The **Picklist** values are Diploma, Degree, and PhD. Select the **Use first value as default value** checkbox.
Text	Name	This field indicates the name of the course. Ensure that the **Required** and **Unique** checkboxes are selected, and set the maximum length to 255 characters.
Text Area	Description	This field gives an optional description of the course.

Finally, we need to set up a field dependency between the **Faculty** and **Faculty Course Area** picklists. This will ensure that when a faculty is selected, only the relevant faculty course areas will be available for selection.

To set up a field dependency, perform the following steps:

1. Navigate to **Setup | Create | Objects**.
2. Click on the **Course** label.
3. Click on the **Field Dependencies** button in the **Custom Fields & Relationships** section.
4. Click on **New** to create a new field dependency.
5. For the **Controlling Field** section, select **Faculty**.
6. For the **Dependent Field** section, select **Faculty Course Area**.
7. Click on **Continue**.
8. In the **Business** column, select **Accounting**, **Management**, and **Marketing**. Click on the **Include Values** button to include them in the **Business** column-dependent values.
9. In the **Science** column, select **Biotechnology**, **Chemistry**, and **Physics**. Click on the **Include Values** button to include them in the **Science** column-dependent values.
10. The output on your screen should resemble the following screenshot:

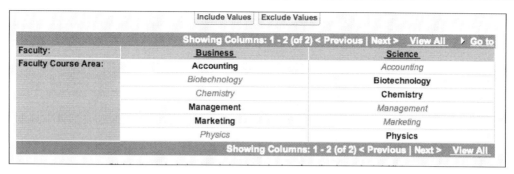

11. Click on **Preview** to display a pop-up dialog, where you can test out your field dependency.

12. When you have finished testing, click on **Close** in the pop-up dialog.

13. Click on **Save**.

> If you look at the **Custom Fields & Relationships** section for the Course object, you will now see that the **Controlling Field** section for **Faculty Course Area** fields has a value of **Faculty**.

Defining the Applicant object

Perform the following steps to configure the Applicant custom object:

1. Navigate to **Setup | Create | Objects**.

2. Click on the **New Custom Object** button.

3. Enter Applicant in the object's **Label** field.

4. Enter Applicants in the **Plural Label** field.

5. Enter A Person applying for a Course in the **Description** field to describe the purpose of the custom object.

6. Enter Applicant Code for the **Record Name** field and change the **Data Type** drop-down menu to **Auto Number**.

7. Enter Applicant-{00000} in the **Display Format** field.

8. Enter 1 in the **Starting Number** field.

9. Select the following checkboxes:

   ◦ **Allow Reports** (an optional feature)

   ◦ **Allow Activities** (an optional feature)

   ◦ **Track Field History** (an optional feature)

   ◦ **Add Notes and Attachments related list to default page layout** (an object creation option)

10. Ensure that the **Deployment Status** section is set to **Deployed**.

11. Click on the **Save** button to create the custom object.

You will now need to configure the custom fields for the **Applicant** object. For this, we will perform the following steps:

1. If you aren't already on the **Applicant** object's detail page, navigate to **Setup Create | Objects**.

2. Click on the **Applicant** label.

3. Click on the **New** button in the **Custom Fields & Relationships** section.

4. Create the fields described in the following table by accepting the default values of the Force.com functionalities for the field-level security and page layout assignments, unless otherwise specified, and clicking on **Save & New** after creating each field:

Field types	Field labels	Comments
Text	Salutation	This field lists the salutation for the applicant, for example, Mr. The maximum length is 50 characters.
Text	Given Names	The fields lists the name of the applicant. Ensure that the **Required** checkbox is selected and the maximum length is set to 255 characters.
Text	Surname	This field lists the surname of the applicant. Ensure that the **Required** checkbox is selected and the maximum length is set to 255 characters.
Picklist	Gender	The field lists the gender of the applicant. The **Picklist** values are Male and Female.

Field types	Field labels	Comments
Date	Date of Birth	This field lists the applicant's date of birth. Ensure that the **Required** checkbox is selected.
Text Area	Address	This field lists the applicant's address. The maximum length of this field is 255 characters. Ensure that the **Required** checkbox is selected.
Phone	Phone	This field lists the applicant's phone number.
Phone	Cell	This field lists the applicant's cell number.
Email	Email	This field lists the applicant's e-mail address.

Defining the Course Application object

Perform the following steps to configure the Course Application custom object:

1. Navigate to **Setup | Create | Objects**.
2. Click on the **New Custom Object** button.
3. Enter Course Application in the object **Label** field.
4. Enter Course Applications in the **Plural Label** field.
5. Enter An application for a course in the **Description** field to describe the purpose of the custom object.
6. Enter Application Number in the **Record Name** field and change the **Data Type** drop-down menu to **Auto Number**.
7. Enter Application-{00000} in the **Display Format** field.
8. Enter 1 in the **Starting Number** field.
9. Select the following checkboxes:
    ◦ **Allow Reports** (an optional feature)
    ◦ **Allow Activities** (an optional feature)
    ◦ **Track Field History** (an optional feature)
    ◦ **Add Notes and Attachments related list to default page layout** (object creation options)
10. Ensure that the **Deployment Status** section is set to **Deployed**.
11. Click on the **Save** button to create the custom object.

You will now need to configure the custom fields for the **Course Application** object. For this, we will perform the following steps:

1. If you aren't already on the **Course Application** detail page, navigate to **Setup** | **Create** | **Objects**.

2. Click on the **Course Application** label.

3. Click on the **New** button in the **Custom Fields & Relationships** section.

4. Create the fields described in the following table by accepting default values for the field-level security and page layout assignments of the Force.com functionalities, unless otherwise specified, and clicking on **Save & New** after creating each field:

Field types	Field labels	Comments
Lookup Relationship	`Applicant`	This field indicates the applicant who is applying for a course. A lookup relationship to the `Applicant` object. Ensure that the **Required** checkbox is selected.
Formula	`Applicant Name`	For this field, the following formula is to used : `Applicant__r.Salutation__c & " " & Applicant__r. Given_Names__c & " " & Applicant__r.Surname__c` In the **Blank Field Handling** section, select **Treat blank fields as blanks**.
Lookup Relationship	`Course`	This field indicates the course that is being applied for. A lookup relationship to the `Course` object. Ensure that the **Required** checkbox is selected. Do not add a related list to the **Course Layout** section in the last step of the wizard.
Formula	`Course Faculty`	For this field, the following formula is to be used: `TEXT(Course__r.Faculty__c)` In the **Blank Field Handling section**, select **Treat blank fields as blanks**. Do not add the field to the **Course Application** page layout.

Field types	Field labels	Comments
Formula	Course Name	For this field, the following formula is to be used: `Course__r.Name__c` In the **Blank Field Handling** section, select **Treat blank fields as blanks**.
Picklist	Application Status	This field indicates the status of the course application. The **Picklist** values are New, Queued For Assessment, Under Assessment, Under Conditional Approval, Closed – Admit Applicant, Closed – Application Denied, Withdrawn by Applicant, and Cancelled by Admissions. Select the **Use first value as default value** checkbox.
Text Area	Personal Qualifications	This field states any personal qualities that the applicant believes are relevant to the application.
Text Area	Academic Qualifications	This field states any academic qualifications that the applicant believes are relevant to the application.
Text Area	Employment Experience	This field states any employment experience that the applicant believes is relevant to the application.
Text Area	Professional Memberships	This field states any professional memberships that the applicant believes are relevant to the application.
Text Area	Decision Notes	This field states any notes relevant to the decision on the application.
Text Area	Decision Conditions	This field states any conditions on the application decision. This field will be mandatory when the status will be Under Conditional Approval.
Text Area	General Comments	This field states any general comments relevant to the application.

We need a validation rule to ensure that the decision conditions are mandatory when the application has a `Under Conditional Approval` status. To set up the validation rule, perform the following steps:

1. If you aren't already on the **Course Application** detail page, navigate to **Setup | Create | Objects**.

2. Click on the **Course Application** label.

3. Click on the **New** button in the **Validation Rules** section.

4. In the **Rule Name** field, enter `Conditional_Approval_Decision_ Conditions`.

5. In the **Description** field, enter `Ensure that Decision Conditions are entered when the application is under conditional approval`.

6. In the **Error Condition Formula** section, enter `ISPICKVAL( Application_ Status__c , "Under Conditional Approval") && ISBLANK( Decision_Conditions__c )`. Your formula on the screen should resemble the one given in the following screenshot:

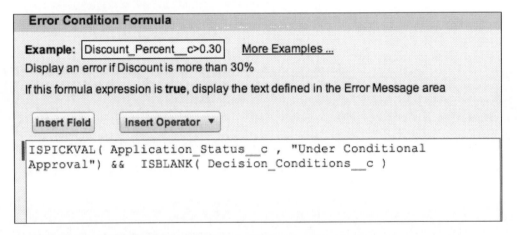

7. For the **Error Message** section, enter `You must enter Decision Conditions when a Course Application is under conditional approval`.

8. Select **Top of Page** for the **Error Location** section.

9. Click on **Save**.

User profiles

We will now configure the following three user profiles in our system:

- Course Administration (for the course administrators)
- Admissions Office (for the admissions office staff)
- Selection Officer (for the faculty selection officers)

This will ensure that only authorized users are able to access the student admissions' data.

The Course Administration profile

To create the Course Administration profile, perform the following steps:

1. Navigate to **Setup | Manage Users | Profiles**. A shortcut is to enter Profiles in the **Search** box.
2. Select the **Clone** link for the **Standard Platform User** profile.

 If your developer organization doesn't have a **Clone** link for the profiles, select the **New Profile** button and select **Standard Platform User** in the existing profiles drop-down list.

3. Enter Course Administration for the **Profile Name** field.
4. Click on **Save**.

We will now need to configure the **Course Administration** profile to restrict access to only those objects that the course administrators will need in the student admissions system. To do this, perform the following steps:

1. Navigate to **Setup | Manage Users | Profiles**.
2. Select the **Edit** link for the **Course Administration** profile.
3. Leave the **Standard Object Permissions** section with the default settings.
4. In the **Custom Object Permissions** section, ensure that the profile has the **Read, Create, Edit, Delete, View All,** and **Modify All** access options available to the **Courses** custom object.

5. Your **Custom Object Permissions** section for the profile should resemble the one in the following screenshot:

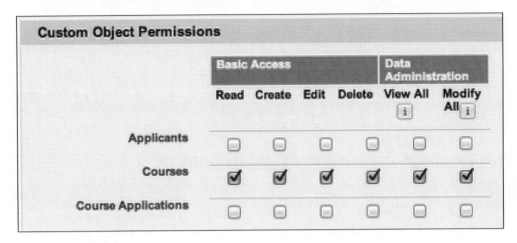

6. Click on **Save**.
7. Click on the **Back to Profile** button.

The Admissions Office profile

To create the Admissions Office profile, perform the following steps:

1. Navigate to **Setup | Manage Users | Profiles**.
2. Select the **Clone** link for the **Standard Platform User** profile.
3. Enter Admissions Office in the **Profile Name** field.
4. Click on **Save**.

We will now need to configure the **Admissions Office** profile to restrict access to only those objects that the admissions office staff will need in the student admissions system. To do this, perform the following steps:

1. Navigate to **Setup | Administer | Manage Users | Profiles**.
2. Select the **Edit** link for the **Admissions Office** profile.
3. Leave the **Standard Object Permissions** section with the default settings.
4. In the **Custom Object Permissions** section, ensure that the profile has **Read, Create, Edit, Delete, View All**, and **Modify All** access options available to the **Applicants** and **Course Applications** custom objects.
5. Ensure that the profile has a **Read** access to the **Courses** custom object.

6. Your **Custom Object Permissions** section for the profile should resemble the one in the following screenshot:

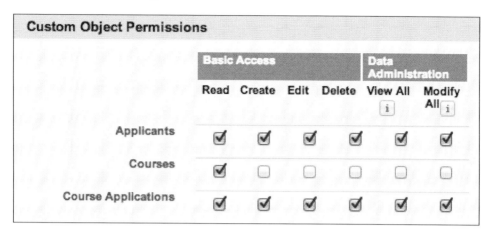

7. Click on **Save**.
8. Click on the **Back to Profile** button.

In a production application, you probably wouldn't allow anyone to have the **Delete** access option to the **Course Applications** object. It is likely that all **Course Applications** would need to be retained for auditing and reporting purposes, or if an applicant appeals against a decision. Instead of using the **Modify All** permission, you will need to use **Sharing Rules** to grant **Edit** access to all **Course Applications** for the **Admissions Office** profile.

The Selection Officer profile

To create the `Selection Officer` profile, perform the following steps:

1. Navigate to **Setup | Manage Users | Profiles**.
2. Select the **Clone** link for the **Standard Platform User** profile.
3. Enter `Selection Officer` in the **Profile Name** field.
4. Click on **Save**.

We will now need to configure the **Selection Officer** profile to restrict access to only those objects that the selection officers will need in the student admissions system. To do this, perform the following steps:

1. Navigate to **Setup | Administer | Manage Users | Profiles**.

2. Select the **Edit** link for the **Selection Officer** profile.

3. Leave the **Standard Object Permissions** section with the default settings.

4. In the **Custom Object Permissions** section, ensure that the profile has a **Read** and **Edit** access option to the **Course Applications** custom object.

5. Ensure that the profile has the **Read** access option to the **Courses** and **Applicants** custom objects.

6. Your **Custom Object Permissions** for the profile should resemble the one in the following screenshot:

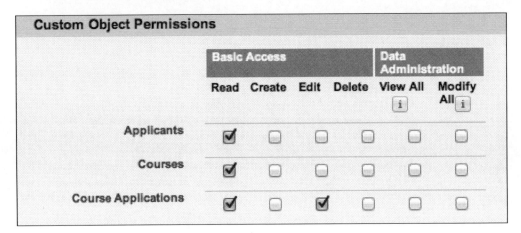

7. Click on **Save**.

8. Click on the **Back to Profile** button.

Organization-Wide Defaults

Now that we have configured the user profiles, we need to configure the **Organization-Wide Defaults** settings for our custom objects. The **Organization-Wide Defaults** values will provide the base-level record-sharing rules that we will build upon in the role hierarchy, which we will be configuring in the next section.

We will be setting the default values for **Applicants** and **Courses** to give all users in the role hierarchy the ability to see the records in the system. The role hierarchy permissions will then determine who can edit the records.

We will be setting the default values for **Course Applications** to the more restrictive private-sharing rule. This limits all record access to the owners of the course application records and users that we enable through the role hierarchy.

To configure the **Organization-Wide Defaults** section, perform the following steps:

1. Navigate to **Administer | Security Controls | Sharing Settings**.
2. In the **Organization-Wide Defaults** section, click on **Edit**.
3. For the **Applicant** object, set **Default Internal Access** to **Public Read Only**.
4. For the **Course** object, set **Default Internal Access** to **Public Read Only**.
5. For the **Course Application** object, set **Default Internal Access** to **Private**.
6. Ensure that **Grant Access Using Hierarchies** is checked for **Applicant**, **Course**, and **Course Application**.
7. Your configuration settings for **Organization-Wide Defaults** should resemble the one in the following screenshot:

8. Click on **Save**.

The role hierarchy

Our final task in configuring security of the users and data is to configure the following role hierarchy:

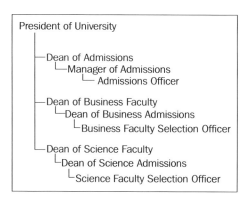

The role hierarchy will allow us to add permissions to the **Organization-Wide Defaults** values to give roles the extra permissions they need to perform their assigned tasks in the system.

Configuring the top-level roles

To configure the top-level role hierarchy, perform the following steps:

1. Navigate to **Setup** | **Administer** | **Manage Users** | **Roles**.

2. If a page titled **Understanding Roles** is displayed, click on **Set Up Roles**.

3. Click on the **+** symbol next to the **CEO** role to see a default role hierarchy generated by Force.com, as shown in the following screenshot:

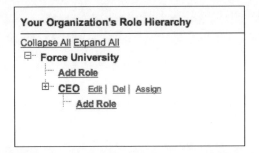

 For simplicity, this sample application we will be leaving the role of **CEO** and its subordinates intact. In a real production application, you would most likely edit the default role hierarchy to suit your needs.

4. Click on the **Add Role** link that is located directly underneath your organization name (in the current example, it is **Force University**).

5. Change the **Label** field to President of University.

6. Make sure that the **Role Name** field defaults to **President_of_University**.

7. Enter President in the **Role Name as displayed on reports** field.

8. Click on **Save**.

9. Return to the role hierarchy by navigating to **Setup** | **Administer** | **Manage Users** | **Roles** (you will need to perform this step after adding each role).

 If the **Understanding Roles** page is redisplayed, it is a good idea to select **Don't show this page again** before selecting **Set Up Roles**.

10. Click on the **Add Role** link located directly underneath the **President of University** role.

11. Change the **Label** field to `Dean of Admissions`. The **Role Name** field should automatically generate **Dean_of_Admissions**.

12. Make sure that the role reports to **President of University**.

13. Enter `Dean of Admissions` for **Role Name as displayed on reports**.

14. Click on **Save**.

15. Return to the role hierarchy and select the **Add Role** link located directly underneath the **President of University** role.

16. Change the **Label** field to `Dean of Business Faculty`. The **Role Name** field should automatically generate **Dean_of_Business_Faculty**.

17. Make sure that the role reports to **President of University**.

18. Enter `Dean of Business` in the **Role Name as displayed on reports** field.

19. Click on **Save**.

20. Return to the role hierarchy and select the **Add Role** link located directly underneath the **President of University** role.

21. Change the **Label** field to `Dean of Science Faculty`. The **Role Name** field should automatically generate **Dean_of_Science_Faculty**.

22. Make sure that the role reports to **President of University**.

23. Enter `Dean of Science` in the **Role Name as displayed on reports** field.

24. Click on **Save**.

25. Return to the role hierarchy. Click on the + button next to **President of University** to expand that branch. Your output on the screen should now resemble the following screenshot:

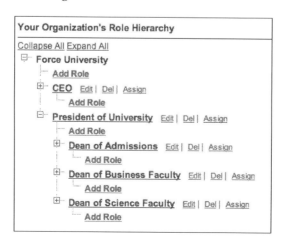

Configuring the admissions office hierarchy

To configure the admissions office hierarchy, perform the following steps:

1. Return to the role hierarchy and select the **Add Role** link located directly underneath the **Dean of Admissions** role.

2. Change the **Label** field to `Manager of Admissions`. The **Role Name** field should automatically generate **Manager_of_Admissions**.

3. Make sure that the role reports to **Dean of Admissions**.

4. Enter `Admissions Manager` in the **Role Name as displayed on** reports field.

5. Click on **Save**.

6. Return to the role hierarchy and expand the **Dean of Admissions** branch. Select the **Add Role** link located directly underneath the **Manager of Admissions** role.

7. Change the **Label** field to `Admissions Officer`. The **Role Name** field should automatically generate **Admissions_Officer**.

8. Make sure that the role reports to **Manager of Admissions**.

9. Enter `Admissions Officer` in the **Role Name as displayed on** reports field.

10. Click on **Save**.

11. Return to the role hierarchy. Click on the **+** button next to the **President of University** role, the **Dean of Admissions** role, and the **Manager of Admissions** role to expand those branches. Your output on the screen should now resemble the following screenshot:

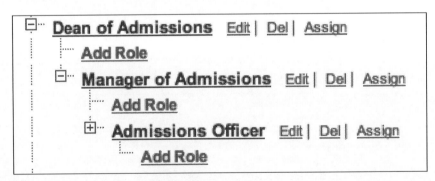

Configuring the business faculty hierarchy

To configure the business faculty hierarchy, perform the following steps:

1. Return to the role hierarchy and select the **Add Role** link located directly underneath the **Dean of Business Faculty** role.

2. Change the **Label** field to `Dean of Business Admissions`. The **Role Name** field should automatically generate **Dean_of_Business_Admissions**.

3. Make sure that the role reports to **Dean of Business Faculty**.

4. Enter `Dean of Business Admissions` in the **Role Name as displayed on reports** field.

5. Click on **Save**.

6. Return to the role hierarchy and expand the **Dean of Business Faculty** branch. Select the **Add Role** link located directly underneath the **Dean of Business Admissions** role.

7. Change the **Label** field to `Business Faculty Selection Officer`. The **Role Name** field should automatically generate **Business_Faculty_Selection_Officer**.

8. Make sure that the role reports to **Dean of Business Admissions**.

9. Enter `Business Selection Officer` in the **Role Name as displayed on reports** field.

10. Click on **Save**.

11. Return to the role hierarchy. Click on the **+** button next to the **President of University** role, the **Dean of Business Faculty** role, and the **Dean of Business Admissions** role to expand those branches. Your output on the screen should now resemble the following screenshot:

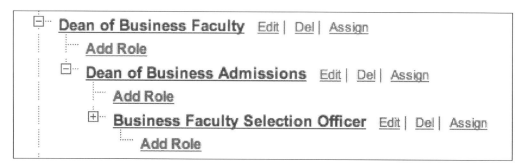

Configuring the science faculty hierarchy

To configure the science faculty hierarchy, perform the following steps:

1. Return to the role hierarchy and select the **Add Role** link located directly underneath the **Dean of Science Faculty** role.

2. Change the **Label** field to `Dean of Science Admissions`. The **Role Name** field should automatically generate **Dean_of_Science_Admissions**.

3. Make sure that the role reports to **Dean of Science Faculty**.

4. Enter `Dean of Science Admissions` in the **Role Name as displayed on reports** field.

5. Click on **Save**.

6. Return to the role hierarchy and select the **Add Role** link located directly underneath the **Dean of Science Admissions** role.

7. Change the **Label** field to `Science Faculty Selection Officer`. The **Role Name** field should automatically generate **Science_Faculty_Selection_Officer**.

8. Make sure the role reports to **Dean of Science Admissions**.

9. Enter `Science Selection Officer` for **Role Name as displayed on reports**.

10. Click on **Save**.

11. The university role hierarchy is complete and should now resemble the following screenshot:

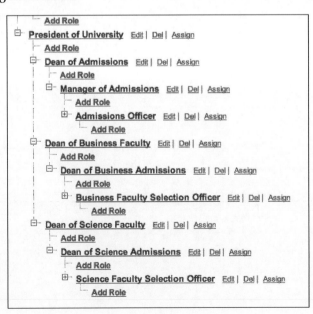

Chatter

Chatter is an integral part of the Force.com platform and the development of applications with social capabilities. The admissions process by its very nature requires collaboration across different areas of the university, so it makes perfect sense to use Chatter in our admissions system.

 In this section, it is assumed that you have already activated Chatter for your Salesforce organization. Note that Chatter is automatically enabled when a developer organization is created.

Enabling the Chatter feeds for Course

To enable the Chatter feeds for the **Course** object, perform the following steps:

1. Navigate to **Setup | Build | Customize | Chatter | Feed Tracking**.
2. In the list of objects being tracked, select **Course**.
3. Select the **Enable Feed Tracking** checkbox.
4. In the list of fields available to be tracked, select **Description**, **Faculty**, **Faculty Course Area**, and **Name**.
5. Click on **Save**.
6. Your Chatter feed tracking for **Course** should now resemble the following screenshot:

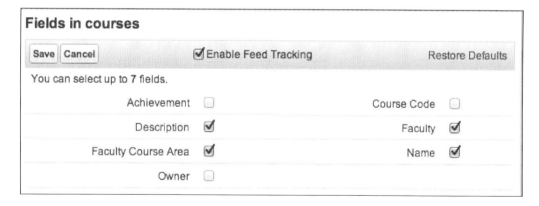

Enabling the Chatter feed for the **Course** object will add it at the top of the **Course** detail page, as shown in the following screenshot:

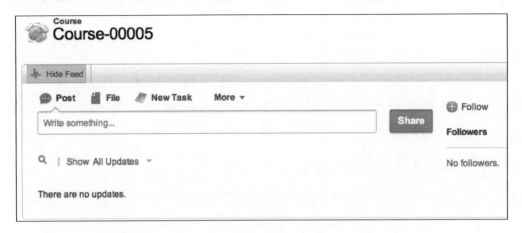

Enabling the Chatter feeds for Applicant

To enable the Chatter feed for the **Applicant** object, perform the following steps:

1. Navigate to **Setup | Build | Customize | Chatter | Feed Tracking**.

2. In the list of objects being tracked, select **Applicant**.

3. Select the **Enable Feed Tracking** checkbox.

4. In the list of fields available to be tracked, select **Address**, **Cell**, **Email**, **Given Names**, **Phone**, and **Surname**.

5. Click on **Save**.

6. Your Chatter feed tracking for **Applicant** should now resemble the following screenshot:

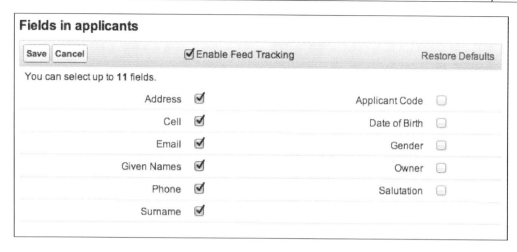

Enabling the Chatter feed for the **Applicant** object will add it at the top of the **Applicant** detail page:

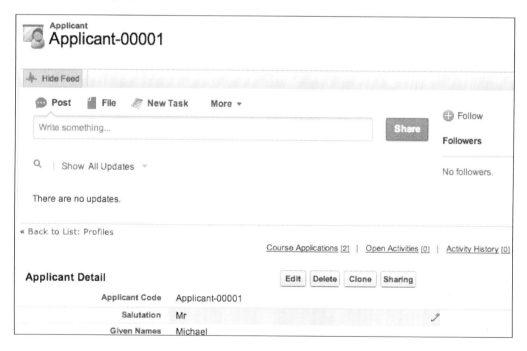

Enabling the Chatter feeds for Course Application

To enable the Chatter feed for the **Course Application** object, perform the following steps:

1. Navigate to **Setup | Build | Customize | Chatter | Feed Tracking**.

2. In the list of objects being tracked, select **Course Application**.

3. Select the **Enable Feed Tracking** checkbox.

4. In the list of fields available to be tracked, select **Academic Qualifications, Applicant, Application Status, Course, Decision Conditions, Decision Notes, Employment Experience, General Comments, Personal Qualifications,** and **Professional Memberships**.

5. Click on **Save**.

6. Your Chatter feed tracker for **Course Application** should now resemble the following screenshot:

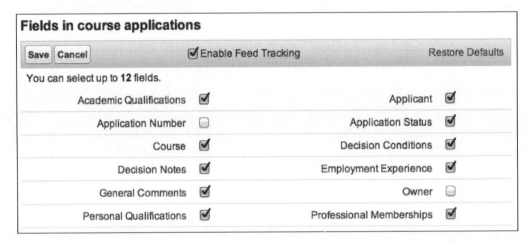

Enabling the Chatter feed for the **Course Application** object will add it at the top of the **Course Application** detail page, as shown in the following screenshot:

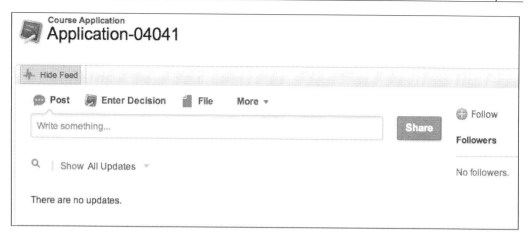

Defining the custom object tabs

To configure the tabs for the custom objects, perform the following steps:

1. Navigate to **Setup | Create | Tabs**.
2. Click on **New** in the **Custom Object Tabs** section.
3. In the **Object** drop-down list, select **Course**.
4. Select the lookup icon to set any unused tab style. Click on **Next**.
5. Select **Tab Hidden** as the default setting for all profiles. Click on **Next**.
6. Deselect all applications (a shortcut is to deselect the **Include Tab** checkbox) to ensure that this tab is not added. Leave **Append tab to user's existing personal customizations** checked.
7. Click on **Save**.
8. Click on **New** in the **Custom Object Tabs** section.
9. In the **Object** drop-down list, select **Applicant**.
10. Select the lookup icon to set any unused tab style. Click on **Next**.
11. Select **Tab Hidden** as the default setting for all profiles. Click on **Next**.
12. Deselect all applications (a shortcut is to deselect the **Include Tab** checkbox) to ensure that this tab is not added. Click on **Save**.
13. Click on **New** in the **Custom Object Tabs** section.
14. In the **Object** drop-down list, select **Course Application**.
15. Select **Tab Hidden** as the default setting for all profiles. Click on **Next**.
16. Accept the default settings for **Add to Profiles** and click on **Next**.

17. Deselect all applications to ensure that this tab is not added. Leave **Append tab to user's existing personal customizations** checked.

18. Click on **Save**.

Setting the tab permissions for profiles

We now need to set the correct tab visibility flags for each profile in the application, and this can be done by performing the following steps:

1. Navigate to **Setup | Administer | Manage Users | Profiles**.

2. Select the **Course Administrator** profile.

3. Click on **Edit**.

4. In the **Tab Settings** section, set the **Courses** tab to **Default On**.

5. Click on **Save**.

6. Select the **Selection Officer** profile.

7. Click on **Edit**.

8. In the **Tab Settings** section, set the **Course Applications** tab to **Default On** and the **Applicants** tab to **Default On**.

9. Click on **Save**.

10. Select the **Admissions Office** profile.

11. Click on **Edit**.

12. In the **Tab Settings** section, set the **Course Applications** tab to **Default On**, the **Courses** tab to **Default On**, and the **Applicants** tab to **Default On**.

13. Click on **Save**.

14. Select the **System Administrator** profile.

15. Click on **Edit**.

16. In the **Tab Settings** section, set the **Course Applications** tab to **Default On**, the **Courses** tab to **Default On**, and the **Applicants** tab to **Default On**.

17. Click on **Save**.

Creating the Force.com application

To define the admissions Force.com application, perform the following steps:

1. Navigate to **Setup | Create | Apps**.

2. Click on the **New** button in the **Apps** section.

3. Select **Custom app** as the type of app to create. Click on **Next**.

4. In the **App Label** field, enter Admissions. The **App Name** field should also be defaulted to **Admissions**. Click on **Next**.

5. Click on **Next** to accept the default logo.

6. Move the **Courses, Applicants**, and **Course Applications** tabs to the **Selected Tabs** list.

7. Leave **Home** as the **Default Landing Tab** option. Click on **Next**.

8. Make the application visible to the **System Administrators, Admissions Office, Course Administration**, and **Selection Officer** profiles.

9. Set **Admissions** as the default application for the **Admissions Office, Course Administration**, and **Selection Officer** profiles.

10. Click on **Save** to create the Force.com application.

The user interface

Now that we have the base Force.com application in place, we can customize the default user interface to make it more intuitive for users.

Applicants

Firstly, we will adjust the **Applicant** page layout by performing the following steps:

1. Navigate to **Setup | Build | Create | Objects**.

2. Click on the **Applicant** label.

3. Scroll down to the **Page Layouts** section and select the **Edit** link next to the **Applicant Layout** option.

4. Scroll down to the **Related Lists** section.

5. Move the list related to **Course Applications** at the top of the **Related Lists** section.

6. Select the wrench icon for the list related to **Course Applications**.

7. Remove the **Applicant Name** option from the **Selected Fields** list.

8. In the **Sort By:** drop-down list, select **Application Number** and **Descending** as the sort order (this will show the most recent applications first in the related list). Click on **OK** to close the **Related List Properties – Course Applications** window, as shown in the following screenshot:

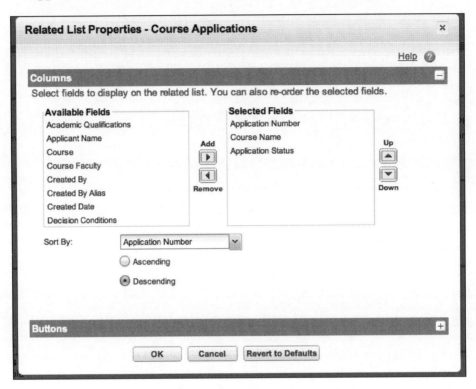

9. Click on **Save**.

The **Lookup Dialog** layout for **Applicants** will also need to be modified; this can be done by completing the following steps:

1. Scroll down to the **Search Layouts** section and select the **Edit** link next to the **Lookup Dialogs** layout.

2. Move the **Salutation, Given Names, Surname**, and **Date of Birth** fields (in this order) to the **Selected Fields** list.

3. Click on **Save**.

Courses

The default page layout for **Courses** will suffice for our needs; however, we will adjust the **Lookup Dialogs** and **Mini View** layouts for **Courses** with the following steps:

1. Navigate to **Setup | Create | Objects**.
2. Click on the **Course** label hyperlink.
3. Scroll down to the **Search Layouts** section and select the **Edit** link next to the **Lookup Dialogs** layout.
4. Move the **Name**, **Achievement**, **Faculty**, and **Faculty Course Area** fields (in this order) to the **Selected Fields** list.
5. Click on **Save**.

The **Mini View** page layout is displayed when you move the cursor over the **Course** field in the **Course Application Detail** page, as shown in the following screenshot:

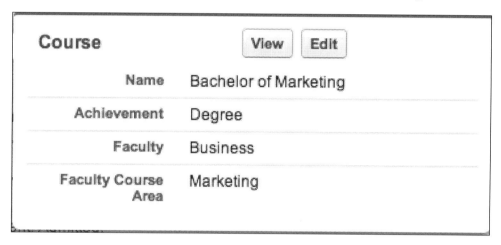

To adjust the **Mini View** page layout, perform the following steps:

1. Scroll down to the **Page Layouts** section and select the **Edit** link next to the **Course Layout** option.

2. Select **Mini Page Layout** from the top-right row of hyperlinks, as shown in the following screenshot:

3. Move the **Name, Achievement, Faculty,** and **Faculty Course Area** fields (in this order) to the **Selected Fields** list.

4. Click on **Save**.

5. Click on **Save** in the page layout editor.

The Course Application page layout

Next, we will adjust the **Course Application** page layout by completing the following steps:

1. Navigate to **Setup | Create | Objects**.

2. Click on the **Course Application** label.

3. Scroll down to the **Page Layouts** section and select the **Edit** link next to **Course Application Layout** option.

4. Drag a new section from the palette. Place it underneath the existing **Information** section and name it Decision Information. Ensure that the new section has two columns. Click on **OK**.

5. Drag the **Decision Notes** field from its existing position on the screen to the **Decision Information** section.

6. Drag the **Decision Conditions** field from its existing position on the screen to the **Decision Information** section.

7. Drag the **General Comments** field from its existing position on the screen underneath the **Decision Notes** field.

8. Drag the **Applicant Name** field from its existing position on the screen next to the **Applicant** field.

9. Drag the **Course Name** field from its existing position on the screen next to the **Course** field.

10. Add a blank space from the palette underneath the **Course** and **Course Name** fields.

11. Add a blank space from the palette next to the **Application Status** field.

12. Add two **Blank Space** components from the palette underneath the **Application Status** field (one in the left-hand side column and one in the right-hand side column).

13. Drag the **Academic Qualifications** field from its existing position on the screen next to the **Personal Qualifications** field.

14. Drag the **Professional Memberships** field from its existing position on the screen next to the **Employment Experience** field.

15. Your **Course Application** page layout should now resemble the following screenshot:

16. Click on **Quick Save**.

17. Select **Mini Page Layout** from the top-right row of hyperlinks.

18. Move the **Application Number** and **Application Status** fields to the **Selected Fields** list in this order (**Applicant** and **Course** should already be in the **Selected Fields** list).

19. Click on **Save**.

20. Click on **Save** in the page layout editor.

The Applicants tab

Similar to the **Courses** tab, we will adjust the **Applicants** tab by completing the following steps:

1. Navigate to **Setup | Create | Objects**.

2. Click on the **Applicant** label.

3. Scroll down to the **Search Layouts** section and select the **Edit** link next to the **Applicants Tab** layout, as shown in the following screenshot:

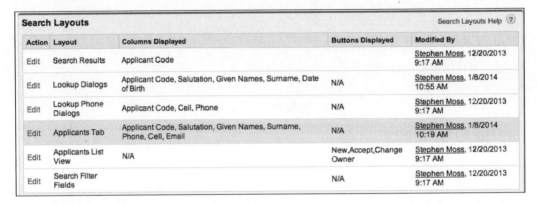

4. Move the **Salutation**, **Given Names**, **Surname**, **Phone**, **Cell**, and **Email** fields (in this order) to the **Selected Fields** list.

5. Click on **Save**.

We will also need to adjust the **Applicants** tab listview columns while viewing all the **Applicant** records by performing the following steps:

1. Select the **Applicants** tab.

2. In the **View:** drop-down list, ensure that **All** is selected (it should be the only item in the list unless you have already created some custom views), and click on the **Edit** hyperlink, as displayed in the following screenshot:

3. Scroll down to the **Step 3. Select Fields to Display** section.

4. Move the **Applicant Code, Salutation, Given Names, Surname, Phone, Cell,** and **Email** fields (in this order) to the **Selected Fields** list.

5. In the **Step 4. Restrict Visibility** section, ensure that **Visible to all users (Includes partner and customer portal users)** is selected.

6. Click on **Save**.

The Courses tab

Next, we will adjust the **Courses** tab by completing the following steps:

1. Navigate to **Setup | Create | Objects**.

2. Click on the **Course** label hyperlink.

3. Scroll down to the **Search Layouts** section and select the **Edit** link next to the **Courses Tab** layout.

4. Move the **Name, Achievement, Faculty,** and **Faculty Course Area** fields (in order) to the **Selected Fields** list (**Course Code** should already be selected).

5. Click on **Save**.

We will also need to adjust the **Courses** tab listview columns while viewing all the **Course** records with the following steps:

1. Select the **Courses** tab.

2. In the **View:** drop-down list, ensure that **All** is selected (it should be the only item in the list unless you have already created some custom views), and click on the **Edit** hyperlink, as shown in the following screenshot:

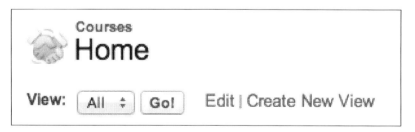

3. Scroll down to the **Step 3. Select Fields to Display** section.

4. Move the **Course Code, Name, Achievement, Faculty,** and **Faculty Course Area** fields (in this order) to the **Selected Fields** list.

5. In the **Step 4. Restrict Visibility** section, ensure that **Visible to all users (Includes partner and customer portal users)** is selected.

6. Click on **Save**.

The Course Applications tab

We will also need to adjust the **Course Applications** tab by completing the following steps:

1. Navigate to **Setup | Create | Objects**.

2. Click on the **Course Application** label.

3. Scroll down to the **Search Layouts** section and select the **Edit** link next to the **Course Applications Tab** layout.

4. Move the **Applicant Name, Course Name**, and **Application Status** fields (in this order) to the **Selected Fields** list.

5. Click on **Save**.

We will also need to adjust the **Course Applications** tab listview columns while viewing all the **Course Application** records:

1. Select the **Course Applications** tab.

2. In the **View:** drop-down list, ensure that **All** is selected (it should be the only item in the list unless you have already created some custom views), and click on the **Edit** hyperlink, as shown in the following screenshot:

3. Scroll down to the **Step 3. Select Fields to Display** section.

4. Move the **Application Number, Applicant Name, Course Name**, and **Application Status** fields (in this order) to the **Selected Fields** list.

5. In the **Step 4. Restrict Visibility** section, ensure that **Visible to all users (Includes partner and customer portal users)** is selected.

6. Click on **Save**.

Queues

In this section, we will create a set of queues that will be instrumental in developing a workflow capability to automatically route the course applications to the various faculties within the university when they are created.

The system administrators public group

The first task is to set up a public group for system administrator user(s). A public group is different from a profile as it contains roles, users, and other public groups. This will become necessary when we start to restrict access to the queues that we will be creating in the later sections. To set up a public group for the system administrators, perform the following steps:

1. Navigate to **Setup** | **Manage Users** | **Public Groups**.
2. Click on **New**.
3. In the **Label** field, enter System Administrators.
4. The **Group Name** field should default to **System_Administrators**.
5. Select **Users** in the **Search:** drop-down list.
6. In the **Available Members** list, select all system administrator users and move them to the **Selected Members** list.
7. Click on **Save**.

The Business Faculty Course Applications queue

To create a queue for the course applications to the business faculty, perform the following steps:

1. Navigate to **Setup** | **Manage Users** | **Queues**.
2. Click on **New**.
3. In the **Label** field, enter Business Faculty Course Applications.
4. The **Queue Name** field should default to **Business_Faculty_Course_Applications**.
5. Enter business@forceuniversity.com for the **Queue Email** field.
6. In the **Supported Objects** section, move **Course Application** to the **Selected Objects** list.
7. In the **Queue Members** section, select **Roles and Internal Subordinates** in the **Search:** drop-down list.

8. In the **Available Members** list, select **Role and Internal Subordinates: Dean of Business Faculty** and move it to the **Selected Members** list.

9. In the **Queue Members** section, select **Public Groups** in the **Search:** drop-down list.

10. In the **Available Members** list, select **Group: System Administrators** and move it to the **Selected Members** list.

11. Click on **Save**.

The Science Faculty Course Applications queue

To create a queue for the course applications to the science faculty, perform the following steps:

1. Navigate to **Setup | Manage Users | Queues**.

2. Click on **New**.

3. In the **Label** field, enter `Science Faculty Course Applications`.

4. The **Queue Name** field should default to **Science_Faculty_Course_Applications**.

5. Enter `science@forceuniversity.com` in the **Queue Email** field.

6. In the **Supported Objects** section, move **Course Application** to the **Selected Objects** list.

7. In the **Queue Members** section, select **Roles and Internal Subordinates** in the **Search:** drop-down list.

8. In the **Available Members** list, select **Role and Internal Subordinates: Dean of Science Faculty** and move it to the **Selected Members** list.

9. In the **Queue Members** section, select **Public Groups** in the **Search:** drop-down list.

10. In the **Available Members** list, select **Group: System Administrators** and move it to the **Selected Members** list.

11. Click on **Save**.

The Course Application Exception queue

In a real-world application, it is frequently necessary to capture exceptions when they occur so that the support and administrative staff can action them where appropriate. To support this, we will create an exceptions queue for the course applications that can't be routed automatically to a faculty.

To create the exceptions queue, perform the following steps:

1. Navigate to **Setup** | **Manage Users** | **Queues**.

2. Click on **New**.

3. In the **Label** field, enter `Course Application Exception Queue`.

4. The **Queue Name** field should default to **Course_Application_Exception_Queue**.

5. Enter `administrator@forceuniversity.com` for the **Queue Email** field.

6. In the **Supported Objects** section, move **Course Application** to the **Selected Objects** list.

7. In the **Queue Members** section, select **Public Groups** in the **Search:** drop-down list.

8. In the **Available Members** list, select **Group: System Administrators** and move it to the **Selected Members** list.

9. Click on **Save**.

Restricting access to the business faculty queue

We only want members of the business faculty to be able to view and access the course applications in their queue. This is achieved by creating a view on the **Course Applications** tab and adjusting the permissions on the view. It is also necessary to ensure that system administrators can access the queue to provide administrative support.

To restrict access to the business faculty queue, perform the following steps:

1. Select the **Course Applications** tab, as shown in the following screenshot:

2. In the **View:** drop-down list, click on the **Create New View** hyperlink, as shown in the following screenshot:

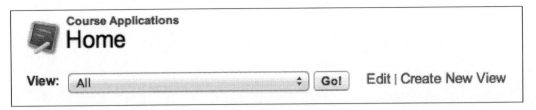

3. The **View Name** field will be highlighted. Enter `Business Faculty Course Applications`.

4. The **View Unique Name** field should default to **Business_Faculty_Course_Applications**, as shown in the following screenshot:

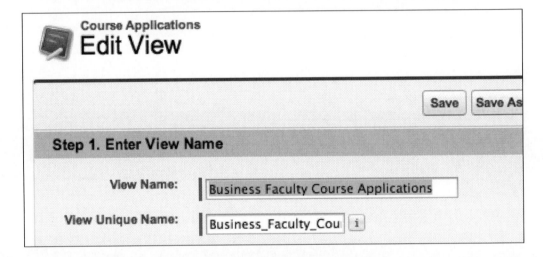

5. In the **Step 2. Specify Filter Criteria** section, select **Queue** and select **Business Faculty Course Applications** from the drop-down list, as shown in the following screenshot:

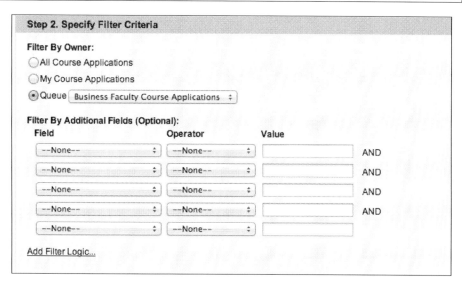

6. Scroll down to the **Step 3. Select Fields to Display** section.

7. Move the **Application Number**, **Applicant Name**, **Course Name**, and **Application Status** fields (in this order) to the **Selected Fields** list, as shown in the following screenshot:

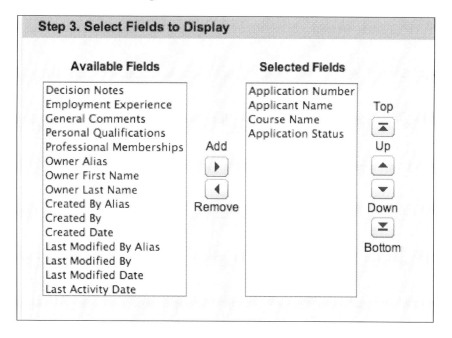

8. In the **Step 4. Restrict Visibility** section, remove **All Internal Users** from the **Shared To** list.

9. Select **Public Groups** in the **Search:** drop-down list.

10. In the **Available Members** list, select **Group: System Administrators** and move it to the **Selected Members** list.

11. In the **Queue Members** section, select **Roles and Internal Subordinates** in the **Search:** drop-down list.

12. In the **Available Members** list, select **Role and Internal Subordinates: Dean of Business Faculty** and move it to the **Shared To** list, as shown in the following screenshot:

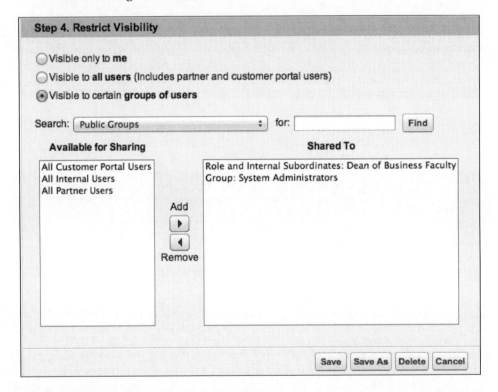

13. Click on **Save**.

Restricting access to the science faculty queue

In a similar vein to the business faculty, we only want members of the science faculty to be able to view and access the course applications in their queue. This is achieved by creating a view on the **Course Applications** tab and adjusting the permissions on the view. Again, it is also necessary to ensure that system administrators can access the queue to provide administrative support.

To restrict access to the science faculty queue, perform the following steps:

1. Select the **Course Applications** tab.

2. In the **View:** drop-down list, click on the **Create New View** hyperlink.

3. The **View Name** field will be highlighted. Enter `Science Faculty Course Applications`.

4. The **View Unique Name** field should default to **Science_Faculty_Course_Applications**, as shown in the following screenshot:

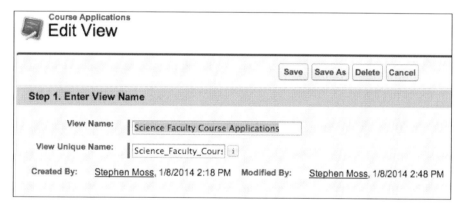

5. In the **Specify Filter Criteria** section, select **Queue** and select **Science Faculty Course Applications** from the drop-down list, as shown in the following screenshot:

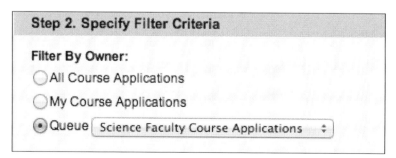

6. Scroll down to the **Step 3. Select Fields to Display** section.

7. Move the **Application Number, Applicant Name, Course Name**, and **Application Status** fields (in this order) to the **Selected Fields** list.

8. In the **Step 4. Restrict Visibility** section; remove **All Internal Users** from the **Shared To** list.

9. Select **Public Groups** in the **Search:** drop-down list.

10. In the **Available Members** list, select **Group: System Administrators** and move it to the **Selected Members** list.

11. In the **Queue Members** section, select **Roles and Internal Subordinates** in the **Search:** drop-down list.

12. In the **Available Members** list, select **Role and Internal Subordinates: Dean of Science Faculty** and move it to the **Shared To** list, as shown in the following screenshot:

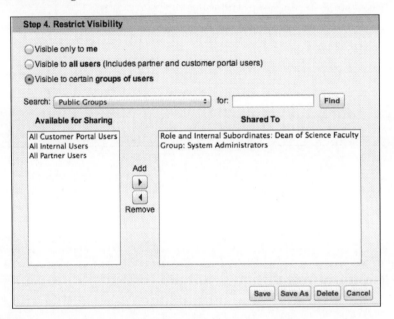

13. Click on **Save**.

Restricting access to the exceptions queue

Finally, it is necessary to ensure that only system administrators can access the exceptions queue. This is achieved by creating a view on the **Course Applications** tab and adjusting the permissions on the view.

To restrict access to the exceptions queue, perform the following steps:

1. Select the **Course Applications** tab.

2. In the **View:** drop-down list, select **Course Applications Exception Queue** and click on the **Create New View** hyperlink.

3. The **View Name** field will be highlighted. Enter Course Application Exception Queue.

4. The **View Unique Name** field should default to **Course_Application_ Exception_Queue**.

5. In the **Specify Filter Criteria** section, select **Queue** and select **Course Application Exception Queue** from the drop-down list, as shown in the following screenshot:

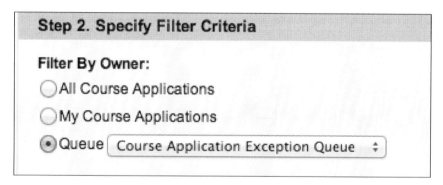

6. Scroll down to the **Step 3. Select Fields to Display** section.

7. Move the **Application Number**, **Applicant Name**, **Course Name**, and **Application Status** fields (in this order) to the **Selected Fields** list.

8. In the **Step 4. Restrict Visibility** section, remove **All Internal Users** from the **Shared To** list.

9. Select **Public Groups** in the **Search:** drop-down list.

10. In the **Available Members** list, select **Group: System Administrators** and move it to the **Selected Members** list, as shown in the following screenshot:

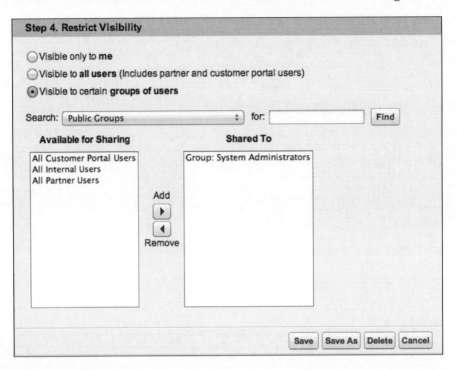

11. Click on **Save**.

Custom settings

We will use the custom settings capability of Force.com to provide a mapping between a faculty and the Force.com queues we have created. This will allow us to simplify our Apex trigger logic that will do the actual assignment to a faculty queue in the next section.

To create the custom settings for the queue mappings, perform the following steps:

1. Go to **Setup | Develop | Custom Settings**.
2. Click on **New**.
3. In the **Label** field, enter Admissions Faculty Queues.
4. In the **Object Name** field, enter FacultyQueueMapping.
5. Select **List** from the **Setting Type** drop-down list.
6. Select **Protected** from the **Visibility** drop-down list.

7. For the **Description** field, enter `Mapping to a Course Application queue for a Faculty`.

8. Click on **Save**.

You will need to add some custom fields to the custom settings, which can be done by completing the following steps:

1. Go to **Setup** | **Develop** | **Custom Settings**.

2. Click on **Admissions Faculty Queues** in the **Label** column.

3. Click on **New** in the **Custom Fields** section.

4. Select **Text** for the **Data Type** section. Click on **Next**.

5. In **Field Label**, enter `Faculty`.

6. Enter `50` in the **Length** field.

7. Ensure that the **Required** checkbox is selected.

8. Ensure that the **Unique** checkbox is selected, and that duplicate matches are set to **case sensitive**.

9. Click on **Next**, and in the final screen, click on **Save & New**.

10. Perform similar steps to create the remaining custom fields specified in the following table:

Field label	Type	Length	Comments
QueueCode	**Text**	100	**Required**: Yes
			Unique: Yes (case sensitive)
Description	**Text**	255	**Required**: No
			Unique: No

Finally, we will create the custom setting entries by completing the following steps:

1. Go to **Setup** | **Build** | **Develop** | **Custom Settings**.

2. Click on **Admissions Faculty Queues** in the **Label** column.

3. Click on **Manage** and then click on **New**.

4. Enter `BusinessFacultyQueue` in the **Name** field.

5. Enter `Business` in the **Faculty** field.

6. Enter `Business_Faculty_Course_Applications` in the **QueueCode** field.

7. Enter `Queue Mapping for Business Faculty Course Applications` in the **Description** field.

8. Click on **Save & New**.

9. Enter `ScienceFacultyQueue` in the **Name** field.

10. Enter `Science` in the **Faculty** field.

11. Enter `Science_Faculty_Course_Applications` in the **QueueCode** field.

12. Enter `Queue Mapping for Science Faculty Course Applications` in the **Description** field.

13. Click on **Save & New**.

14. Enter `ExceptionQueue` in the **Name** field.

15. Enter `Exception` in the **Faculty** field.

16. Enter `Course_Application_Exception_Queue` in the **QueueCode** field.

17. Enter `Queue Mapping for exceptioned Course Applications` in the **Description** field.

18. Click on **Save**.

The Course Application routing logic

Now that the queues are in place, we can complete the logic required to automatically route a course application to the relevant faculty within the university.

Building the faculty assignment Apex trigger

We will use an Apex trigger on the before insert event of a course application to route it to a faculty queue. The primary responsibilities of the trigger will be to determine the faculty to Force.com queue mappings and route the course application to the correct faculty queue. The faculty assignment will be determined by the course that the applicant is applying for.

To create the faculty assignment Apex trigger, perform the following steps:

1. Navigate to **Setup | Develop | Apex Triggers**.

2. All of the Apex triggers for your organization will be displayed. Click on **Developer Console**.

3. Go to **File | New | Apex Trigger** in the developer console.

4. Enter `assignToFacultyQueue` in the **Name** field.

5. Select **Course_Application__c** in the **sObject** drop-down list and click on **Submit**, as shown in the following screenshot:

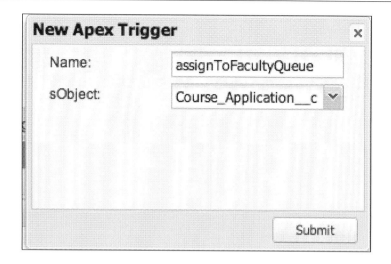

6. In the code download for this chapter, locate the `assignToFacultyQueue.trigger` file.

7. Clear the existing code, copy, and paste the contents of `assignToFacultyQueue.trigger` to the developer console code-editing window, as shown in the following screenshot:

```
Code Coverage: None                                                              Go To
 1 trigger assignToFacultyQueue on Course_Application__c (before insert) {
 2
 3     System.debug(LoggingLevel.DEBUG, '*** Executing Apex Trigger assignToFacultyQueue...');
 4
 5     try {
 6
 7         // retrieve the queue information
 8         System.debug(LoggingLevel.DEBUG, '*** Retrieving Force.com Queues...');
 9         List<Group> queues = [SELECT Id, DeveloperName, Type
10                               FROM Group
11                               WHERE Type = 'Queue'];
12
13         // Map to hold Queue information mapped to each queue code
14         Map<string, Group> facultyQueues = new Map<string, Group>();
15
```

8. Navigate to **File | Save**.

How the faculty queue assignment trigger works

For this, we will start by retrieving the Force.com queues that we configured earlier with the following code:

```
// retrieve the queue information
List<Group> queues = [SELECT Id, DeveloperName, Type
                      FROM Group
                      WHERE Type = 'Queue'];
```

We then load the queue information onto Map, keyed by DeveloperName for each queue (which corresponds to the queue name we used when we configured the queues) with the following code:

```
// Map to hold Queue information mapped to each queue code
Map<string, Group> facultyQueues = new Map<string, Group>();

// construct the map of Faculty Queues
for (Group queue : queues) {
  facultyQueues.put(queue.DeveloperName, queue);
}
```

Next, we define Map which will hold the unique queue identifier for each faculty with the following code:

```
// Map to hold Queue Mappings
// string = the Faculty the queue is assigned to
// string = the Force.com unique Id for the queue
Map<string, string> facultyQueueMappings = new Map<string,
  string>();
```

The final piece of information we need to complete the faculty to queue mappings are the custom settings we defined earlier, and this is done by using the following code:

```
// get the custom setting information
List<FacultyQueueMapping__c> facultyQueueMappingsList =
  FacultyQueueMapping__c.getAll().values();
```

Now, we can map each faculty to a corresponding Force.com queue using the following code:

```
for (FacultyQueueMapping__c facultyQueueMapping :
            facultyQueueMappingsList) {
  Group facultyQueue =                    facultyQueues.
get(facultyQueueMapping.QueueCode__c);
```

```
    // if the queue exists, map it to the Faculty
    if (facultyQueue != null) {
      facultyQueueMappings.put(
            facultyQueueMapping.Faculty__c,                 facultyQueue.
  Id);
    }
  }
```

With the faculty to queue mappings in place, we can now assign the course application to the correct faculty by using the following code:

```
for (Course_Application__c courseApplication : trigger.new) {
    // assign Course Application to Faculty queue
    string queueId = facultyQueueMappings.get(
          courseApplication.Course_Faculty__c);
    if (queueId != null) {
      courseApplication.OwnerId = queueId;
    } else {
      // assign Course Application to Exception Queue
      string exceptionQueueId =                 facultyQueueMappings.
  get('Exception');
      courseApplication.OwnerId = exceptionQueueId;
    }
}
```

 Even though currently we expect only a single course application to be processed at a time, we are still using a **bulkified** trigger, which is a Salesforce best practice. You should always write your triggers in this fashion.

Testing the faculty queue assignment trigger

As a bonus, I've included the `testFacultyQueueAssignment.cls` file in the code download for this chapter. This is the test class that I used to test the faculty assignment trigger while developing the application for this chapter.

To create the faculty assignment Apex trigger, perform the following steps:

1. Navigate to **Setup | Develop | Apex Classes**.
2. All of the Apex classes for your organization will be displayed. Click on **New**.
3. In the code download for this chapter, locate the `testFacultyQueueAssignment.cls` file.
4. Copy and paste the contents of `testFacultyQueueAssignment.cls` to the Apex code editor in your Force.com window.

5. Click on **Save**.

 I highly recommend that you take time to study the code in `testFacultyQueueAssignment.cls` as there are quite a few things you need to take into account while writing the code to test the custom settings and assign records to a queue.

A decision entry publisher action

As a final touch, we will add a publisher action to the **Course Application** object. This will allow a selection officer to quickly enter a selection decision against an application.

Enabling the publisher actions

If the publisher actions are not enabled already, you will need to enable them in your organization. To enable the publisher actions, perform the following steps:

1. Navigate to **Setup** | **Customize** | **Chatter** | **Settings**.

2. Click on **Edit**.

3. Scroll down to **Publisher Actions** and select the **Enable Publisher Actions** checkbox, as shown in the following screenshot:

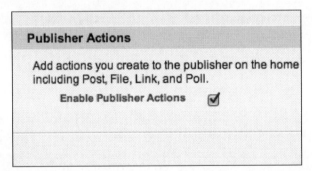

4. Click on **Save**.

Developing the publisher action

Now we can develop a publisher action for an entry of a decision. While developing a publisher action, you need to think about what the user is trying to achieve, and the bare minimum of information that needs to be added or updated. Also, to make life easier for users (especially on mobile devices), you can specify the default values that are independent of those defined for a Force.com object.

To develop the publisher action, perform the following steps:

1. Navigate to **Setup | Create | Objects**.
2. Click on the **Course Application** label.
3. Scroll down to the **Buttons, Links, and Actions** section.
4. Click on **New Action**.
5. Select **Update a Record** from the **Action Type** drop-down list.
6. Specify `Enter Decision` in the **Label** field.
7. Leave **None** selected in the **Standard Label Type** field.
8. In the **Description** field, enter `Publisher Action to allow a Selection Officer to quickly enter a decision`.
9. Your screen should now resemble the following screenshot:

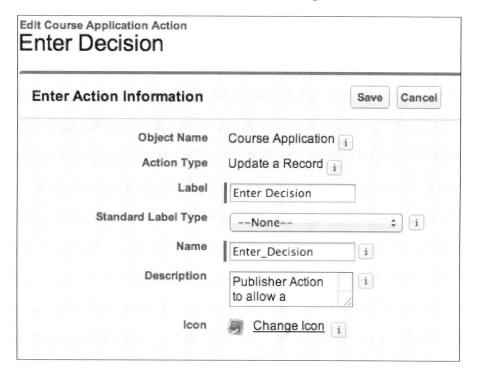

10. Click on **Save**.

11. You will now be directed to the publisher layout editor. Add the **Blank Space**, **Application Status**, **Decision Notes**, and **Decision Conditions** fields and rearrange the fields in the layout so that your publisher layout editor resembles the following screenshot:

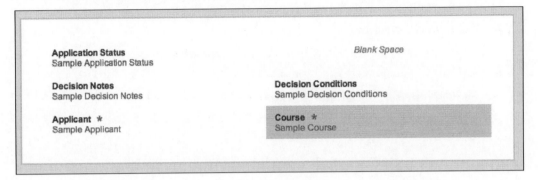

12. Click on **Save**.

13. You will now be returned to the **Enter Decision** detail page.

14. Click on **New** in the **Predefined Field Values** section.

15. Select **Application Status** in the **Field Name** drop-down list.

16. Select **Closed – Admit Applicant** in the **A specific value** drop-down list.

17. Click on **Save**.

Adding the publisher action to the Chatter feed

To add the **Enter Decision** action to the Chatter feed for the course application, perform the following steps:

1. Navigate to **Setup | Create | Objects**.

2. Click on the **Course Application** label.

3. Scroll down to the **Page Layouts** section and select the **Edit** link next to **Course Application Layout**.

4. In the **Publisher Actions** section, click on the **override the global publisher layout** link.

5. From the **Actions** section of the page layout editor, drag the **Enter Decision** action and place it between the **Post** and **File** actions.

6. Your **Publisher Actions** window should resemble the following screenshot:

7. Click on **Save**.

Try out the publisher action

The **Enter Decision** action is now ready for us to try out. This can be done with the following steps:

> Before using the publisher action, you will need some existing course applications in your organization. I have provided some sample data for **Applicants** and **Courses** in the code download for this chapter that you can import. You can then create some course applications to try out the publisher action.

1. Select the **Course Applications** tab.

2. Open an existing course application, as shown in the following screenshot:

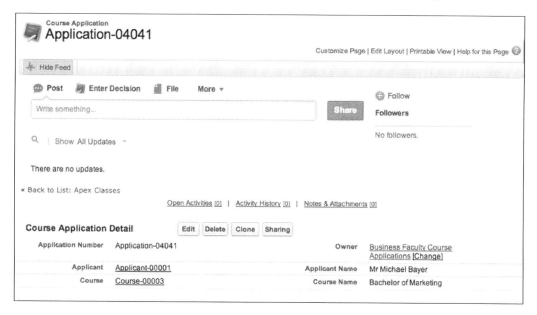

3. Click on **Enter Decision** in the Chatter feed. The following layout will now be displayed:

4. Fill in the **Decision Notes** field with a comment and click on **Update**.

5. You will see a flash message that indicates the record has been successfully updated.

6. If you refresh the page or reopen the course application, you will see that it has been updated and a post is automatically added to the Chatter feed, as shown in the following screenshot:

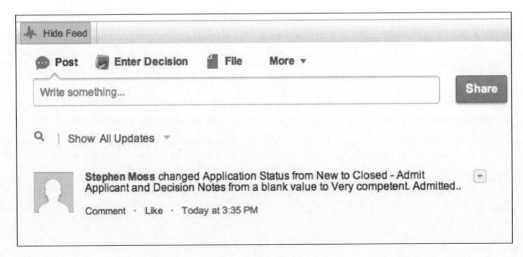

You can also use a Visualforce page for a publisher action, which provides quite a powerful platform for development. Refer to the **Salesforce1 App Developer Guide** page for more details at `https://developer.salesforce.com/docs/atlas.en-us.salesforce1.meta/salesforce1/salesforce1_guide_introduction.htm`.

Congratulations! Our admissions application is now complete!

Summary

In this chapter, we have built a comprehensive CRM system using a major portion of the Force.com platform functionalities. I sincerely hope that the application we have built can be used as a starting blueprint for your real-world projects.

Hopefully, you can now appreciate the ease with which we can tap into the vast amount of power contained within the platform as well as extend it when required.

Even though the application is fairly complete, there are still a few improvements that you can make, and they are listed as follows:

- Add a custom logo to the application to refine it a bit
- Implement an approvals process for conditionally approved course applications
- Implement a workflow to send the result of a course application, when a decision is made, to the applicant (you may also need to use an Apex trigger for this)
- Implement a set of reports and dashboards to aid the university staff in tracking and managing the admissions process.

Building a Reporting System

Reporting is a crucial requirement for any business. The old adage, *If you cannot measure it, you cannot improve it*, is as true today as it was when Lord Kelvin coined the term.

Force.com provides extremely powerful analytics and reporting capabilities out of the box. The standard details, summary and matrix reports, and charts and dashboards should suffice for the majority of business reporting needs.

However, as powerful as the standard reporting capabilities are, there will be times when the standard reporting isn't enough. At this stage, a business usually has two choices:

1. Download a reporting system from AppExchange or export data from Salesforce to a more powerful data warehouse / operational reporting environment to build custom reports. Examples of this are the IBM Cognos or the Oracle Business Intelligence suite of tools.

2. Build a custom reporting capability in Force.com using Visualforce and Apex.

If you work in an enterprise environment and you have an existing data warehouse / operational reporting capability and the available budget, the first option could be a feasible option.

For smaller-or medium-sized businesses that don't have the luxury of a data warehouse, the second option becomes much more attractive. This will be the subject of this chapter.

Our customer will be **Force Majeure Insurance Brokers**, a fictional insurance brokerage firm, which negotiates insurance policies for clients in home and property, personal liability, motor vehicle, and marine.

Force Majeure has recently adopted Salesforce to track their customer accounts and policy information. The management would now like an executive dashboard to allow them to track business performance. In this chapter, we will build the executive dashboard that they require.

Reporting system overview

The reporting system will be responsible for generating an on-demand **Executive Information System (EIS)** Dashboard for Force Majeure management to quickly assess the performance of their insurance broker operations.

This will allow Force Majeure executives to monitor business performance against a set of **Key Performance Indicators (KPIs)** and, if required, to make informed decisions to improve operational performance.

Reporting requirements

The following criteria will be used for the executive dashboard:

- Date from
- Date to
- Policy type

The following KPIs will be displayed for the policies being renewed:

KPIs	Description
Terminating renewals	The policy amount ($) and number of renewal policies in the selected date range for the selected policy type
Unsuccessful renewals	The policy amount ($) and number of policies that were not renewed in the selected date range for the selected policy type
Successful renewals	The policy amount ($) and number of renewal policies that were successfully renewed in the selected date range for the selected policy type
Renewal success rate	The success rate of renewals in the policy amount ($) and number of renewal policies in the selected date range for the selected policy type
New policies won	The policy amount ($) and number of new policies that were won in the selected date range for the selected policy type

KPIs	Description
Total policies won	The combined policy amount ($) and number of policies won (new and renewals) in the selected date range for the selected policy type
Policy growth percentage	The percentage growth of the policy amount ($) and number of policies from the total due for renewal in the selected date range

The following KPIs will be displayed for the new policies:

KPIs	Description
New policy requests received	The policy amount ($) and number of new policies that were requested in the selected date range for the selected policy type
New policy requests quoted	The policy amount ($) and number of new policies that were quoted on in the selected date range for the selected policy type
New policy request quote rate	The percentage of new policy requests that were quoted on (the policy amount ($) and number of new policies) in the selected date range
New policy success rate	The success rate of new policies in the policy amount ($) and number of policies in the selected date range for the selected policy type

Reporting system design

In this section, we will examine the components that will be required to build the EIS Dashboard:

- The BrokerPolicy custom object
- KPIs' formulae
- The EIS Dashboard Visualforce page
- The EIS Dashboard custom controller

The EIS Dashboard custom object

The EIS Dashboard custom object will contain summarized insurance policy information for new policies being sold and existing policies that are being renewed. The main information we will be interested in is whether a policy has won or lost, if it has been quoted on, and the policy amount.

> In a real-life production environment, your customer will most probably be using **Sales Cloud** and **Opportunities** for this type of application. If this is the case, I recommend you use a monthly **Analytical Snapshot** to populate a custom object similar to the EIS Dashboard object we are using in this chapter for this type of application. For information on how to configure and use Analytical Snapshots, refer to `http://help.salesforce.com/apex/HTViewHelpDoc?id=data_about_analytic_snap.htm`.

KPI formulae

Each KPI will require a specific set of data or formula. The following tables list each KPI and describe the set of data or formula required.

The following are the KPI formulae for the policies being renewed (all formulae assume the selected date range and a policy type):

KPIs	Formulae
Terminating renewals	• Sum of policy amount where policy renewal is `True`
	• Count of policies where policy renewal is `True`
Unsuccessful renewals	• Sum of policy amount where policy renewal is `True` and status is `Lost`
	• Count of policies where policy renewal is `True` and status is `Lost`
Successful renewals	• Sum of policy amount where policy renewal is `True` and status is `Won`
	• Count of policies where policy renewal is `True` and status is `Won`
Renewal success rate	• (Successful renewals policy amount / Terminating renewals policy amount) * 100
	• (Successful renewals number of policies / Terminating renewals number of policies) * 100

KPIs	Formulae
New policies won	• Sum of policy amount where policy renewal is `False` and status is `Won`
	• Count of policies where policy renewal is `False` and status is `Won`
Total policies won	• **Policy amount**: (Terminating renewals - unsuccessful renewals) + new policies won
	• **Number of policies**: (Terminating renewals - unsuccessful renewals) + new policies won
Policy growth percentage	• Policy amount: ((Total policies won – terminating renewals) / terminating renewals) * 100
	• Number of policies: ((Total policies won – terminating renewals) / terminating renewals) * 100

The following are the KPI formulae for the new policies (all formulae assume the selected month/year):

KPIs	Formulae
New policy requests received	• Sum of policy amount where policy renewal is `False`
	• Count of policies where policy renewal is `False`
New policy requests quoted	• Sum of policy amount where policy renewal is `False` and quoted is `True`
	• Count of policies where policy renewal is `False` and quoted is `True`
New policy request quote rate	• **Policy amount**: (New policy requests quoted / new policy requests received) * 100
	• **Number of policies**: (New policy requests quoted / new policy requests received) * 100
New policy success rate	• **Policy amount**: (New policies won / new policy requests received) * 100
	• **Number of policies**: (New policies won / new policy requests received) * 100

The EIS Dashboard Visualforce page

The EIS Dashboard Visualforce page will be responsible for receiving report criteria from a user and then presenting the EIS Dashboard results. The Visualforce page will also present a range of Visualforce charts to present selected dashboard data in a graphical format.

The EIS Dashboard custom controller

We will use a custom controller for the EIS Dashboard Visualforce page. The main responsibility of the custom controller will be issuing the SOQL queries against the database and performing the calculations required to generate the report results for the EIS Dashboard.

Reporting system build

Now that our analysis and design is complete, we can start to build the EIS Dashboard.

 This chapter assumes you are quite familiar with Apex programming. If you haven't done a lot of Apex programming, I advise you to complete the Apex Workbook from the developer Force site at http://wiki. developerforce.com/page/Force.com_workbook.

Defining the EIS Dashboard custom object

To configure the custom object that we will be using for the EIS Dashboard, perform the following steps:

1. Navigate to **Setup** | **Create** | **Objects**.
2. Press the **New Custom Object** button.
3. Enter EIS Policy for **Label**.
4. Enter EIS Policies for the **Plural Label**.
5. Select the **Starts with vowel sound** checkbox.
6. Enter a **Description** to describe the purpose of the custom object.
7. Enter EIS Policy Code for the **Record Name** and change the **Data Type** to **Auto Number**.
8. Enter Policy-{00000} in the **Display Format** field.
9. Enter 1 in the **Starting Number** field.

10. Select the **Allow Reports** checkbox only (we are assuming this object will be used for reporting purposes only).

11. Ensure that the **Deployment Status** is set to **Deployed**.

12. Click on the **Save** button to create the custom object.

You will now need to configure the custom fields for the object:

1. Navigate to **Setup | Create | Objects**.

2. Click on the **EIS Policy** hyperlink.

3. Click on the **New** button in the **Custom Fields & Relationships** section.

4. Create the fields described in the following table, accepting the Force.com defaults for field level security and page layouts unless otherwise specified:

Field Type	Field Label	Comments
Picklist	Status	This is the status of the policy. Picklist values are Won and Lost. Select the **Use first value as default value** checkbox.
Picklist	Policy Type	This is the type of policy. Picklist values are Home and Property, Personal Liability, Motor Vehicle, and Marine. Select the **Use first value as default value** checkbox.
Checkbox	Renewal	If true, the policy is a renewal. If the checkbox is not selected, the policy is a new business.
Checkbox	Quoted	If true, policy has been quoted on.
Currency	Policy Amount	This is the cost of the policy.
Date	Policy Date	This is the date of the policy.

Creating the skeleton EIS Dashboard application

Next, we will create a skeleton EIS Dashboard application. This will consist of an Application Tab, and a basic Visualforce page.

Creating the initial Visualforce page

To create the initial version of the EIS Dashboard page, perform the following steps:

1. Navigate to **Setup | Develop | Pages**.
2. All of the Visualforce pages for your organization will be displayed. Click on **New**.
3. In the **Page Information** section, enter EIS Dashboard Page in the **Label** field.
4. Enter EIS_Dashboard_Page in the **Name** field.
5. Enter EIS Dashboard Visualforce Page in the **Description**.
6. Accept the default markup in the **Visualforce Page Editor**.
7. Click on **Save**.

Defining the application tabs

To define the application tabs, perform the following steps:

1. Navigate to **Setup | Create | Tabs**.
2. Click on **New** in the **Custom Object Tabs** section.
3. In the **Object** drop-down list select **EIS Policy**.
4. Select the Lookup icon to set a **Tab Style** (a suggestion is **Trophy**). Click on **Next**.
5. Accept the defaults for **Add to Profiles** and click on **Next**.
6. Deselect all applications to ensure this tab is not added. Click on **Save**.
7. Click on **New** from the **Visualforce Tabs** section.
8. Select **EIS Dashboard Page** for the **Visualforce Page**.
9. Enter EIS Dashboard for the **Tab Label**.
10. Enter EIS_Dashboard for the **Tab Name**.
11. Select the Lookup icon to set a **Tab Style** (a suggestion is **PDA**). Click on **Next**.
12. Accept the defaults for **Add to Profiles** and click on **Next**.
13. Deselect all applications to ensure this tab is not added. Click on **Save**.

Creating the EIS Dashboard application

To define the EIS Dashboard application, perform the following steps:

1. Navigate to **Setup** | **Create** | **Apps**.
2. Click on the **New** button.
3. Select **Custom app** as the type of app to create. Click on **Next**.
4. For the **App Label**, enter EIS. The **App Name** should also be defaulted to **EIS**. Click on **Next**.
5. Click on **Next** to accept the default logo.
6. Move **EIS Policies** and **EIS Dashboard** to the **Selected Tabs** list.
7. Leave **Home** as **Default Landing Tab**. Click on **Next**.
8. Make the application visible to **System Administrator** and click on **Save**.

Importing EIS policy data

The code download for the chapter contains the eis_policy_sample_data.csv file in the sample_data folder. This contains some sample data you can use while you are developing and testing your reports. Refer to *Chapter 2, The E-Commerce Framework*, for details on loading data into your Force.com organization.

We have now completed the skeleton application. If you select EIS from the Force.com application dropdown, your screen should resemble the following screenshot:

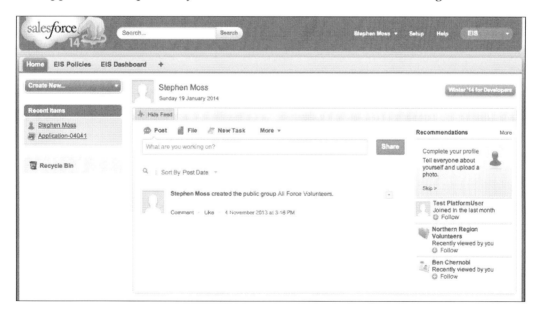

Building the final reporting application

With the skeleton EIS application in place, we can commence the build of the final application.

The application will display a Visualforce page, accept the **Date From** and **Date To** inputs, and allow the user to select a **Policy Type** (or all policy types) from a drop-down list. When the user selects a **Generate** button, the EIS Dashboard will be generated and displayed on the Visualforce page.

To support this functionality, we will build the following components:

- EIS Dashboard custom controller
- EIS Dashboard Visualforce page
- EIS Dashboard charts

The EIS Dashboard custom controller

This custom controller will be responsible for generating the KPIs for the EIS Dashboard. To create the EIS Dashboard custom controller, perform the following steps:

1. Navigate to **Setup | Develop | Apex Classes**.
2. All of the Apex classes for your organization will be displayed. Click on **New**.
3. In the code download for the chapter, locate the `EISDashboardController.cls` file in the `force_com` folder.
4. Copy and paste the contents of `EISDashboardController.cls` into the **Apex Code Editor** in your **Force.com** window, as shown in the following screenshot.
5. Click on **Save**.

Working of the EIS Dashboard controller

The first step in the controller is to declare the properties that we will need to store the dashboard criteria entered by the user:

```
// Date From
public Date dateFrom {get; set;}

// Date To
public Date dateTo {get; set;}

// Policy Type picklist values
public List<selectOption> policyTypeOptions {get; set;}

// selected value in picklist
public string selectedPolicyType {get; set;}
```

The `dateFrom` and `dateTo` controller properties will hold the selected date range for the dashboard entered by the user on the EIS Dashboard Visualforce page. We will be populating the drop-down list for the policy type manually and adding an **All** option to support generating the dashboard for all policy types. The `policyTypeOptions` property will hold this list of values. Note the `List<selectOption>` property type that directly corresponds to a list of the `<apex:selectOption>` elements on a Visualforce page. Finally, we declare the string variable `selectedPolicyType`, which will store the policy type the user has actually selected in the drop-down list.

The next set of properties we declare will hold the KPIs for policies being renewed:

```
// Terminating Renewal Totals
public decimal totalTerminatingRenewalsPolicyAmount {get; set;}
public decimal totalTerminatingRenewalsPolicyCount  {get; set;}

// Successful Renewal Totals
public decimal totalSuccessfulRenewalsPolicyAmount {get; set;}
public decimal totalSuccessfulRenewalsPolicyCount  {get; set;}

// Unsuccessful Renewal Totals
public decimal totalUnsuccessfulRenewalsPolicyAmount {get; set;}
public decimal totalUnsuccessfulRenewalsPolicyCount  {get; set;}

// Renewal Success Rate
public decimal renewalSuccessRatePolicyAmount { get; set;}
public decimal renewalSuccessRatePolicyCount  { get; set;}

// Total Policies Won
public decimal totalPoliciesWonPolicyAmount { get; set;}
public decimal totalPoliciesWonPolicyCount  { get; set;}

// Policy Growth Rate
public decimal policyGrowthRatePolicyAmount { get; set;}
public decimal policyGrowthRatePolicyCount  { get; set;}
```

The next set of properties we declare will hold the KPIs for new policies:

```
// New Policy Request Totals
public decimal totalNewPolicyRequestAmount {get; set;}
public decimal totalNewPolicyRequestCount  {get; set;}

// New Policies Won Totals
public decimal totalNewPolicyRequestWonAmount {get; set;}
public decimal totalNewPolicyRequestWonCount  {get; set;}

// New Policy Request Quoted Totals
public decimal totalNewPolicyRequestQuotedAmount {get; set;}
public decimal totalNewPolicyRequestQuotedCount  {get; set;}

// New Policy Quote Rate
public decimal newPolicyQuoteRateAmount { get; set;}
public decimal newPolicyQuoteRateCount  { get; set;}

// New Policy Success Rate
public decimal newPolicySuccessRateAmount { get; set;}
public decimal newPolicySuccessRateCount  { get; set;}
```

Finally, we declare a set of properties that will hold the data series for the Visualforce charts:

```
// Chart Data Series for Renewals Charts
public List<ChartData> renewalPieData {get; set;}
public List<ChartData> renewalGaugeData {get; set;}

// Chart Data for New Policy Charts
public List<ChartData> newPolicyGaugeData {get; set;}
public List<ChartData> newPolicyPieData {get; set;}
```

The ChartData type is a simple wrapper class to hold a series of data points for a chart and is also declared in the controller:

```
// Wrapper class for Chart Data
public class ChartData {

    public String name { get; set; }
    public Integer data { get; set; }

    public ChartData(String name, Integer data) {
        this.name = name;
        this.data = data;
    }

    public ChartData(String name, decimal data) {
        this.name = name;
        this.data = integer.valueOf(data);
    }
}
```

The EIS Dashboard controller constructor

The constructor method for the controller is used to initialize the controls displayed on the Visualforce page:

```
public EISDashboardController() {

    // initialize values for "Policy Type" picklist
    policyTypeOptions = new List<selectOption>();
    policyTypeOptions.add(new selectOption('All','All'));
    List<Schema.PicklistEntry> policyTypes =
    EIS_Policy__c.fields.Policy_Type__c
                            .getDescribe().getpicklistvalues();

    for (Schema.PicklistEntry a : policyTypes) {
```

```
            policyTypeOptions.add(new selectOption(a.getValue(),
                                          a.getLabel())));
    }


    // set initial value for Policy Type to 'All'
    selectedPolicyType = 'All';

    // initialize dashboard values
    initializeEISDashboard();


}
```

We begin by initializing the `policyTypeOptions` list and then adding a new element for the **All** drop-down list option. The next line of code defines a list of the `Schema.PicklistEntry` objects. The `Schema.PicklistEntry` class is defined in the `Schema` namespace in the *Apex Developers Guide (Reference Section)* (`http://www.salesforce.com/us/developer/docs/apexcode/index_Left.htm`) and represents a picklist entry for a Force.com object picklist field. We then call the `getDescribe()` method on the **Policy Type** field of the **EIS Policy** object, which returns an instance of `Schema.SObjectType` representing the field. A further call to the `getpicklistvalues()` method then returns the **Policy Type** picklist values.

Now that the list contains the picklist values for the policy type, we can iterate through it in the succeeding `for` loop and load them into the `policyTypeOptions` list.

Finally, we set the `selectedPolicyType` property to `All` as its default value and call the `initializeEISDashboard()` method to set all KPI-related properties to `0`.

Generating the button click handler method

The next method we define is `startGenerateEISDashboard()`, which handles the click event for the **Generate** button on the EIS Dashboard Visualforce page:

```
// start EIS Dashboard generation
public PageReference startGenerateEISDashboard() {
  if (dateFrom != null && dateTo != null) {
    if (dateTo >= dateFrom) {
      generateEISDashboard();
    } else {
      // display custom page message
      ApexPages.Message myMsg = new ApexPages.Message(ApexPages.
Severity.ERROR,'Date To must be greater than or equal to Date From!');
        ApexPages.addMessage(myMsg);
    }
  } else {
    // display custom page message
```

```
      ApexPages.Message myMsg = new ApexPages.Message(ApexPages.
  Severity.ERROR,'You must select a Date From and a Date To!');
          ApexPages.addMessage(myMsg);
    }
    return null;
  }
```

First, we check that values for **Date From** and **Date To** have been entered. If either of them contains a null value, we construct an appropriate error message and rerender the EIS Dashboard Visualforce page. If **Date From** and **Date To** have been entered, we then check that **Date To** occurs after **Date From**. If both validations are passed, we call the `generateEISDashboard()` method, which will commence generating the KPIs for the dashboard. If any of the validations fail, we construct an appropriate error message and rerender the EIS Dashboard Visualforce page.

Generating the EIS Dashboard

The `generateEISDashboard()` method itself calls a set of methods to generate the dashboard:

```
// generate the dashboard
private void generateEISDashboard() {
  initializeEISDashboard();
  generateRenewals();
  generateNewPolicies();
  generateSuccessIndicators();
  generateCharts();
}
```

As described earlier, `initializeEISDashboard()` sets all KPI values to 0. This is important, especially if the dashboard has previously been generated in the current session (we don't want to accidentally display any old values from a previous generation of the dashboard).

The `generateRenewals()` method generates renewal-policy-related KPIs. The `generateNewPolicies()` method generates new-policy-related KPIs. The `generateSuccessIndicators()` method then uses the KPIs generated by `generateRenewals()` and `generateNewPolicies()` to calculate success indicators such as success rates and growth rates of policies.

Generating the renewal totals

The `generateRenewals()` method performs a set of SOQL queries and processes the results to generate the renewal-policy-related KPIs. First, we define a map we will use throughout the method to store the totals from a SOQL query:

```
Map<string, decimal> renewalQueryTotals = new Map<string, decimal>();
```

We then perform a SOQL query to retrieve the policy amount and policy count to terminate renewals:

```
// get amounts for Terminating Renewals
List<AggregateResult> renewalsAggregateResult =
    [SELECT SUM(Policy_Amount__c) totalRenewalsAmount,
     COUNT(Id) totalRenewalsCount, Policy_Type__c
     FROM EIS_Policy__c
     WHERE Renewal__c = true
     AND Policy_Date__c >= :dateFrom AND Policy_Date__c <= :dateTo
     GROUP BY Policy_Type__c];
```

There is quite a bit happening in this SOQL query, so we will examine it in greater detail:

1. In the SELECT statement, we are retrieving the SUM value of terminating renewals through the **Policy Amount** field and the number of terminating renewals by applying the COUNT aggregator to the **Id** field. We also retrieve the **Policy Type** field, as we will use it to group the results of the query.

2. In the WHERE statement, we are specifying that we are only interested in policies where the **Renewal** field is `true`, and the **Policy Date** occurs between the **Date From** and **Date To** values.

3. Finally, we specify the GROUP BY clause on the **Policy Type** field. This will return `renewalsAggregateResult`, which is a list of `AggregateResult` objects, with one `AggregateResult` object for each **Policy Type**. Each `AggregateResult` object will contain the total policy amount and number of policies for an individual policy type.

Now that we have the query results in the `renewalsAggregateResult` list, we can call the `calculateAggregateTotals()` generic method to calculate the dashboard values for us:

```
// get the Terminating Renewal totals
renewalQueryTotals =
    calculateAggregateTotals(renewalsAggregateResult,
      'totalRenewalsAmount',
      'totalRenewalsCount');
```

We pass the `renewalsAggregateResult` list and the string identifiers for the total policy amount and policy count elements within the `renewalsAggregateResult` object. Note that the string identifiers are an exact match to the aliases we defined for the fields in the SOQL query.

The `calculateAggregateTotals` method is defined as follows:

```
// generic function to calculate totals from an AggregateResult
private Map<string, decimal>
   calculateAggregateTotals(List<AggregateResult> results,
     string amountString, string countString) {

     decimal policyAmount = 0;
     decimal policyCount = 0;

     // Loop through aggregate results returned and get totals
     for (AggregateResult a : results) {
        if (selectedPolicyType == 'All') {
           policyAmount =
             decimal.valueOf(String.valueOf(a.get(amountString)));
           policyCount =
             decimal.valueOf(String.valueOf(a.get(countString)));
        } else {
           if (String.valueOf(a.get('Policy_Type__c')) ==
               selectedPolicyType) {
             policyAmount =
               decimal.valueOf(String.valueOf(
                                   a.get(amountString)));
             policyCount =
               decimal.valueOf(String.valueOf(
                                   a.get(countString)));
           }
        }
     }

     // construct Map and return it
     Map<string, decimal> resultMap = new Map<string, decimal>();
     resultMap.put(amountString, policyAmount);
     resultMap.put(countString, policyCount);

     return resultMap;

}
```

The method begins by declaring the `policyAmount` and `policyCount` variables, which will hold the total policy amount and policy count, respectively.

We then begin a `for` loop to iterate through the list of the `AggregateResult` objects passed into the method (one per policy type).

Within the `for` loop, we check if the user has selected **All** in the **Policy Type** drop-down list on the Visualforce page. If so, we add the policy amount and policy count for the current policy type to the `policyAmount` and `policyCount` variables, respectively.

If the user hasn't selected **All** in the **Policy Type** drop-down list, we then check if the policy type for the current `AggregateResult` object matches the user-selected policy type. If the policy type values match, we add the policy amount and policy count for the policy type to the `policyAmount` and `policyCount` variables.

In a nutshell, the `for` loop provides the following behavior:

- If the user selects **All** in the **Policy Type** drop-down list, the policy amount and policy count values for every policy type returned by the SOQL query are added together to give a grand total for all policy types.
- If the users select a specific policy type from the drop-down list, only the policy amount and policy count for the selected policy type are included in the total.

Once the `for` loop is completed, we construct a map with an element for the total policy amount and total policy count keyed by the string identifiers we passed into the `calculateAggregateTotals()` method. The map is then passed back to the `generateRenewals()` method.

Back in the `generateRenewals()` method, we retrieve the values from the map and assign them to the EIS Dashboard values:

```
totalTerminatingRenewalsPolicyAmount =
   renewalQueryTotals.get('totalRenewalsAmount');
totalTerminatingRenewalsPolicyCount =
   renewalQueryTotals.get('totalRenewalsCount');
```

We then use similar logic to calculate the totals for successful renewals, using a different SOQL query and alias values:

```
////// get amounts for Successful Terminating Renewals
List<AggregateResult> successfulRenewalsAggregateResult =
   [SELECT SUM(Policy_Amount__c) successfulRenewalsAmount,
   COUNT(Id) successfulRenewalsCount, Policy_Type__c
   FROM EIS_Policy__c
   WHERE Renewal__c = true
   AND Status__c = 'Won'
   AND Policy_Date__c >= :dateFrom AND Policy_Date__c <= :dateTo
   GROUP BY Policy_Type__c];

// get the successful Terminating Renewals Totals
```

```
renewalQueryTotals =
  calculateAggregateTotals(successfulRenewalsAggregateResult,
  'successfulRenewalsAmount',
  'successfulRenewalsCount');
  totalSuccessfulRenewalsPolicyAmount =
  renewalQueryTotals.get('successfulRenewalsAmount');
  totalSuccessfulRenewalsPolicyCount =
  renewalQueryTotals.get('successfulRenewalsCount');
```

As we have the total and successful renewals' values, we can simply calculate the unsuccessful renewals:

```
totalUnsuccessfulRenewalsPolicyAmount =
  totalTerminatingRenewalsPolicyAmount -
  totalSuccessfulRenewalsPolicyAmount;
totalUnsuccessfulRenewalsPolicyCount =
  totalTerminatingRenewalsPolicyCount -
  totalSuccessfulRenewalsPolicyCount;
```

Generating the new policy totals

The generateNewPolicies() method uses very similar logic to the generateRenewals() method. First, we declare a map to hold the totals from an SOQL query:

```
Map<string, decimal> newPolicyQueryTotals = new Map<string,
decimal>();
```

Then, we execute an SOQL query and process its results to get the totals of new policies:

```
// get amounts for New Policies
List<AggregateResult> newPolicyAggregateResult =
  [SELECT SUM(Policy_Amount__c) totalNewPolicyAmount,
  COUNT(Id) totalNewPolicyCount, Policy_Type__c
  FROM EIS_Policy__c
  WHERE Renewal__c = false
  AND Policy_Date__c >= :dateFrom AND Policy_Date__c <= :dateTo
  GROUP BY Policy_Type__c];

// get the New Policy Totals
newPolicyQueryTotals =
  calculateAggregateTotals(newPolicyAggregateResult,
  'totalNewPolicyAmount',
  'totalNewPolicyCount');
totalNewPolicyRequestAmount =
```

```
  newPolicyQueryTotals.get('totalNewPolicyAmount');
totalNewPolicyRequestCount =
  newPolicyQueryTotals.get('totalNewPolicyCount');
```

We execute another SOQL query and process its results to get the totals of the new policies that won:

```
// get amounts for New Policies
List<AggregateResult> newPolicyAggregateResult =
  [SELECT SUM(Policy_Amount__c) totalNewPolicyAmount,
  COUNT(Id) totalNewPolicyCount, Policy_Type__c
  FROM EIS_Policy__c
  WHERE Renewal__c = false
  AND Policy_Date__c >= :dateFrom AND Policy_Date__c <= :dateTo
  GROUP BY Policy_Type__c];

// get the New Policy Totals
newPolicyQueryTotals = calculateAggregateTotals(newPolicyAggregateRes
ult,
  'totalNewPolicyAmount',
  'totalNewPolicyCount');
totalNewPolicyRequestAmount =
  newPolicyQueryTotals.get('totalNewPolicyAmount');
totalNewPolicyRequestCount =
  newPolicyQueryTotals.get('totalNewPolicyCount');
```

Our final task in `generateNewPolicies()` is to get the totals for new policies that have been quoted:

```
// get amounts for New Policies Quoted
List<AggregateResult> newPolicyQuotedAggregateResult =
  [SELECT SUM(Policy_Amount__c) totalNewPolicyQuotedAmt,
  COUNT(Id) totalNewPolicyQuotedCount, Policy_Type__c
  FROM EIS_Policy__c
  WHERE Renewal__c = false
  AND Quoted__c = true
  AND Policy_Date__c >= :dateFrom AND Policy_Date__c <= :dateTo
  GROUP BY Policy_Type__c];

// get the New Policy Totals
newPolicyQueryTotals =
  calculateAggregateTotals(newPolicyQuotedAggregateResult,
  'totalNewPolicyQuotedAmt',
  'totalNewPolicyQuotedCount');
  totalNewPolicyRequestQuotedAmount =
    newPolicyQueryTotals.get('totalNewPolicyQuotedAmt');
```

```
totalNewPolicyRequestQuotedCount =
   newPolicyQueryTotals.get('totalNewPolicyQuotedCount');
```

Generating KPIs

The `generateSuccessIndicators()` method uses the data generated in the `generateRenewals()` and `generateNewPolicies()` methods to calculate the KPIs related to success and growth rate.

First, we calculate the success rate for the renewal policies:

```
// Renewals Success Rate
if (totalTerminatingRenewalsPolicyAmount != 0 &&
   totalSuccessfulRenewalsPolicyAmount != 0) {
   renewalSuccessRatePolicyAmount =
      (totalSuccessfulRenewalsPolicyAmount /
      totalTerminatingRenewalsPolicyAmount) * 100;
   renewalSuccessRatePolicyCount =
      (totalSuccessfulRenewalsPolicyCount /
      totalTerminatingRenewalsPolicyCount) * 100;
}
```

Note that we check for zero values in the `totalTerminatingRenewalsPolicyAmount` and `totalSuccessfulRenewalsPolicyAmount` properties to guard against a division by zero runtime error.

Next, we calculate the total policies won, which takes into account the number of successful renewals, unsuccessful renewals, and new policies won:

```
// Total Policies Won
totalPoliciesWonPolicyAmount =
   totalTerminatingRenewalsPolicyAmount -
   totalUnsuccessfulRenewalsPolicyAmount +
   totalNewPolicyRequestWonAmount;

totalPoliciesWonPolicyCount =
   totalTerminatingRenewalsPolicyCount -
   totalUnsuccessfulRenewalsPolicyCount +
   totalNewPolicyRequestWonCount;
```

The overall policy growth rate calculates the overall rate in policy growth across both, renewals and new policies:

```
// Policy Growth Rate
if (totalTerminatingRenewalsPolicyAmount != 0 &&
         totalPoliciesWonPolicyAmount != 0) {
   policyGrowthRatePolicyAmount =
```

```
         ((totalPoliciesWonPolicyAmount -
                  totalTerminatingRenewalsPolicyAmount) /
                  totalTerminatingRenewalsPolicyAmount) * 100;

    policyGrowthRatePolicyCount =
       ((totalPoliciesWonPolicyCount -
                  totalTerminatingRenewalsPolicyCount) /
                  totalTerminatingRenewalsPolicyCount) * 100;
}
```

The policy-quoted rate calculates the percentage of new policy requests that have been quoted:

```
// New Policy Quoted Rate
if (totalNewPolicyRequestQuotedAmount != 0 &&
                  totalNewPolicyRequestAmount != 0) {
    newPolicyQuoteRateAmount =
              (totalNewPolicyRequestQuotedAmount /
               totalNewPolicyRequestAmount) * 100;
    newPolicyQuoteRateCount =
              (totalNewPolicyRequestQuotedCount /
               totalNewPolicyRequestCount) * 100;
}
```

Finally, we calculate the success rate of new policies:

```
// New Policy Success Rate
if (totalNewPolicyRequestWonAmount !=0 &&
                  totalNewPolicyRequestAmount !=0) {
    newPolicySuccessRateAmount =
              (totalNewPolicyRequestWonAmount /
               totalNewPolicyRequestAmount) * 100;

    newPolicySuccessRateCount =
              (totalNewPolicyRequestWonCount /
               totalNewPolicyRequestCount) * 100;
}
```

Generating the Visualforce charts

The final method in the controller takes care of generating the data for the Visualforce charts, which will be displayed with the dashboard:

```
private void generateCharts() {

    // Renewals Pie Chart
    renewalPieData = new List<ChartData>();
    renewalPieData.add(new ChartData('Successful $',
```

```
                            totalSuccessfulRenewalsPolicyAmount));
        renewalPieData.add(new ChartData('Unsuccessful $',
                            totalUnsuccessfulRenewalsPolicyAmount));

        // Renewals Success Rate Gauge
        renewalGaugeData = new List<ChartData>();
        renewalGaugeData.add(new ChartData('Success Rate %',
                            renewalSuccessRatePolicyAmount));

        // New Policy Success Rate Gauge
        newPolicyGaugeData = new List<ChartData>();
        newPolicyGaugeData.add(new ChartData('Success Rate %',
                            newPolicySuccessRateAmount));

        // New Policy Quoted Amount Pie Chart
        newPolicyPieData = new List<ChartData>();
        newPolicyPieData.add(new ChartData('Quoted $',
                            totalNewPolicyRequestQuotedAmount));
        newPolicyPieData.add(new ChartData('Not Quoted $',
                        totalNewPolicyRequestAmount
                            - totalNewPolicyRequestQuotedAmount));

    }
```

Testing the controller

I've included the testEISDashboardController.cls file in the code download for the chapter. This is the test class that I used to test the EIS Dashboard custom controller during the development of the application for this chapter.

To create the test class for the controller, perform the following steps:

1. Navigate to **Setup | Develop | Apex Classes**.
2. All of the Apex classes for your organization will be displayed. Click on **New**.
3. In the code download for the chapter, locate the testEISDashboardController.cls file.
4. Copy and paste the contents of testEISDashboardController.cls into the **Apex Code Editor** in your **Force.com** window.
5. Click on **Save**.

EIS Dashboard Visualforce page

To create the final version of the EIS Dashboard page, perform the following steps:

1. Navigate to **Setup** | **Develop** | **Pages**.
2. All of the Visualforce pages for your organization will be displayed.
3. Click on **EIS Dashboard Page** in the **Label** column.
4. In the code download for the chapter, locate the EIS_Dashboard_Page.page file in the force_com folder.
5. Clear the default markup in the **Visualforce Page Editor**.
6. Copy and paste the contents of EIS_Dashboard_Page.page into the **Visualforce Page Editor** in your **Force.com** window.
7. Click on **Save**.

How the Dashboard Visualforce page works

We begin with the page declaration that introduces a few elements we haven't yet used in this book:

```
<apex:page readOnly="true" controller="EISDashboardController"
    docType="html-5.0" tabStyle="EIS_Dashboard__tab"
    sidebar="false" >
```

The readOnly attribute relaxes the following restrictions for our Visualforce page, and by extension, the custom controller we are using:

- Allows us to perform unrestricted queries against the Force.com database
- Removes the limit on the number of rows returned for a request (allows up to a million rows to be returned)

However, the following restrictions are introduced:

- Code cannot perform DML operations
- Calls to future methods are not allowed
- Sending of e-mails from code is not allowed

Fortunately for us, the restrictions introduced by using readOnly have no impact on our application while we can definitely take advantage of the relaxed restrictions for queries and number of returned rows.

Setting the docType attribute to html-5.0 allows us to take advantage of new features introduced as part of the HTML 5 specification (http://www.w3.org/TR/html5/). In particular, we will be using HTML 5 when we declare some date picker fields that aren't bound to a Force.com object field.

We also declare a few inline CSS styles we will use throughout the page:

```
<style>
    .centerHeader { text-align:center;}
</style>
<style>
    .centerHeaderBold { text-align:center; font-weight:bold; }
</style>
```

Declaring the input criteria controls

We start the actual page structure by declaring form and pageBlock for the Visualforce page. We also declare a pageMessages component to display any errors:

```
<apex:form >
  <apex:pageBlock title="EIS Dashboard">
    <apex:pageMessages id="messages" ></apex:pageMessages>
```

The first pageBlock section we declare will hold the Visualforce controls to allow the user to enter criteria for the dashboard:

```
<apex:pageBlockSection title="Enter Criteria" columns="1">
```

Then, we declare the dashboard criteria controls themselves:

```
<apex:panelGroup >
    <apex:outputLabel value="Date From" />
    <apex:input label="Date From" value="{!dateFrom}"
        type="auto" />
    <apex:outputLabel value="Date To" />
    <apex:input label="Date To" value="{!dateTo}" type="auto" />
    <apex:outputLabel value="Policy Type" />
    <apex:selectList label="Policy Type"
                        value="{!selectedPolicyType}" size="1">
        <apex:selectOptions
            value="{!policyTypeOptions}">
        </apex:selectOptions>
    </apex:selectList>
    <apex:commandButton value="Generate"
                        action="{!startGenerateEISDashboard}" />
</apex:panelGroup>
```

We use `apex:panelGroup` to present the controls on a single line. The `Date From` and `Date To` controls take advantage of the `html-5.0` declaration for the `docType` attribute and will actually present a date picker control, because they are linked to the `dateFrom` and `dateTo` date type properties in the controller. The following screenshot shows a date picker in action using the Google Chrome browser:

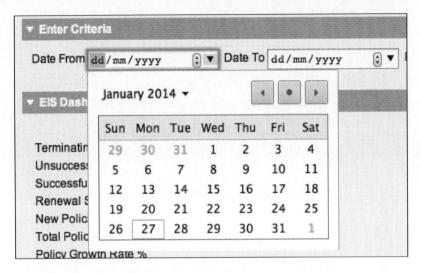

The **Policy Type** picklist is linked to the `selectedPolicyType` property in the controller. Therefore, whenever a picklist item is selected, it will be stored in the controller property. The picklist items themselves are supplied by the `policyTypeOptions` controller property. Remember that this is a `List<selectOption>` type of property that we initialize in the constructor for the controller.

With all the controls in place, our dashboard criteria section resembles the following screenshot:

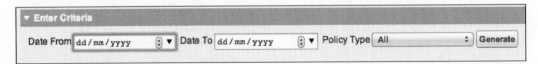

Displaying the renewal KPIs

Now, we close the current `pageBlockSection` for the dashboard criteria and start a new `pageBlockSection` for the textual dashboard results:

```
</apex:pageBlockSection>
<apex:pageBlockSection title="EIS Dashboard" columns="2">
```

We have declared a two-column `pageBlockSection`. The first column will hold the renewal-related dashboard results and the second column will hold the new-policy-related dashboard results.

We begin declaring the first column using an `apex:panelGrid` control, using the inline CSS styles declared earlier to format the column headings:

```
<apex:panelGrid columns="3" width="100%"
               columnClasses=",centerHeaderBold,centerHeaderBold">
    <apex:outputText value="" />
    <apex:outputText value="Amount" />
    <apex:outputText value="# Policies" />
```

The `apex:panelGrid` control is rendered as an HTML table when the Visualforce page is generated. Therefore the `apex:outputText` controls declared above will be rendered as a table row `<tr>` element and a series of `<td>` elements for each table cell.

> You might be wondering how `apex:panelGrid` knows when to render a new table row. If you look at the `apex:panelGrid` definition, you will see that the `columns` attribute has been set to a value of `3`. This means that after every third control in `panelGrid`, Visualforce will render a new table row.

We then render the renewal KPIs required to calculate and display the success rate for renewals:

```
<apex:outputText value="Terminating Renewals" />
<apex:outputText value="{0,number,$###,###,##0}">
  <apex:param value="{!totalTerminatingRenewalsPolicyAmount}" />
</apex:outputText>
<apex:outputText value="{0,number,###,###,##0}">
  <apex:param value="{!totalTerminatingRenewalsPolicyCount}" />
</apex:outputText>
<apex:outputText value="Unsuccessful Renewals" />
<apex:outputText value="{0,number,$###,###,##0}">
  <apex:param value="{!totalUnsuccessfulRenewalsPolicyAmount}" />
</apex:outputText>
<apex:outputText value="{0,number,###,###,##0}">
  <apex:param value="{!totalUnsuccessfulRenewalsPolicyCount}" />
</apex:outputText>
<apex:outputText value="Successful Renewals" />
<apex:outputText value="{0,number,$###,###,##0}">
  <apex:param value="{!totalSuccessfulRenewalsPolicyAmount}" />
</apex:outputText>
<apex:outputText value="{0,number,###,###,##0}">
```

```
    <apex:param value="{!totalSuccessfulRenewalsPolicyCount}" />
</apex:outputText>
<apex:outputText value="Renewal Success Rate %" />
<apex:outputText value="{0,number,##0.00}">
  <apex:param value="{!renewalSuccessRatePolicyAmount}" />
</apex:outputText>
<apex:outputText value="{0,number,##0.00}">
  <apex:param value="{!renewalSuccessRatePolicyCount}" />
</apex:outputText>
```

To make the code easier to read, I have highlighted every second row of the KPI values. For each row, we are displaying an apex:outputText control containing the description for the row, an apex:outputText control containing the KPI value for the policy amount, and finally an apex:outputText control containing the KPI value for the policy count.

You will notice that the currency values are formatted using a format mask in the value field for the apex:outputText control, which then passes the value from an apex:param control that contains the KPI value from the controller we are displaying and formatting.

We adopt a similar pattern for the remaining renewal KPI rows and add the closing tag for apex:panelGrid, as shown in the next code. This completes the first column.

```
<apex:outputText value="New Policies Won" />
<apex:outputText value="{0,number,$###,###,##0}">
  <apex:param value="{!totalNewPolicyRequestAmount}" />
</apex:outputText>
<apex:outputText value="{0,number,###,###,##0}">
  <apex:param value="{!totalNewPolicyRequestCount}" />
</apex:outputText>
<apex:outputText value="Total Policies Won" />
<apex:outputText value="{0,number,$###,###,##0}">
  <apex:param value="{!totalPoliciesWonPolicyAmount}" />
</apex:outputText>
<apex:outputText value="{0,number,###,###,##0}">
  <apex:param value="{!totalPoliciesWonPolicyCount}" />
</apex:outputText>
<apex:outputText value="Policy Growth Rate %" />
<apex:outputText value="{0,number,##0.00}">
  <apex:param value="{!policyGrowthRatePolicyAmount}" />
</apex:outputText>
<apex:outputText value="{0,number,##0.00}">
  <apex:param value="{!policyGrowthRatePolicyCount}" />
</apex:outputText>

</apex:panelGrid>
```

Displaying the new policy KPIs

The second column contains the KPI values for new policies. We declare another `apex:panelGrid` and display the values using the same pattern as the first column:

```
<apex:panelGrid columns="3" width="100%"
                columnClasses=",centerHeaderBold,centerHeaderBold">
  <apex:outputText value="" />
  <apex:outputText value="Amount" />
  <apex:outputText value="# Policies" />
  <apex:outputText value="New Policy Requests Received" />
  <apex:outputText value="{0,number,$###,###,##0}">
    <apex:param value="{!totalNewPolicyRequestAmount}" />
  </apex:outputText>
  <apex:outputText value="{0,number,###,###,##0}">
    <apex:param value="{!totalNewPolicyRequestCount}" />
  </apex:outputText>
  <apex:outputText value="New Policy Requests Quoted" />
  <apex:outputText value="{0,number,$###,###,##0}">
    <apex:param value="{!totalNewPolicyRequestQuotedAmount}" />
  </apex:outputText>
  <apex:outputText value="{0,number,###,###,##0}">
    <apex:param value="{!totalNewPolicyRequestQuotedCount}" />
  </apex:outputText>
  <apex:outputText value="New Policy Requests Quote Rate" />
  <apex:outputText value="{0,number,##0.00}">
    <apex:param value="{!newPolicyQuoteRateAmount}" />
  </apex:outputText>
  <apex:outputText value="{0,number,##0.00}">
    <apex:param value="{!newPolicyQuoteRateCount}" />
  </apex:outputText>
  <apex:outputText value="New Policy Success Rate %" />
  <apex:outputText value="{0,number,##0.00}">
    <apex:param value="{!newPolicySuccessRateAmount}" />
  </apex:outputText>
  <apex:outputText value="{0,number,##0.00}">
    <apex:param value="{!newPolicySuccessRateCount}" />
  </apex:outputText>
</apex:panelGrid>
```

Next, we close the `apex:pageBlockSection` for the dashboard textual values:

```
</apex:pageBlockSection>
```

When the Visualforce page is first rendered, the EIS Dashboard's `pageBlockSection` will resemble the following screenshot:

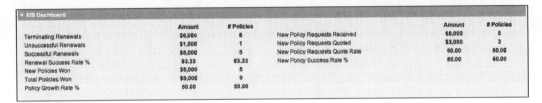

When an EIS Dashboard is generated, the values will be displayed and formatted as per the defined format masks, as illustrated in the following screenshot:

	Amount	# Policies		Amount	# Policies
Terminating Renewals	$6,000	6	New Policy Requests Received	$8,000	5
Unsuccessful Renewals	$1,000	1	New Policy Requests Quoted	$3,000	3
Successful Renewals	$5,000	5	New Policy Requests Quote Rate	60.00	60.00
Renewal Success Rate %	83.33	83.33	New Policy Success Rate %	80.00	80.00
New Policies Won	$5,000	5			
Total Policies Won	$9,000	9			
Policy Growth Rate %	50.00	50.00			

Displaying the renewal dashboard charts

In the next `apex:pageBlockSection`, we will display the renewals-related Visualforce charts. We begin by declaring the beginning of `pageBlockSection`:

```
<apex:pageBlockSection title="Renewals Charts" columns="2">
```

Next, we declare `pageBlockSectionItem` to display the pie chart for the share between successful and unsuccessful renewals:

```
<apex:pageBlockSectionItem >
  <apex:panelGroup >
    <apex:chart height="350" width="400" data="{!renewalPieData}">
      <apex:pieSeries dataField="data" labelField="name"/>
      <apex:legend position="right"/>
    </apex:chart>
    <apex:outputText value="Share of Renewals" />
  </apex:panelGroup>
</apex:pageBlockSectionItem>
```

The key elements in the chart declaration are highlighted. The data attribute of the `apex:chart` control points to the `renewalPieData` controller property, which you will recall is a list of the `ChartData` elements. Subsequently, the `dataField` attribute of the `apex:pieSeries` control points to the `data` element in each `ChartData` instance, which contains the value for each occurrence of the `renewalPieData` data series. In a similar fashion, the `labelField` attribute holds the label for each occurrence of `renewalPieData`.

Similarly, we declare another `pageBlockSectionItem` to display the gauge chart for the renewal success rate:

```
<apex:pageBlockSectionItem >
    <apex:chart height="350" width="650"
                        animate="true" data="{!renewalGaugeData}">
        <apex:axis type="Gauge" position="gauge"
                        title="Renewal Success Rate"
                        minimum="0" maximum="100" steps="10"/>
        <apex:gaugeSeries dataField="data" donut="50"
                                        colorSet="#78c953,#ddd"/>
    </apex:chart>
</apex:pageBlockSectionItem>
```

The only difference is that we don't require a `labelField` attribute for each data series value in a gauge chart.

With both `pageBlockSectionItem` controls declared, we can close the `pageBlockSection` for the renewal charts:

```
</apex:pageBlockSection>
```

The following screenshot shows some example renewal charts when an EIS Dashboard is generated:

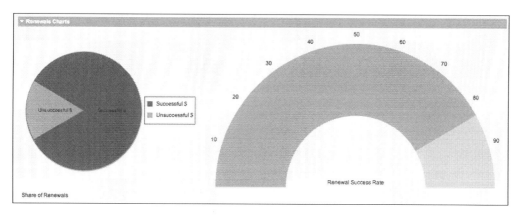

Displaying the New Policy Dashboard Charts

The final `apex:pageBlockSection` we declare will display the new-policy-related Visualforce charts. We begin by declaring the beginning of the `pageBlockSection`:

```
<apex:pageBlockSection title="New Policy Charts" columns="2">
```

We then declare `pageBlockSectionItem` to display a gauge chart for the new policy success rate:

```
<apex:pageBlockSectionItem >
  <apex:chart height="350" width="650" animate="true"
                          data="{!newPolicyGaugeData}">
    <apex:axis type="Gauge" position="gauge"
                          title="New Policy Success Rate"
                          minimum="0" maximum="100" steps="10"/>
    <apex:gaugeSeries dataField="data" donut="50"
                                colorSet="#78c953,#ddd"/>
  </apex:chart>
</apex:pageBlockSectionItem>
```

The final `pageBlockSectionItem` will display a pie chart showing the share of quoted and unquoted new policies:

```
<apex:pageBlockSectionItem >
  <apex:panelGroup >
    <apex:chart height="350" width="400"
                            data="{!newPolicyPieData}">
      <apex:pieSeries dataField="data" labelField="name"/>
      <apex:legend position="right"/>
    </apex:chart>
    <apex:outputText value="Share of Quoted Policies" />
  </apex:panelGroup>
</apex:pageBlockSectionItem>
```

The following screenshot shows an example of new policy charts when an EIS Dashboard is generated:

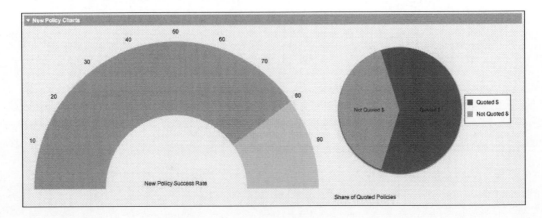

With all of the Visualforce elements in place, we declare all of the remaining closing tags for the page:

```
    </apex:pageBlockSection>

   </apex:pageBlock>

  </apex:form>

 </apex:page>
```

Congratulations! The EIS Dashboard reporting system is now complete.

Summary

In this chapter, we have built a dashboard-style reporting system using Visualforce and Apex. Once again, we started by defining the application requirements and design and building a base application to serve as a starting point.

We then built out the remaining application functionality in a modular manner, implementing tests where appropriate. I hope you have noticed this development pattern used throughout the book. By following this pattern, you will greatly increase your chances of building high-quality applications that are easier to maintain.

Along the way, we have learnt how to build a Visualforce page and custom controller that are well suited to querying data (through the use of the readOnly attribute). We have also used some grouped SOQL queries and generic controller logic to calculate the dashboard results. Finally, we added some graphical representations of data using the Visualforce charting feature.

As always, there are a few improvements you can make to the application:

- Implement some Force.com Ajax functionality to generate the dashboard without requiring a total page refresh every time.

- Experiment with some different types of charts to include in the dashboard. I suggest you consult the *Visualforce Developers Guide* for some further examples.

- Attempt to implement an analytical snapshot to populate an object to serve as the data source for a report.

5
The Force.com
Mobile SDK Application

The release of the iPhone in 2007 and the iPad in 2010 have fueled a mobile computing revolution. The market for smartphones and tablets has experienced an explosive period of growth, to the point that shipments of these devices are beginning to consistently outstrip the demand for traditional desktop PCs.

There has been a corresponding surge in the amount and breadth of mobile applications being built by developers around the world. Millions of mobile applications are available for mobile devices, with more being added every day.

Salesforce has recognized that mobile devices are here to stay and with the release of Salesforce1, has provided a huge level of support and toolkits for established and emerging mobile technologies. In Salesforce1, there are three main options available when developing Force.com mobile applications, as follows:

- HTML5
- Hybrid (iOS and Android, based on Apache Cordova)
- Native (iOS and Android software development kits)

Each option has its strengths and weaknesses, and the future dominant mobile development platform is yet to be defined. However, it is obvious that the demand for mobile applications will only increase in the future. If you haven't dipped your feet into mobile development with Salesforce yet, you better start now!

In this chapter, we will be building a Salesforce Mobile SDK HTML5 application using the AngularJS JavaScript Framework and Twitter Bootstrap, powered by Node.js running on Heroku.

The application will display the Salesforce opportunity information, and present nearby opportunities on a Google map. We have a lot to get through, so let's get started.

Mobile application overview

To help put the chapter into context, we will take a quick tour of the mobile application. There is a fair bit of code to write in this chapter, and it is always easier to build something when we can visualize the end result. By performing the following steps, we can get an overview of the mobile application:

1. First, we will be presented with a screen to log into Salesforce, as shown in the following screenshot:

2. Clicking on the **Login** button will start the Salesforce **Open Authorization** (**OAuth**) authentication process, as shown in the following screenshot:

A good introduction to the Salesforce OAuth protocol is provided on the developer Force website at `https://wiki.developerforce.com/page/Digging_Deeper_into_OAuth_2.0_on_Force.com`.

3. After a successful login, we will be asked to confirm the mobile application permissions, as illustrated in the following screenshot:

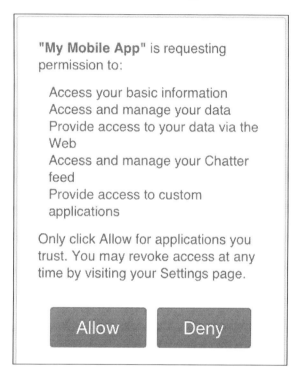

4. After granting the mobile application permissions, we will be presented with a list of open Salesforce opportunities, as shown in the following screenshot:

5. Tapping on an opportunity will display a screen containing further information, as displayed in the following screenshot:

6. We will also build a page to display the nearby opportunities on a Google map, as shown in the following screenshot:

7. Finally, tapping on an opportunity on the map will display an information window, as shown in the following screenshot:

Building a base AngularJS HTML5 application

Initially, we will be building a basic HTML5 application and deploying it to Heroku. The aim is to assemble the majority of required technical components for the application and ensure that they are successfully integrated before diving in to build the final, fully functional version.

In the base application, we will be assembling the following technical components:

- Salesforce Mobile SDK JavaScript libraries
- AngularJS
- Twitter Bootstrap
- jQuery
- Salesforce AngularJS Mobile Pack

Downloading AngularJS

We will be using the AngularJS framework to build the bulk of the application. AngularJS is a JavaScript Framework, maintained by Google, which is well suited to build single-page web applications using the **Model-View-Controller (MVC)** paradigm.

To download AngularJS, perform the following steps:

1. Navigate your web browser to the AngularJS home page at `http://angularjs.org`.

2. Click on the **Download** button.

3. For the **Branch** option, select **1.2.x (legacy)**, as shown in the following screenshot:

4. For the **Build** option, select **Zip** to download all AngularJS files.

5. Click on the **Download** button.

6. Expand the `.zip` file contents to a working folder for the chapter. The AngularJS version used for this chapter is v1.2.16.

> For a great introduction to AngularJS, I highly recommend that you watch an introductory video by Dan Wahlin at `https://www.youtube.com/watch?v=i9MHigUZKEM`.

Downloading Twitter Bootstrap

We will be using Twitter Bootstrap to provide a more attractive interface for our application (well, much more attractive than my HTML UI skills!). Twitter Bootstrap is a responsive web design framework developed by Mark Otto and Jacob Thornton to standardize the user interface development. In August 2011, Twitter released the framework as an open source project, and it is now used by a multitude of web developers across the world.

To download Twitter Bootstrap, perform the following steps:

1. Navigate your web browser to the Twitter Bootstrap home page at `http://getbootstrap.com`.

2. Click on the **Download Bootstrap** button.

3. From the available download choices, select **Download source**, as shown in the following screenshot:

Download

Bootstrap has a few easy ways to quickly get started, each one appealing to a different skill level and use case. Read through to see what suits your particular needs.

Bootstrap

Compiled and minified CSS, JavaScript, and fonts. No docs or original source files are included.

Download Bootstrap

Source code

Source Less, JavaScript, and font files, along with our docs. **Requires a Less compiler and** some setup.

Download source

Sass

Bootstrap ported from Less to Sass for easy inclusion in Rails, Compass, or Sass-only projects.

Download Sass

4. Expand the `.zip` file contents to a working folder for the chapter. The Twitter Bootstrap version used for this chapter is v3.1.0.

The *Getting started* section of the `getbootstrap.com` site contains a great introduction as well as some downloadable samples that you can also use to kick start your applications. It is well worth checking them out.

Downloading jQuery

The Salesforce Mobile SDK we will be using requires jQuery. To download it, perform the following steps:

1. Navigate your web browser to the jQuery home page at `http://jquery.com`.

2. Click on the **Download jQuery** button.

3. Select the link to download the uncompressed, development version of jQuery 2.x (at the time of writing, the version was 2.1.0) to a working directory.

 If you haven't used jQuery before, there is a ton of information on the web. A great place to start is the jQuery Learning Center at `http://learn.jquery.com/`.

Downloading the Salesforce AngularJS Mobile Pack

As described earlier, we will be using AngularJS to build the user interface for the application. To make accessing Salesforce data easier, we will be using the AngularJS Mobile Pack for Salesforce.

To download the AngularJS Mobile Pack for Salesforce, perform the following steps:

1. Navigate your web browser to the AngularJS Mobile Pack GitHub repository at `https://github.com/developerforce/MobilePack-AngularJS`.

2. Select the **Download ZIP** button.

3. Expand the `.zip` file contents to a working folder for the chapter.

Building a base HTML5 application structure

We will now build the folder structure required for the HTML5 application. In a base folder for the chapter, set up a folder structure as per the following screenshot:

In the **js** folder, set up two additional folders as per the following screenshot:

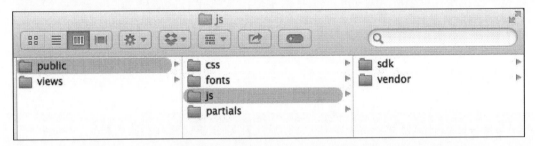

Copying the base HTML5 application files

We will now copy the base Salesforce Mobile SDK, JavaScript Framework, and Twitter Bootstrap files for the HTML5 application by completing the following steps.

 For the rest of the chapter, I will be referring to the `MyMobileApp` folder created in the previous section as the `application base` folder.

1. Navigate to the folder where you unzipped the Salesforce AngularJS Mobile Pack.

2. Navigate to the `samples/AngularHerokuBootstrapNode` folder.

3. Copy the following files to the `application base` folder: `app.js`, `package.json`, and `Procfile`.

4. Navigate to the `samples/AngularHerokuBootstrapNode/public/js/sdk` folder.

5. Copy the following files to the `application base/public/js/sdk` folder: `angular-force.js`, `forcetk.mobilesdk.js`, `forcetk.ui.js`, and `smartsync.js`.

6. Navigate to the `samples/AngularHerokuBootstrapNode/public/js/vendor` folder.

7. Copy the following file to the `application base/public/js/vendor` folder: `underscore-1.4.4.min.js`.

8. Navigate to the folder where you have unzipped Twitter Bootstrap.

9. Navigate to the `dist/css` folder.

10. Copy the following files to the `application base/public/css` folder: `bootstrap-theme.css` and `bootstrap.css`.

11. Navigate to the `dist/fonts` folder.

12. Copy the following files to the `application base/public/fonts` folder: `glyphicons-halflings-regular.eot`, `glyphicons-halflings-regular.svg`, `glyphicons-halflings-regular.ttf`, and `glyphicons-halflings-regular.woff`.

13. Navigate to the folder where you unzipped jQuery.

14. Copy the `jQuery 2.x` file that you have downloaded earlier to the `application base/public/js/vendor` folder (at the time of writing, my filename was `jquery-2.1.0.js`).

15. Navigate to the folder where you unzipped AngularJS.

16. Copy the following files to the `application base/public/js/vendor` folder: `angular.js` and `angular-route.js`.

Building a base HTML5 Heroku application

At this point, we have all of the building blocks in place to build our HTML5 application. As we will be using Heroku to host our application, now is a good time to verify if we can deploy to Heroku successfully.

 I'm assuming that you have completed the e-commerce Heroku application in *Chapter 2, The E-Commerce Framework*, so I won't be going into detail about the commands used to initialize a git repository and deploy an application to Heroku.

First, we will need a user interface for our base application. Create a file named `index.ejs` in the `application base/views` folder and add the following code:

```html
<!doctype html>

<html>
<head>
  <meta name="viewport" content="width=device-width, initial-scale=1.0">
  <!-- set 60 pixel padding for top bar -->
  <style>
    body {
      padding-top: 60px;
    }

    .button {
      text-align: center;
    }
  </style>
  <link href="css/bootstrap.css" rel="stylesheet">
  <link href="css/bootstrap-theme.css">
</head>

<body>

  <div class="navbar navbar-inverse navbar-fixed-top">
    <div class="navbar-inner">
      <div class="container">
        <a class="navbar-brand" href="#">My Mobile App</a>
      </div>
    </div>
  </div>

  <div class="container">
    <div>
      <h1>Hello from Twitter Bootstrap!</h1>
      <p>This is a Test Mobile Application powered by Heroku and Node.js</p>
    </div>
  </div>

  <script type="text/javascript">
```

```
    var configFromEnv = {
      client_id: '<%= client_id %>',
      app_url: '<%= app_url %>'
    };
    console.log('***client_id = ' + configFromEnv.client_id);
    console.log('***app_url = ' + configFromEnv.app_url);

    </script>

  <!-- references for jquery and angularjs -->
  <script src="js/vendor/jquery-2.1.0.js"></script>
  <script src="js/vendor/underscore-1.4.4.min.js"></script>
  <script src="js/vendor/angular.js"></script>
  <script src="js/vendor/angular-route.js"></script>

  <!-- references for the Force.com Libraries -->
  <script src="js/sdk/forcetk.mobilesdk.js"></script>
  <script src="js/sdk/smartsync.js"></script>
  <script src="js/sdk/angular-force.js"></script>
  <script src="js/sdk/forcetk.ui.js"></script>

  </body>
  </html>
```

 You may need to adjust the version number of some script libraries if they are different to the code listing.

Now, we will need to initialize a local git repository for the application. Open a terminal window and issue the following commands from the application base folder:

```
$ git init
$ git add -A
$ git commit -m 'Base HTML5 application'
```

Now, you will need to create a new Heroku application by using the following commands:

```
$ heroku login
$ heroku apps:create
```

Make a note of your Heroku application's name and ensure that you substitute your Heroku application's name when required.

Configuring a remote access application

To be able to access Force.com data from our mobile application, we need to configure a remote access application in Force.com. This will give us the authentication and authorization information, which we need to be able to configure our mobile application. To configure the remote access application, perform the following steps:

1. Navigate to **Setup | Create | Apps**.

2. Scroll down to the **Connected Apps** section and click on **New**.

3. Enter `My Mobile App` for the **Connected App Name** field.

4. The **API Name** field will be autopopulated.

5. Enter your e-mail address in the **Contact Email** field.

6. Enter `Mobile app to access Salesforce.com data` for the **Description** field.

7. Select the **Enable OAuth Settings** checkbox. A new set of fields will be displayed.

8. Enter `https://<<your Heroku App Name>>/#/callback` for the **Callback URL** field. For example, `https://limitless-sierra-9138.herokuapp.com/#/callback`.

9. From the **Available OAuth Scopes** list, move all the options to the **Selected OAuth Scopes** list.

10. Click on **Save**.

The key information that you will need from this screen to connect the mobile application to Force.com is the consumer key. This is the key that will connect your mobile application to the Salesforce remote access application, as shown in the following screenshot:

Deploying the HTML5 base application to Heroku

Now, we are ready to deploy the HTML5 base application to Heroku. To do this, complete the following steps:

1. Set the Heroku environment variables for the HTML5 application client ID and URL by issuing the following commands:

   ```
   $ heroku config:add app_url="https://[your Heroku Application URL]"

   $ heroku config:add client_id="[your Connected Application Consumer Key]"


   for example:


   $ heroku config:add app_url="https://limitless-sierra-9138.herokuapp.com"

   $ heroku config:add client_id="3MVG9A....."
   ```

Make sure that when copying your consumer key from the browser, you don't inadvertently include a newline character. If you start getting errors in your browser console regarding illegal or unexpected characters, this is likely the root cause for those errors.

2. Issue the following command to deploy the application to Heroku:

   ```
   $ git push heroku master
   ```

3. Open the application in your browser by issuing the following command:

   ```
   $ heroku open
   ```

4. You can also use a mobile device to navigate to the application and view the application, as shown in the following screenshot:

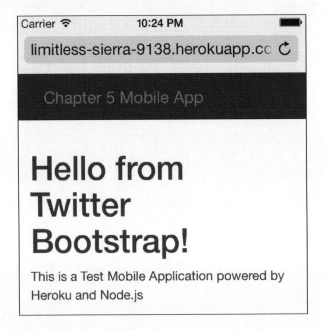

Congratulations! We now have a solid base to start building our final HTML5 application.

How the base application works

Even though the application is only in its basic form, it is worth examining how it works, especially if you are new to Node.js and are wondering how the page is rendered.

The key is the three files that we copied to the `application base` folder earlier.

The `package.json` file tells Heroku which Node.js modules to load when we deploy the application to Heroku. In this case, the key modules that we are interested in are express, which provides web server support; and ejs, which provides a rendering engine for our web pages.

The `Procfile` mechanism is used by Heroku to start the application and consists of the following one line of code:

```
web: node app.js
```

This instructs Heroku to start up Node.js and use `app.js` as the startup script.

The `app.js` file is the bootstrap script for the Node.js application. It sets up the web server environment using the express module, and initializes the ejs module as the default page renderer. It then extracts the Heroku configuration variables for `client_id` and `app_url` so that they can be made available to our `index.ejs` page. Finally, the script sets up a route for the base application URL to render `index.ejs`, and passes through the `app_url` and `client_id` information.

The `index.ejs` page is a fairly straightforward Twitter Bootstrap HTML page, except for the following script block:

```
<script type="text/javascript">

  var configFromEnv = {
    client_id: '<%= client_id %>',
    app_url: '<%= app_url %>'
  };
  console.log('***client_id = ' + configFromEnv.client_id);
  console.log('***app_url = ' + configFromEnv.app_url);

</script>
```

The highlighted lines of code show where we are extracting the `client_id` and `app_url` parameters provided by `app.js` and making them available to our application through ejs substitution. These variables will be required when authenticating against Salesforce using OAuth in our final application.

Building the final AngularJS HTML5 application

Now that we have proven that our technical environment is functioning correctly, we can proceed to build the final, fully functional version of the application.

We will be adding the following features:

- Ability to authenticate and log in to Salesforce

- Adding a page to display a list of opportunities

- Adding a detail page to display information about a single opportunity

- Adding a page to display a Google map showing opportunities within a 5 mile radius of your current location

I am assuming that you have at least a basic understanding of HTML5, JavaScript, AngularJS, jQuery, the Google Maps Geocoding API, and the Google Maps v3 API. If any of these areas are unfamiliar, I recommend that you take some time to familiarize yourself with the technology before attempting to build the final application. For information on AngularJS and jQuery learning resources, check their respective download sections in this chapter. For HTML5 and JavaScript tutorials, check out `http://www.w3schools.com/`. For learning resources for the Google Maps API, check out `https://developers.google.com/maps/documentation/javascript/`, and for the Google Geocoding API check out `https://developers.google.com/maps/documentation/geocoding/`.

Finalizing the application folder structure

To finalize the application folder structure, create the following folders: `application base/public/js/controller`, `application base/public/js/model`, `application base/public/js/service`, `application base/public/partials`, and `application base/public/partials/opportunity`.

Finalizing the application landing page

The first step in finalizing the application logic is to enhance `application base/views/index.ejs`. We will add some AngularJS elements; import the required JavaScript files; and add some structural page elements for the AngularJS application, logout, and navigation.

The inline CSS styles have been modified where necessary to ensure that all `<div>` containers use 100 percent of the available height. This ensures that our Google map will be rendered correctly. This process can be done using the following code:

```
<!doctype html>

<html>
<head>
  <meta name="viewport" content="width=device-width, initial-
scale=1.0">
  <!-- set 60 pixel padding for top bar -->
  <style>
    html { height: 100%; }
    body {
      padding-top: 60px;
      height: 100%;
    }

    .button {
      text-align: center;
    }
    #map-canvas { height: 100%; }
  </style>
  <link href="css/bootstrap.css" rel="stylesheet">
  <link href="css/bootstrap-theme.css">

</head>
```

The `ng-app` directive declares our AngularJS application and informs the framework that we will be using an AngularJS module named `MyMobileApp` to provide the logic for the application.

The new `navbar` items provide links for the opportunity list, opportunity map, and application logout respectively. We have used the `glyph` icons of Twitter Bootstrap for the opportunity list and map links, with a button for the application logout. The `ng-show='isLoggedIn()'` directive ensures that these elements will only be displayed when a user is successfully authenticated against Salesforce. This process can be done by using the following code:

```
<!-- app reference for AngularJS -->
<body ng-app="MyMobileApp">

  <div class="navbar navbar-inverse navbar-fixed-top">
    <div class="navbar-inner">
      <div class="container">
```

```
        <a class="navbar-brand" href="#">My Mobile App</a>
        <!-- Set up Logout Link -->
        <div ng-show='isLoggedIn()' class="pull-right">
            <a href="#/opportunities"><span class="glyphicon glyphicon-
list"></span></a> 
            <a href="#/map"><span class="glyphicon glyphicon-globe"></
span></a> 
            <button class="btn btn-xs btn-primary" ng-
click="logout()">Logout</button>
        </div>
      </div>
    </div>
  </div>
```

The `<div>` element will be the main container for the application itself immediately after the `navbar` item. The `ng-view` directive instructs AngularJS to manage the content for the application. In effect, we have defined a **Single Page Application (SPA)**, where AngularJS will manage the application data (model), display the correct HTML page fragments (view), and manage the application business logic (controller). Do you notice a familiar pattern here? The following code presents the `<div>` element immediately after the `navbar` item, which will be the main container for the application itself:

```
<div class="container-fluid" style="height: 100%">
  <!-- Display Container for AngularJS application -->

  <div ng-view style="height: 100%"></div>
</div>

</body>

<script type="text/javascript">

var configFromEnv = {
  client_id: '<%= client_id %>',
  app_url: '<%= app_url %>'
};
console.log('***client_id = ' + configFromEnv.client_id);
console.log('***app_url = ' + configFromEnv.app_url);

</script>

<!-- references for jquery and angularjs -->
<script src="js/vendor/jquery-2.1.0.js"></script>
<script src="js/vendor/underscore-1.4.4.min.js"></script>
```

```
<script src="js/vendor/angular.js"></script>
<script src="js/vendor/angular-route.js"></script>

<!-- references for the Force.com Libraries -->
<script src="js/sdk/forcetk.mobilesdk.js"></script>
<script src="js/sdk/smartsync.js"></script>
<script src="js/sdk/angular-force.js"></script>
<script src="js/sdk/forcetk.ui.js"></script>
```

The final script declarations in the following code import the Google Maps v3 API and the AngularJS code that we will be creating as we work through the chapter:

```
<!-- Google Maps API -->
<script type="text/javascript"
  src="https://maps.googleapis.com/maps/api/js?key=[Your API key
here]&sensor=false">
</script>

<!-- AngularJS files -->
<script src="js/MyMobileApp.js"></script>
<script src="js/model/Opportunity.js"></script>
<script src="js/service/ReflectionService.js"></script>
<script src="js/service/LocationService.js"></script>
<script src="js/controller/HomeController.js"></script>
<script src="js/controller/LoginController.js"></script>
<script src="js/controller/LogoutController.js"></script>
<script src="js/controller/CallbackController.js"></script>
<script src="js/controller/OppListController.js"></script>
<script src="js/controller/OppViewController.js"></script>
<script src="js/controller/MapViewController.js"></script>

</html>
```

 For your convenience, I have highlighted the differences in the base application version of the file.

Initializing the AngularJS application

In the `application base/public/js` folder, create a file named `MyMobileApp.js` and enter the code from this section.

The following line in `application base/views/index.ejs` initializes the AngularJS application:

```
<!-- app reference for AngularJS -->
<body ng-app="MyMobileApp">
```

Correspondingly, in `MyMobileApp.js`, we bootstrap the application by declaring the `app` variable, which will be the `MyMobileApp` application module for our application (as defined in the `<body>` tag). In AngularJS, an application module is a container for application logic artifacts such as controllers, services, and model-related code. We also use the context dependency injection to inject the dependencies that the application requires to run. In this instance, `AngularForce`, `AngularForceObjectFactory`, and `ngRoute`. `AngularForce` and `AngularForceObjectFactory` are AngularJS modules, which are defined in the Salesforce AngularJS Mobile Pack and provide a wrapper around the lower-level Salesforce Mobile SDK JavaScript libraries. This makes authenticating against Salesforce and retrieving Salesforce data a lot easier than if we had to code against the Salesforce Mobile SDK libraries directly. The `ngRoute` module provides support that will enable us to define the RESTful AngularJS routes for our application, as mentioned in the following code:

```
/* This file initializes the AngularJS app
   and includes the necessary Force.com
   SDK Libraries
*/

// initialize base AngularJS module
var app = angular.module('MyMobileApp', ['AngularForce',
'AngularForceObjectFactory', 'ngRoute']);
```

We then proceed to define the `SFConfig` object, which is a key component of our application. This object will hold the OAuth session token and authentication information required by the application to retrieve data from Salesforce. To initialize `SFConfig`, a call is made to `getSalesforceConfig()`, which checks that we have defined the required environment configuration variables for the Heroku application URL and the Salesforce connected application consumer key. If the variables are defined, we store them in the `SFConfig` object. Finally, we populate `SFConfig` with the URL required to authenticate against Salesforce. The object is then stored as an application constant that can be used throughout the application. This is done with the following code:

```
// get Salesforce Configuration
var SFConfig = getSalesforceConfig();

// set maximum list size
```

```
SFConfig.maxListSize = 25;

// define a constant for the AngularJS app
app.constant('SFConfig', SFConfig);
```

The next block of code defines the RESTful routing for our application. For each application route, we define the route pattern (for example, '/'), the AngularJS controller that will be used to handle the request (for example, 'HomeController'), and the HTML page fragment that will be displayed in the application container for the route (for example, 'partials/home.html'):

```
/****************************
  Configure AngularJS routes
 ****************************/
app.config(function ($routeProvider) {
$routeProvider
   .when('/', {controller: 'HomeController', templateUrl:
                                       'partials/home.html'})
   .when('/login', {controller: 'LoginController', templateUrl:
                                       'partials/login.html'})
   .when('/logout', {controller: 'LogoutController',
                      templateUrl: 'partials/logout.html'})
   .when('/callback', {controller: 'CallbackController',
                      templateUrl: 'partials/callback.html'})
   .when('/opportunities', {controller: 'OppListController',
                   templateUrl: 'partials/opportunity/list.html'})
   .when('/view/:oppId', {controller: 'OppViewController',
                   templateUrl: 'partials/opportunity/view.html'})
   .when('/map', {controller: 'MapViewController', templateUrl:
                                       'partials/map.html'})
   .otherwise({redirectTo: '/'});
});
```

The initApp() method is called when the application user is successfully authenticated against Salesforce (as described later in the *The Salesforce authentication components* section). This method takes the information returned from the authentication process and uses it to initialize the Salesforce Mobile SDK Force toolkit. Once the Force.init method is called, the SFConfig object has all the information it needs to connect to Salesforce and retrieve data. This process is done with the following code:

```
/**********************************************
  initApp - called when authentication successful
 **********************************************/
function initApp(options, forcetkClient) {
  // initialize options object to hold Salesforce
```

```
  // access and configuration information
  options = options || {};
  options.loginUrl = SFConfig.sfLoginURL;
  options.clientId = SFConfig.consumerKey;
  options.apiVersion = 'v29.0';
  options.userAgent = 'SalesforceMobileUI/alpha';
  options.proxyUrl = options.proxyUrl || SFConfig.proxyUrl;

  // initialize forcetk toolkit
  Force.init(options, options.apiVersion, forcetkClient);

}


/***********************************
 Salesforce Configuration Functions
 ***********************************/

function getSalesforceConfig() {
  // first check if environment configuration variables are set
  if (!configFromEnv || configFromEnv.client_id == "" ||
      configFromEnv.client_id == "undefined" ||
      configFromEnv.app_url == "" ||
      configFromEnv.app_url == "undefined") {
      throw 'Environment variable client_id and/or app_url is
missing. Please set them before you start the app';
  }
  // return config information for login URL, OAuth information and
proxy URL
  return {
    sfLoginURL: 'https://login.salesforce.com/',
    consumerKey: configFromEnv.client_id,
    oAuthCallbackURL: removeTrailingSlash(configFromEnv.app_url) +
'/#/callback',
    proxyUrl: removeTrailingSlash(configFromEnv.app_url) + '/proxy/'
  }
}

//Helper
function removeTrailingSlash(url) {
  return url.replace(/\/$/, "");
}
```

Finally, by using the following code, we declare two functions that will be available globally to the application. The `isLoggedIn()` function will determine whether a user is successfully logged in, and `logout()` will be used to log a user out of Salesforce, and the application itself:

```
/*****************************
 Authentication Functions to
 check if user logged in, and
 log user out
*****************************/

// return authentication status
app.run(function (AngularForce, $rootScope) {
  $rootScope.isLoggedIn = function() {
    return AngularForce.authenticated();
  }
});


// logout user
app.run(function (AngularForce, $rootScope, $location) {
  $rootScope.logout = function() {
    AngularForce.logout();
    // Now go to logout page
    $location.path('/logout');
  }
});
```

The Salesforce authentication components

We will now build the AngularJS application components necessary to execute the OAuth process that will enable the application users to authenticate against Salesforce.

Home controller

In the `application base/public/js/controller` folder, create a file named `HomeController.js` and enter the following code:

```
// AngularJS Controller for Home Page
app.controller('HomeController', function($scope, AngularForce,
$location, $routeParams) {
  // check if user authenticated
  var isAuthenticated = AngularForce.authenticated();

  if (AngularForce.refreshToken)
```

```
  {
    // try to relogin using refresh token
    AngularForce.login(function() {
      $location.path('/opportunities');
    });
  } else {
    $location.path('/login');
  }

});
```

In the `application base/public/partials` folder, create a file named `home.html`. Leave this file blank as we will not be displaying any content for this HTML page fragment.

How the home controller works

The home controller commences by calling the `AngularForce.refreshToken()` method to check for a refresh token from a successful login. If a refresh token is found, the `AngularForce.login()` method is called to relogin to Salesforce and refresh the session token. Once the login is completed successfully, the application presents a list of opportunities using the `/opportunities` AngularJS route.

If the user isn't logged in, they are redirected to the `/login` AngularJS route to allow them to authenticate against Salesforce using the OAuth process.

The login controller

In the `application base/public/js/controller` folder, create a file named `LoginController.js` and enter the following code:

```
app.controller('LoginController', function($scope, AngularForce,
$location) {

  // check if authenticated
  if (AngularForce.authenticated()) {
    return $location.path('/opportunities');
  }

  // login to Salesforce
  $scope.login = function() {
    AngularForce.login();
  };

});
```

In the `application base/public/partials` folder, create a file named `login.html` and enter the following code:

```
<div class="span4 well">
  <p>Please log into Salesforce.</p>
  <p style='text-align: center;padding-bottom: 30px;'>
    <button class="btn btn-large btn-primary" ng-
click="login()">Login</button>
  </p>

</div>
```

How the login controller works

The login controller first checks if the user is logged in by calling the `AngularForce.authenticated()` method. If the user is logged in, they are redirected to the `/opportunities` AngularJS route.

If the user isn't logged in, the `login.html` page is displayed. The **Login** button is linked to the AngularJS `$scope.login()` event handler. When the button is clicked, the `AngularForce.login()` method is called to start the Salesforce OAuth authentication process.

The callback controller

In the `application base/public/js/controller` folder, create a file named `CallbackController.js` and enter the following code:

```
app.controller('CallbackController', function($scope, AngularForce,
$location) {
  AngularForce.oauthCallback(document.location.href);

  // set hash to empty before setting path to /opportunities
  $location.hash('');
  $location.path('/opportunities');

});
```

In the `application base/public/partials` folder, create a file named `callback. html` and enter the following code:

```
<p>You are successfully logged into Salesforce.</p>
```

How the callback controller works

The callback controller is executed when the `/callback` route is invoked after a user is successfully authenticated against Salesforce (as defined in our Salesforce connected application). The authentication information (session token and Salesforce REST API endpoint) is included as parameters to the callback URL. The controller calls the `AngularForce.oauthCallback()` method and passes it in the URL information. Behind the scenes, this invokes the `initApp()` method defined in `MyMobileApp.js`.

The method then proceeds to remove the authentication information from the URL (by removing the hash) and redirect the user to the opportunities list page.

The logout controller

In the `application base/public/js/controller` folder, create a file named `LogoutController.js` and enter the following code:

```
app.controller('LogoutController', function($scope, AngularForce,
$location, ReflectionService) {

    $location.path('/');

});
```

In the `application base/public/partials` folder, create a file named `logout.html` and enter the following code:

```
<p>You are now logged out of the application.</p>
```

How the logout controller works

When the user clicks on the **Logout** button in the application, the `logout()` method defined in `MyMobileApp.js` is invoked. This logs the users out of the application and redirects them to the `/logout` route. At this point, the message defined in `logout.html` is displayed to the users and they are redirected to the application's home page.

The opportunity display components

We will now build the application components necessary to retrieve and display the Salesforce opportunities in our mobile application.

The opportunity factory

The opportunity AngularJS factory contains the following three methods that provide opportunities to the application:

Method	Description
`getOpportunityList`	This method returns a list of open opportunities
`getOpportunity`	This method returns information about a single opportunity
`getOpportunitiesWithinRadius`	This method returns opportunities within a 5 mile radius of the user's current location

Each method follows the AngularJS promise pattern. This is a pattern used to define methods that return results asynchronously. First, we declare the `deferred` variable to set up the AngularJS promise context. The method initially returns a `deferred.promise` object to the calling method as a placeholder for the results when they arrive. When the results are ready, they are returned to the calling method through the `deferred.resolve()` method. If an error occurs, the `deferred.reject()` method is used to return the error details to the calling method. We will see how the calling method handles the AngularJS promise when we examine the *The opportunity list controller* section.

In the `application base/public/js/model` folder, create a file named `Opportunity.js` and enter the following code from this section:

```
app.factory('Opportunity', function($q, AngularForceObjectFactory,
ReflectionService) {

  var factory = {};

  // get a list of opportunities
  factory.getOpportunityList = function() {

    var deferred = $q.defer();
```

The `objQuery` object is initialized through JSON and defines the Salesforce object to be queried, the fields to be returned, the `where` filtering clause, the field(s) to sort by, and the maximum number of rows to be returned. This is done by using the following code:

```
// Configure Opportunity Object Criteria
var objQuery = {
  type: 'Opportunity',
  fields: ['Id', 'Name', 'Account.Name', 'StageName', 'Amount',
    'CloseDate'],
  where: "StageName <> 'Closed Won' AND StageName <> 'Closed
    Lost'",
  orderBy: 'Id',
  limit: 20
};
```

The `Opportunity` object is defined next, passing in the `objQuery` object into the constructor by using the following code. The `query()` method is then called. When the query results are returned, the success function returns the results to the calling method. If an error occurs, the error information is passed back to the calling method:

```
var Opportunity = AngularForceObjectFactory(objQuery);

Opportunity.query(function(data) {
  var opportunities = data.records;
  deferred.resolve(opportunities);
}, function(error) {
  deferred.reject(error);

});

// return promise to controller to deliver deferred results
return deferred.promise;

};
```

The `getOpportunity()` method uses a similar pattern. The only difference is the `Where` clause, which uses the `id` parameter to extract a single opportunity. This is explained in the following code:

```
// get a single opportunity
factory.getOpportunity = function(id) {

  var deferred = $q.defer();

  // Configure Opportunity Object Criteria
  var objQuery = {
    type: 'Opportunity',
    fields: ['Id', 'Name', 'Account.Name', 'Account.Phone',
      'StageName', 'Amount', 'CloseDate'],
    where: "Id = '" + id + "'",
    orderBy: 'Id',
    limit: 20
  };

  var Opportunity = AngularForceObjectFactory(objQuery);

  Opportunity.query(function(data) {
    var opportunity = data.records;
    deferred.resolve(opportunity);
```

```
  }, function(error) {
    deferred.reject(error);

  });

  // return promise to controller to deliver deferred results
  return deferred.promise;
};
```

The following code from the getOpportunitiesWithinRadius() method is of particular interest, which uses a geolocation SOQL query to find opportunities within the 5 mile radius. We will see how the location-related data is populated in Salesforce when we will examine the *The opportunity map components* section:

```
// get a list of opportunities within a given map radius
factory.getOpportunitiesWithinRadius = function(currLat, currLng) {

  var deferred = $q.defer();

  // Configure Opportunity Object Criteria
  var objQuery = {
    type: 'Opportunity',
    fields: ['Id', 'Name', 'Account.Name', 'Account.Phone',
          'Account.BillingStreet',
          'Account.BillingCity', 'Account.BillingState',
          'Account.BillingCountry',
          'Account.BillingPostalCode',
          'Account.Location__Latitude__s',
          'Account.Location__Longitude__s'],
    where: "DISTANCE (Account.Location__c, GEOLOCATION(" +
          currLat +
          "," + currLng + "),'mi') < 5",
    orderBy: 'Id',
    limit: 20
  };

  var Opportunity = AngularForceObjectFactory(objQuery);

  Opportunity.query(function(data) {
    var opportunity = data.records;
    deferred.resolve(opportunity);
  }, function(error) {
    deferred.reject(error);
  });
```

```
    // return promise to controller to deliver deferred results
    return deferred.promise;
};


return factory;


});
```

The opportunity list controller

In the `application base/public/js/controller` folder, create a file named `OppListController.js` and enter the following code:

```
// AngularJS Controller for Opportunity List
'use-strict';
app.controller('OppListController', function($scope, $rootScope,
AngularForce, $location, Opportunity, ReflectionService) {

  // set flag to display progress message
  $scope.isWorking = true;

  if ($rootScope.isLoggedIn()) {

    Opportunity.getOpportunityList().then(function(data) {
      // model for view
      $scope.isWorking = false;
      $scope.opportunityList = data;

    }, function(data) {
      console.log('***OppListController.js - Error Retrieving
        Opportunity List...');
      console.log('readyState = ' + data.readyState);
      console.log('responseText = ' + data.responseText);
      console.log('responseJSON = ' + data.responseJSON);
      console.log('status = ' + data.status);
      console.log('statusText = ' + data.statusText);

    });

  } else {
    // re-direct to login page
    $location.path('/');
  }

});
```

In the `application base/public/partials/opportunity` folder, create a file named `list.html` and enter the following code:

```
<div ng-show='isWorking'>
  <p>Retrieving Opportunities...</p>
</div>

<!-- responsive table (class="hidden-xs") -->
<div ng-show='!isWorking'>
  <table width="80%" class="table">
    <thead>
      <tr>
        <th>Name</th>
        <th class="hidden-xs">Account</th>
        <th>Amount</th>
        <th class="hidden-xs">Stage</th>
        <th>Closes</th>
      </tr>
    </thead>
    <tbody>
      <tr ng-repeat='opportunity in opportunityList'>
        <td><a href="#/view/{{opportunity.Id}}">{{opportunity.Name}}</a></td>
        <td class="hidden-xs">{{opportunity.Account.Name}}</td>
        <td>{{opportunity.Amount | currency:"USD$"}}</td>
        <td class="hidden-xs">{{opportunity.StageName}}</td>
        <td>{{opportunity.CloseDate | date:"shortDate"}}</td>
      </tr>
    </tbody>
  </table>
</div>
```

How the opportunity list controller works

The opportunity list controller first ensures that the user is logged in. If so, the `Opportunity.getOpportunityList()` method is called. This illustrates the other half of the AngularJS promise pattern. The block of code contained in the `.then()` block is executed after the query results or error information is returned by the `deferred.resolve()` or `deferred.reject()` methods in the opportunity factory method. In the case of a successful query, the results are injected into the current AngularJS scope so that they can be accessed by the AngularJS view.

If the user isn't logged in, they are redirected back to the application home page.

The view consists of an HTML table, augmented with some Twitter Bootstrap responsive CSS classes and AngularJS directives. The `hidden-xs` class causes bootstrap to automatically hide columns on smaller displays.

The ng-repeat directive is then used to render a table row for each opportunity that is returned. The opportunity values are inserted into HTML using AngularJS substitution. AngularJS filters are applied to the opportunity amount and close date to format them as US dollars and a short date, respectively.

The opportunity detail view controller

In the application base/public/js/controller folder, create a file named OppViewController.js and enter the following code:

```
// AngularJS Controller for Opportunity View
'use-strict';
app.controller('OppViewController', function($scope, $rootScope,
AngularForce, $routeParams, $location, Opportunity, ReflectionService)
{

  // set flag to display progress message
  $scope.isWorking = true;

  if ($rootScope.isLoggedIn()) {
    Opportunity.getOpportunity($routeParams.oppId).then(function(data)
{
      // model for view
      $scope.isWorking = false;
      $scope.opportunity = data[0];
    }, function(data) {
      console.log('***OppListController.js - Error Retrieving
        Opportunity...');
      console.log('readyState = ' + data.readyState);
      console.log('responseText = ' + data.responseText);
      console.log('responseJSON = ' + data.responseJSON);
      console.log('status = ' + data.status);
      console.log('statusText = ' + data.statusText);

    });

  } else {
    $location.path('/');
  }

});
```

In the `application base/public/partials/opportunity` folder, create a file named `view.html` and enter the following code:

```
<style>

a[href^="tel:"]:before {
    content: "\260E";
    display: block;
    margin-right: 0.5em;
}
</style>
<div ng-show="isWorking">
  <p>Retrieving Opportunity...</p>
</div>

<div ng-show="!isWorking">
  <h3>{{opportunity.Name}}</h3>
  <p>for {{opportunity.Account.Name}}</p>
  <p><a href="tel:{{opportunity.Account.Phone}}">{{opportunity.
Account.Phone}}</a></p>
  <p>Value: {{opportunity.Amount  | currency:"USD$"}}</p>
  <p>Stage: {{opportunity.StageName}}</p>
  <p>Closes: {{opportunity.CloseDate | date:"shortDate"}}</p>
  <a href="#/opportunities">Back to List</a>
</div>
```

How the opportunity detail view controller works

The opportunity detail controller follows the same pattern as the opportunity list controller. The `Opportunity.getOpportunity()` method is called, passing in the opportunity `id` received in the route.

The view uses AngularJS substitution to inject the opportunity values into HTML. Again, filters are applied to the opportunity amount and close date. Note the inline CSS style, which is used to display a Unicode telephone character in the HTML output.

The opportunity map components

We will now build the application components necessary to retrieve and display Salesforce opportunities on a Google map.

Adding a geolocation trigger to the Account object

We will need to add a trigger to the Account object to geolocate the account addresses. This will allow us to display the location of an opportunity for an account on a Google map in our mobile application.

 The geolocation trigger functionality that is built in this section was inspired by a blog article located at http://blog.internetcreations.com/2012/09/creating-a-geolocation-trigger-in-salesforce-winter-13/.

First, you need to obtain an API key for Google Maps and a geolocation API by using the following steps:

1. Visit https://code.google.com/apis/console and sign in with your Google account (assuming that you already have one).

2. Click on the **Create project...** button.

3. Enter My Mobile Project in the **Project name** field.

4. Accept the default value for the **Project ID** field.

5. Click on **Create**.

6. Click on **APIs & auth** from the left-hand side navigation bar.

7. Set the **Geocoding API** field to **ON**, as shown in the following screenshot:

8. Also, set **Google Maps Javascript API v3** to **ON**, as shown in the following screenshot:

9. Select **Credentials** and click on **CREATE NEW KEY**.

10. Click on the **Browser Key** button.

11. Click on **Create new Server key...** to generate the key. Make a note of the API key, as shown in the following screenshot:

Simple API Access
Use API keys to identify your project when you do not need to access user data. Learn more

Key for browser apps (with referers)
API key:

Referers: Any referer allowed

Activated on: Feb 11, 2014 4:42 PM

Activated by: – you

Create new Server key... Create new Browser key... Create new Android key... Create new iOS key...

Now, we need to add a Salesforce remote site for the Google Maps API by performing the following steps:

1. Navigate to **Setup | Security Controls | Remote Site Settings**.
2. Click on the **New Remote Site** button.
3. Enter Google_Maps_API in the **Remote Site Name** field.
4. Enter https://maps.googleapis.com for the **Remote Site URL** field.
5. Ensure that the **Active** checkbox is checked
6. Click on **Save**.
7. Your **Remote Site Detail** screen should resemble the following screenshot:

Next, we need to add a Location field to the **Account** object:

1. Navigate to **Setup | Customize | Accounts | Fields**.
2. Click on the **New** button in the **Custom Fields & Relationships** section.
3. Select **Geolocation** for the **Data Type** field. Click on **Next**.
4. Enter Location for **Field Label**. The **Field Name** should also default to **Location**.

5. Select **Decimal** for the **Latitude and Longitude Display Notation** section.

6. Enter 7 for the **Decimal Places** field. Click on **Next**.

7. Click on **Next** to accept the default settings for **Field-Level Security**.

8. Click on **Save** to add the field to all account-related page layouts.

Next, we need an Apex utility class to geocode an address using the Google Geocoding API by completing the following steps:

1. Navigate to **Setup | Develop | Apex Classes**.

2. All of the Apex classes for your organization will be displayed. Click on **New**.

3. In the code download for the chapter, locate the `AccountGeocodeAddress.cls` file in the `force_com` folder.

4. Copy and paste the contents of `AccountGeocodeAddress.cls` into the Apex code editor in your Force.com window.

5. Insert your Google API key in the following line of code:

```
String geocodingKey = '[Your API Key here]';
```

6. Click on **Save**.

Finally, we need to implement an Apex trigger class to geocode the billing address when an account is added or updated. For this, perform the following steps:

1. Navigate to **Setup | Develop | Apex Triggers**.

2. All of the Apex triggers for your organization will be displayed. Click on **Developer Console**.

3. Navigate to **File | New | Apex Trigger** in the developer console.

4. Enter `geocodeAccountAddress` in the **Name** field.

5. Select **Account** in the **sObject** drop-down list and click on **Submit**, as shown in the following screenshot:

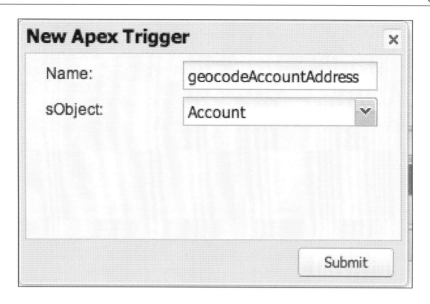

6. In the code download for the chapter, locate the geocodeAccountAddress. trigger file in the force_com folder.

7. Copy and paste the contents of geocodeAccountAddress.trigger into the Apex code editor in your developer console window. Go to **File | Save**.

How the geolocation trigger works

We begin by declaring the Apex class that will perform the geocoding by using the following code:

```
public with sharing class AccountGeocodeAddress {
```

A static variable is then declared to flag whether the geocoding has already been performed in the current execution context by using the following code:

```
private static Boolean geocodingCalled = false;
```

A problem can potentially occur when you geocode an address as a result of an update to an account. For example, account A is updated, which invokes the after update trigger, which in turn invokes a future method to perform the geocoding operation. The geocoding operation within the future method then updates account A by adding/updating the **Location** field coordinates. This in turn calls the after update trigger on account A again, which invokes another future method to perform the geocoding operation. This will trigger an error because you cannot invoke a future method from within a future method.

The following code prevents this from happening:

```
public static void DoAddressGeocode(id accountId) {
  if (geocodingCalled || System.isFuture()) {
    System.debug(LoggingLevel.WARN, '***Address Geocoding Future
Method Already Called - Aborting...');
    return;
  }

  // if not being called from future context, geocode the address
  geocodingCalled = true;
  geocodeAddress(accountId);
}
```

Then, we will declare a future method using the following code that will accept an account ID as a parameter and geocode the billing address against the Google API:

```
// we need a future method to call Google Geocoding API
@future (callout=true)
static private void geocodeAddress(id accountId) {
```

We then declare some variables by using the following code to hold our Google Maps API key and the Account object we are geocoding:

```
// Key for Google Maps Geocoding API
String geocodingKey = '[Your API Key here]';

// get the passed in address
Account geoAccount = [SELECT BillingStreet, BillingCity, BillingState,
BillingCountry, BillingPostalCode
        FROM Account
        WHERE id = :accountId];
```

A quick check is then performed by using the following code to ensure that we have enough information to geocode the address:

```
// check that we have enough information to geocode the address
if ((geoAccount.BillingStreet == null) ||
        (geoAccount.BillingCity == null)) {
  System.debug(LoggingLevel.WARN, 'Insufficient Data to Geocode
Address');
  return;
}
```

The billing address for the Account object is then inspected to build a string representation of the address by using the following code:

```
// create a string for the address to pass to Google Geocoding API
String geoAddress = '';
```

```
if (geoAccount.BillingStreet != null)
  geoAddress += geoAccount.BillingStreet + ', ';
if (geoAccount.BillingCity != null)
  geoAddress += geoAccount.BillingCity + ', ';
if (geoAccount.BillingState != null)
  geoAddress += geoAccount.BillingState + ', ';
if (geoAccount.BillingCountry != null)
  geoAddress += geoAccount.BillingCountry + ', ';
if (geoAccount.BillingPostalCode != null)
  geoAddress += geoAccount.BillingPostalCode;
```

The address string is then URL encoded by using the following code so that it can be included in the call to the Google Geocoding API:

```
// encode the string so we can pass it as part of URL
geoAddress = EncodingUtil.urlEncode(geoAddress, 'UTF-8');
```

We then declare an instance of the Apex `Http` class to initiate the HTTP request and response. We also declare and build an instance of the `HttpRequest` class to represent the GET request to the Google Maps API by using the following code:

```
Http http = new Http();
HttpRequest request = new HttpRequest();
request.setEndpoint('https://maps.googleapis.com/maps/api/geocode/
json?address='
    + geoAddress + '&key=' + geocodingKey
    '&sensor=false');
request.setMethod('GET');
request.setTimeout(60000);
```

With the HTTP request constructed, we then proceed to make the call from within a try-catch block by using the following code:

```
try {
  // make the http callout
  HttpResponse response = http.send(request);
```

We have requested a response from the Geocoding API in JSON format. Therefore, we create an Apex JSON parser to process the JSON format returned from the API. We also declare two variables to hold the latitude and longitude of the address by using the following code:

```
JSONParser responseParser = JSON.createParser(response.getBody());

// initialize co-ordinates
double latitude = null;
double longitude = null;
```

With everything now in place, we can parse the response from the Geocoding API and extract the latitude and longitude of the address by using the following code:

```
while (responseParser.nextToken() != null) {
   if ((responseParser.getCurrentToken() == JSONToken.FIELD_NAME) &&
(responseParser.getText() == 'location')) {
 responseParser.nextToken();
 while (responseParser.nextToken() != JSONToken.END_OBJECT)    {
    String locationText = responseParser.getText();
    responseParser.nextToken();
    if (locationText == 'lat')
       latitude = responseParser.getDoubleValue();
    else if (locationText == 'lng')
  longitude = responseParser.getDoubleValue();
 }
  }
}
```

Finally, we check if we have received co-ordinates from the API. If so, we update the Account object and close the try-catch block, as shown in the following code:

```
// update co-ordinates on address if we get them back
if (latitude != null) {
  geoAccount.Location__Latitude__s = latitude;
  geoAccount.Location__Longitude__s = longitude;
  update geoAccount;
}
} catch (Exception e) {
  System.debug(LoggingLevel.ERROR, 'Error Geocoding Address - ' +
e.getMessage());
}
```

The Account after insert / Account after update trigger itself is relatively simple. If the **Location** field is blank or the billing address has been updated, a call is made to the AccountGeocodeAddress.DoAddressGeocode method to geocode the address against the Google Maps geocoding API with the following code:

```
trigger geocodeAccountAddress on Account (after insert, after update)
{

   // bulkify trigger in case of multiple accounts
   for (Account account : trigger.new) {

      // check if Billing Address has been updated
      Boolean addressChangedFlag = false;
      if (Trigger.isUpdate) {
```

```
        Account oldAccount = Trigger.oldMap.get(account.Id);
    if ((account.BillingStreet != oldAccount.BillingStreet) ||
      (account.BillingCity != oldAccount.BillingStreet) ||
      (account.BillingCountry != oldAccount.BillingCountry) ||
      (account.BillingPostalCode != oldAccount.BillingPostalCode)) {
      addressChangedFlag = true;
      System.debug(LoggingLevel.DEBUG, '***Address changed for - ' +
        oldAccount.Name);
    }
      }


      // if address is null or has been changed, geocode it
      if ((account.Location__Latitude__s == null) || (addressChangedFlag
== true)) {
    System.debug(LoggingLevel.DEBUG, '***Geocoding Account - ' +
account.Name);
      AccountGeocodeAddress.DoAddressGeocode(account.id);
      }
    }
}
```

Location service

In the `application base/public/js/service` folder, create a file named
`LocationService.js` and enter the following code:

```
/******************************
 Location Services for
 Application
 ******************************/

console.log('***LocationService.js - Initializing
LocationService...');
app.service('LocationService', function($q) {

  this.getCurrentLocation = function() {
    var deferred = $q.defer();

    // default co-ordinates are Sydney, Australia
    var defaultLatitude = -34.397;
    var defaultLongitude = 150.644;

    var success = function(position) {
      deferred.resolve(position);
    }
```

```
      var error = function() {
        var defaultPosition = {
          latitude: defaultLatitude,
          longitude: defaultLongitude
        };
        deferred.reject(defaultPosition);
      }

      if (navigator.geolocation) {
        navigator.geolocation.getCurrentPosition(success, error);
      } else {
        error();
      }

      // return promise to controller to deliver deferred results
      return deferred.promise;
    }

});
```

How it works

Once again, we use the AngularJS promise pattern to determine the user's current location. We start by setting some default co-ordinates, in case the device can't determine the current location, or the user does not grant permission for us to use it.

We then set up a success function for a successful attempt to search for a location. This function returns the user's current position to the calling method using the `deferred.resolve()` method. Next, an error handler function is set up in case of an unsuccessful location find attempt. In this case, we return the default co-ordinates to the calling method using `deferred.reject()`.

Finally, we check if the current device supports finding the user's location by checking the browser's `navigator.geolocation` property. If so, we call the `navigator.geolocation.getCurrentPosition()` method to find the user's current location. If the browser doesn't support geolocation, we invoke the error handler method to return the default co-ordinates.

The map view controller

The map view controller is the most complicated controller in the entire application, so we will take some time to examine it in a greater level of detail.

In the `application base/public/js/controller` folder, create a file named
`MapViewController.js` and enter the following code from this section.

```
app.controller('MapViewController', function($scope, $rootScope,
    AngularForce, $location, $routeParams, LocationService,
Opportunity, ReflectionService) {
```

We begin with a check to ensure that the user is logged in, and initialize the map
position and the map itself by using the following code:

```
if ($rootScope.isLoggedIn()) {

    var mapLocation = {
        latitude: 0,
        longitude: 0
    };

    var map = null;
```

We then use an AngularJS promise to get the user's current location. If the location
find attempt is successful, we store the co-ordinates in the `mapLocation` object. In the
event that it is unsuccessful, we store the default co-ordinates in the `mapLocation`
object. For this, we use the following code:

```
    // use LocationService to get current position or default
    // co-ordinates
LocationService.getCurrentLocation().then(function(position) {
        mapLocation.latitude = position.coords.latitude;
        mapLocation.longitude = position.coords.longitude;
    }, function(defaultPosition) {
        defaultPosition.latitude;
        mapLocation.longitude = defaultPosition.longitude;
    })
```

We then use another `.then()` block to execute the following code after the users'
location has been determined. Here, we are also initializing the Google map and
placing a marker on it to show the users' current location:

```
    .then(function() {
        var mapOptions = {
            center: new google.maps.LatLng(mapLocation.latitude,
                mapLocation.longitude),
            zoom: 15,
            mapTypeId: google.maps.MapTypeId.ROADMAP
        };
        map = new google.maps.Map(document.getElementById("map-canvas"),
            mapOptions);
```

```
      // mark current position on map
      var marker = new google.maps.Marker({
        position: new google.maps.LatLng(mapLocation.latitude,
          mapLocation.longitude),
        map: map
      });
    })
```

Now that we have the Google map initialized with the users' current location, we are ready to add markers for the opportunities within a 5 mile radius. We use another `.then()` block to execute the following code:

```
.then(function() {
  // select any opportunities within a 5 mile radius and plot
  // them on the map
  Opportunity.getOpportunitiesWithinRadius(
          mapLocation.latitude, mapLocation.longitude).then(
```

We make a call to the `Opportunity.getOpportunitiesWithinRadius()` method and pass in the user's current location. What is important to note here is that the `getOpportunitiesWithinRadius()` method is also asynchronous in nature, so we need to start another AngularJS promise within the current `.then()` block to ensure that we process the results in the correct sequence.

Next, we will process the `getOpportunitiesWithinRadius()` results when they are returned, by using the following code:

```
function(data) {
  // LatLng Bounds Object to determine zoom level
  var bounds = new google.maps.LatLngBounds();
  // flag to determine whether to adjust default boundary
  var extendBounds = false;

  $.each(data, function(i, val) {
    // add marker to map
    var oppMarker = new google.maps.Marker({
      position: new
    google.maps.LatLng(val.Account.Location__Latitude__s,
                val.Account.Location__Longitude__s),
      map: map,
      icon: 'http://gmaps-samples.googlecode.com/svn/trunk/
        markers/green/blank.png'
    });
```

First, we initialize the `bounds` object. This will help us to ensure that the zoom level of the Google map is set correctly to ensure that all opportunities are displayed. We also set up the `extendBounds` flag, which will tell us whether we need to trigger a map resizing once the opportunities have been processed. We give it an initial value of `false` because we haven't processed any opportunities yet.

A very cool feature of AngularJS is that it plays nicely with jQuery. We take advantage of this by using a jQuery for-each loop to place a marker on the map at the location of each opportunity using the `Account.Location` field. We use a `green` marker to differentiate them from the users' current location marker.

Still within the jQuery for-each loop, we set up an information window to be displayed when the user taps on an opportunity marker, by using the following code:

```
// info window for the marker
(function(i, oppMarker, val) {
  // Event listener has access to values of i and
  // marker as they were during marker creation
  google.maps.event.addListener(oppMarker, 'click',
  function() {
      var infoWindow = new google.maps.InfoWindow({
        content: '<strong>' + val.Name +
          '</strong><br />'
          + val.Account.Name + '<br />'
        + val.Account.BillingStreet + '<br />'
        + val.Account.BillingCity + '<br />'
        + val.Account.BillingState + ' '
        + val.Account.BillingPostalCode + '<br />'
        + val.Account.BillingCountry + '<br />'
        + '<a href="tel:' + val.Account.Phone + '">'
        + val.Account.Phone + '</a><br />'
      });
      infoWindow.open(map, oppMarker);
    });
}) (i, oppMarker, val);
```

At this point, we have placed an opportunity marker and its associated information window on the map. In the following code, we will also adjust the `bounds` object to encapsulate the geographical area of the current marker by calling the `bounds.extend()` method. We also set the `extendBounds` flag to `true` to indicate that we need to adjust the map viewport:

```
// Extend bounds object with each opportunity
bounds.extend(new
  google.maps.LatLng(val.Account.Location__Latitude__s,
                val.Account.Location__Longitude__s));
extendBounds = true;
});
```

Now that the for-each loop has been completed, we have placed all of the markers on the map. At this point, we call the `map.fitBounds()` method to adjust the map viewport to ensure that all opportunity markers are displayed. This is done by using the following code:

```
// if we have at least 1 opportunity adjust the boundary
// to fit all opportunities
if (extendBounds) {
  map.fitBounds(bounds);
}
```

We then complete the AngularJS promise with the standard error handling function. Finally, if the user isn't logged in, we redirect them to the application home page, by using the following code:

```
}, function(data) {
    console.log('***MapViewController.js - Error Retrieving
        Opportunity List...');
    console.log('readyState = ' + data.readyState);
    console.log('responseText = ' + data.responseText);
    console.log('responseJSON = ' + data.responseJSON);
    console.log('status = ' + data.status);
    console.log('statusText = ' + data.statusText);


    });
  });

} else {
  // re-direct to login page
  $location.path('/');
}

});
```

In the `application base/public/partials/opportunity` folder, create a file named `map.html` and enter the following code:

```
<!-- Google Map Canvas -->
<div id="map-canvas">

</div>
```

JavaScript object reflection service

In the `application base/public/js/service` folder, create a file named `ReflectionService.js` and enter the following code:

```
/******************************
 Reflection Services for
 Javascript objects
 ******************************/

app.service('ReflectionService', function() {

  // This is some fantastic utility code to get properties of
  // a Javascript object using reflection
  this.Reflector = function(obj) {
    this.getProperties = function() {
      var properties = [];
      for (var prop in obj) {
        if (typeof obj[prop] != 'function') {
          properties.push(prop);
        }
      }
      return properties;
    };
  }
});
```

The reflection service is a utility that I use to display the properties of JavaScript objects such as `SFConfig` and the data returned by the opportunity factory. The purpose was mainly to debug JavaScript objects and log their property values to the JavaScript console during development. I have included it as part of the application as I think it will be a handy utility that you can use in your own AngularJS projects.

Deploying an application to Heroku

Now that the development of the final application is complete, we can update our local git repository and deploy the application to Heroku by issuing the following commands:

```
$ git add .
$ git commit -m "Final HTML5 Application for Chapter 5"
$ git push heroku master
```

To see the application in action, navigate your web browser to your Heroku application URL or issue the following command:

```
$ heroku open
```

Congratulations! It has been quite a journey but you now have a fully functional HTML5-based mobile SDK application running on Heroku.

Summary

The aim of an effective mobile application is to present relevant information to a user based on their current context. Don't fall into the trap of trying to completely replicate the desktop functionality on a mobile device. We have achieved both of these aims by providing key opportunity data using the mobile application, and presented context-aware information by placing nearby opportunities on a Google map.

Along the way, we have combined an impressive array of technologies to form a fully working application.

Although, at the time of writing, AngularJS is a relatively new JavaScript Framework, I hope this chapter has convinced you that it is an extremely promising technology. In particular, its native support of context dependency injection and the AngularJS promise construct make life a lot easier for JavaScript developers. If you have ever had to debug nested JavaScript functions more than two levels deep, you should know what I mean!

The application itself should give you a good idea of the power of the Salesforce1 mobile SDK, and how you can apply it to your real-world applications. The sheer breadth of the Salesforce1 mobile SDK is extremely impressive, and I encourage you to explore it in more detail.

As always, following are some suggestions on how you can extend the application:

- You can add some limited update functionality to the application, for example, to change the status of an opportunity.
- You could change the color of the opportunity map markers based on the value of an opportunity to give the user a visual cue.
- The HTML5 application forms a perfect base to migrate it to a hybrid app using the Apache Cordova mobile SDK. Try to implement the application in the platform of your choice (iOS or Android).

6
Cloud-connected Applications

In this chapter, we will connect a Force.com application to Microsoft Windows Azure. In a similar vein to mobile devices, cloud computing adoption has skyrocketed in recent years (with Salesforce leading the charge) and shows no signs of slowing down.

Windows Azure is Microsoft's cloud computing environment and provides an impressive array of cloud-based services. We will be connecting a Force.com application to the Azure Service Bus, which offers a feature called **Notification Hubs**.

Notification Hubs offer a service to send mobile device push notifications to iOS, Android, and Windows mobile devices. The service exposes this functionality through a REST API, which can be accessed from Force.com.

The real strength of this feature is that it abstracts the lower-level details of each platform's notification service, relieving us from complex details, such as load balancing, queuing, and in the case of Google Cloud messaging, exponential back off. All we need to do is supply the required credentials for the mobile platform(s) we wish to target, and use the REST API to start sending push notifications.

Fortunately for us, Force.com provides a robust toolkit to access cloud computing platforms such as Azure, and integrates their functionality into our applications.

In this chapter, we will be building the following two applications:

- The first application will be a Force.com application called `Force Notify`. This application will present a Visualforce page to a Salesforce administrator and allow the administrator to broadcast mobile push notification messages to registered Android mobile device users within their organization. The push notifications will be delivered through a Windows Azure Notification Hub.

- Secondly, we will build an accompanying Android application using the Salesforce Android Native Mobile SDK. This application will receive and process push notifications posted from the Windows Azure Notification Hub, and post them in the Android device notification area.

It goes without saying that we have a lot to do in this chapter, so let's begin!

The development process overview

The application we will be building in this chapter will be quite complex, and involves extensive configuration and development. Taking this into account, it is prudent at this point to examine the following components in our development process at a high level:

- **Development environment**: We will begin by configuring the development tools we will require (in addition to Force.com). The toolset we will be using is Node.js, Android Developer Tools, and the Salesforce Android Native Mobile **Software Development Kit (SDK)**.

- **Salesforce-connected application**: We are required to configure a Salesforce-connected application to allow our Android application to connect to Salesforce.

- **Google Cloud Messaging**: We need to configure Google Cloud Messaging to allow push notifications to be sent to our Android application.

- **Azure Notification Hub**: Next, we will configure a Notification Hub in Windows Azure, which we will be connecting to from our Force.com application. In addition, we will gather the credentials that we will need to connect to Azure from Force.com and Android, and download the Azure Android SDK.

- **Android application**: At this point, we are ready to begin developing the Android application that will be receiving our push notifications.

- **Force.com application**: Finally, we will build a Force.com application that will be used to send push notifications to our Android application through the Azure Notification Hub.

Configuring the development environment

The first step in building the application is to configure the development tools we will need. We will need to install Node.js, the Android Developer Tools, and the Salesforce Native Android Mobile SDK.

Installing Node.js

Node.js is a JavaScript platform well-suited to building fast, scalable network applications. The Native Android Mobile SDK requires Node.js. To download and install Node.js, perform the following steps:

1. Navigate your web browser to the Node.js homepage at `http://nodejs.org`.

2. Click on the **INSTALL** link to download the installer for your platform.

3. Start the installer and install Node.js on your system.

4. Take note of the Node.js install locations and ensure that they are part of your system path. For example, the path to Node.js on my system is `/usr/local/bin/node`.

5. Start a terminal window and issue the following commands to verify that Node.js was installed successfully:

```
$ node --version
$ npm --version
```

6. Each command should result in the version number of Node.js and the Node.js package manager being reported. At the time of writing, the Node.js version was v0.10.25 and the Node.js Package Manager version was 1.3.24.

Installing Android Developer Tools

Android Developer Tools (**ADT**) provides a development environment to build Android applications. To develop the Android application for this chapter, we will use the ADT Bundle, which provides a version of the Eclipse IDE with essential Android SDK components preinstalled.

To install ADT, navigate your web browser to `http://developer.android.com/sdk/index.html` and download the ADT Bundle for your operating system. Once you have downloaded the ADT Bundle, follow the instructions at `http://developer.android.com/sdk/installing/bundle.html` to install the ADT environment.

Installing the Android SDK

We need to ensure that we have the correct version of the Android SDK installed for our application. The steps to do this are as follows:

1. Click on the **Android SDK Manager** toolbar button from the ADT toolbar, as shown in the following screenshot:

2. In the **Android SDK Manager** window, ensure that the items displayed in the following screenshot are selected for the **Android 4.4.2** platform and click on **Install**:

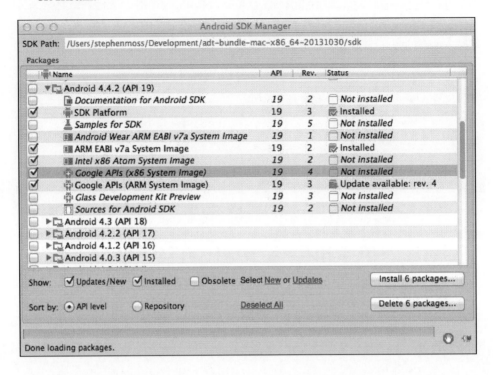

3. When the installation is complete, close the **Android SDK Manager** window.

Configuring an Android virtual device

The next item of configuration for the ADT is to set up an Android virtual device to test our application. The steps to do this are as follows:

1. Click on the **Android Virtual Device Manager** toolbar button from the ADT toolbar, as shown in the following screenshot:

2. In the **Android Virtual Device Manager** window, click on the **New...** button, as shown in the following screenshot:

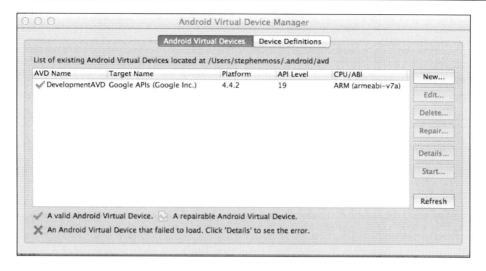

3. Configure the Android virtual device settings, as per the following screenshot:

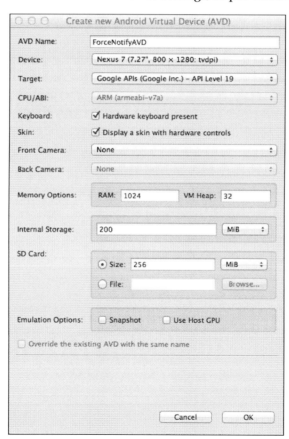

4. Click on **OK** to create the Android virtual machine. The new virtual machine will now appear in the **Android Virtual Device Manager** window, as shown in the following screenshot:

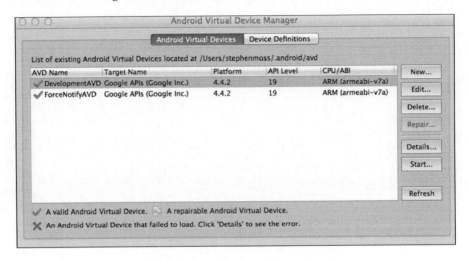

Signing in to the Android virtual device

The final item of configuration is to sign in to the newly created Android virtual device with a Google account (assuming you already have one) so that we can register the virtual device to receive push notifications. The steps to do this are as follows:

1. Assuming that you still have the **Android Virtual Device Manager** window open, highlight your newly created virtual machine and click on the **Start...** button, as shown in the following screenshot:

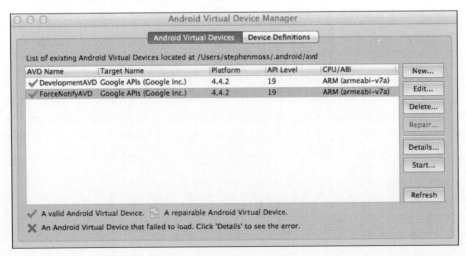

2. From the **Launch Options** dialog window, click on **Launch**, as shown in the following screenshot:

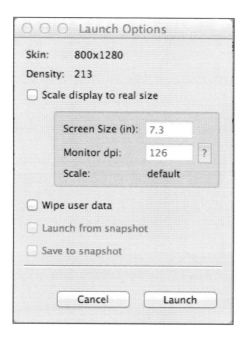

3. The virtual device will be launched (this may take a while!). From the **Home** screen, select the **Applications** icon, as shown in the following screenshot:

4. From the list of applications, choose **Settings**, as shown in the following screenshot:

5. Choose the **Add account** option, as shown in the following screenshot:

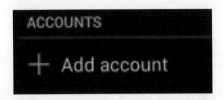

6. Select **Google** from the list of account types, as shown in the following screenshot:

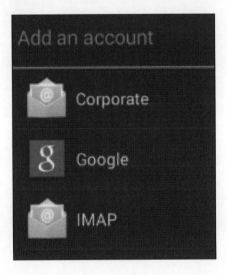

7. Choose to add an existing Google account, as shown in the following screenshot:

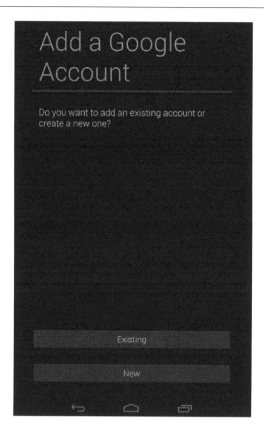

8. Follow the sign-in process with your Google e-mail and password, as shown in the following screenshot:

9. Once you have signed in, the configuration of your Android environment is complete.

 If you haven't developed an Android application before, I recommend that you complete the tutorial located at `http://developer.android.com/training/basics/firstapp/index.html`.

Installing the Salesforce Android Native Mobile SDK

The Salesforce Android Native Mobile SDK is a toolkit that enables developers to build Android applications that securely connect to the Force.com platform. To install the Salesforce Android Native Mobile SDK, perform the following steps:

1. Start a terminal window and issue the following command:

```
$ sudo npm install forcedroid -g
```

 Windows users should omit `sudo` and use `npm install forcedroid -g`.

2. Issue the following command to verify that the SDK was installed successfully:

```
$ forcedroid
```

3. If the command runs and displays a list of options, the SDK has been installed successfully, as shown in the following screenshot:

```
apples-air:~ stephenmoss$ forcedroid
Usage:


forcedroid create
    --apptype=<Application Type> (native, hybrid_remote, hybrid_local)
    --appname=<Application Name>
    --targetdir=<Target App Folder>
    --packagename=<App Package Identifier> (com.my_company.my_app)
    --startpage=<Path to the remote start page> (/apex/MyPage — Only required/us
ed for 'hybrid_remote')
    [--usesmartstore=<Whether or not to use SmartStore> ('true' or 'false'. fals
e by default)]

OR

forcedroid samples
    --targetdir=<Target Samples Folder>
apples-air:~ stephenmoss$ 
```

If you are located on a corporate network, you may need to configure the proxy settings to enable npm to download the SDK. For example, `npm config set proxy http://proxy.company.com:8080` and `npm config set-https-proxy http://proxy.company.com:8080`. You may need to contact a network administrator for the proxy server address and port number.

Configuring a Salesforce-connected application

We will also need a Salesforce-connected application to allow our Android application to access Salesforce data. A connected app is different to a traditional Force.com application as it is designed to allow external applications to securely access your Salesforce organization. To configure the remote access application, perform the following steps:

1. Navigate to **Setup | Create | Apps**.

2. Scroll down to the **Connected Apps** section and click on **New**.

3. Enter `MyNotificationApp` in the **Connected App Name** field.

4. The **API Name** field will be autopopulated.

5. Enter your e-mail address in the **Contact Email** field.

6. Enter `Mobile app to receive Salesforce.com Push Notifications` in the **Description** field.

7. Select the **Enable OAuth Settings** checkbox from the **API** section. A new set of fields will be displayed.

8. Enter `testsfdc:///mobilesdk/detect/oauth/done` in the **Callback URL** field.

9. From the **Available OAuth Scopes** list, move all options to the **Selected OAuth Scopes** list.

10. Leave all of the other unspecified fields blank.

11. Click on **Save**.

12. Make a note of the consumer key and callback URL as you'll need these later.

Configuring Google Cloud Messaging

Google Cloud Messaging is the Google API service used to deliver push notifications to Android devices. We will need to configure Google Cloud Messaging so that we can connect to it from Windows Azure and our Android application. To configure Google Cloud Messaging, perform the following steps:

1. Visit `https://code.google.com/apis/console` and sign in with your Google account (assuming you already have one).
2. If you aren't automatically redirected there, navigate to `https://console.developers.google.com/project`.
3. Click on the **Create Project...** button.
4. Enter `My Notification Project` in the **Project name** field.
5. Accept the default value for the **Project ID** field.
6. Click on **Create**.
7. Click on **APIs & auth** from the left-hand side navigation bar.
8. Set the **Google Cloud Messaging for Android** option to **ON**, as shown in the following screenshot:

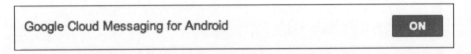

9. Select **Credentials** and click on **CREATE NEW KEY**.
10. Click on the **Server Key** button.
11. Click on **Create** to generate the key. Make a note of the API key, as shown in the following screenshot:

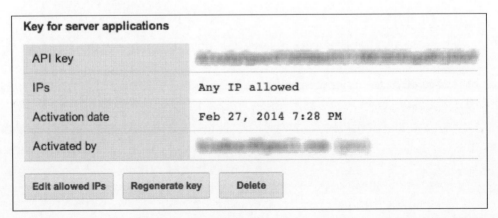

Configuring the Azure Notification Hub

We will now need to configure the Azure Notification Hub we will be using to send the push notifications.

 If you don't have one already, you must sign up for a Windows Azure account to complete the steps in this section.

To configure an Azure Notification Hub, perform the following steps:

1. If you don't have a Windows Azure account, sign up at `http://www.windowsazure.com/en-us/`. Note that a 30-day free trial is available.

2. Log on to your Windows Azure Management Portal at `https://manage.windowsazure.com`.

3. Click on the **NEW** button in the bottom-left corner of the screen.

4. Navigate to **APP SERVICES | SERVICE BUS | NOTIFICATION HUB | QUICK CREATE**, as shown in the following screenshot:

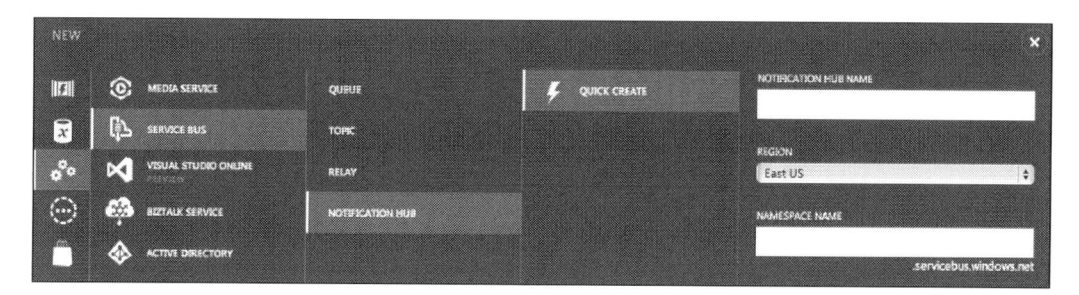

5. Enter a name for your Notification Hub and select the region closest to your location. Note that the name in the **Namespace Name** field is automatically generated and must be unique, as shown in the following screenshot:

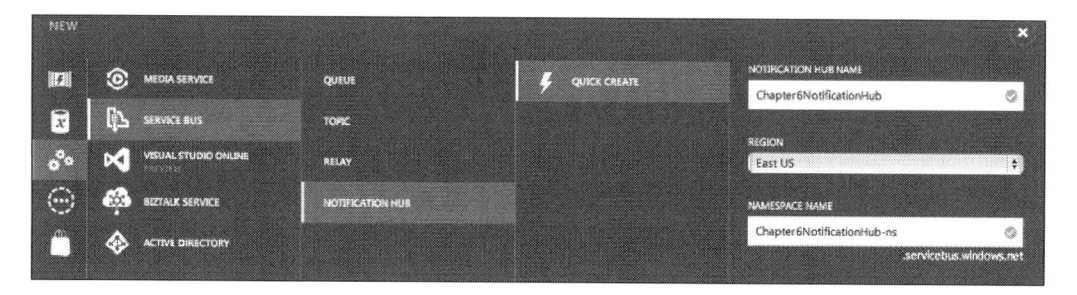

6. Click on **CREATE A NEW NOTIFICATION HUB,** as shown in the following screenshot:

7. Your Notification Hub will be created and your namespace name will appear in your **service bus** list, as shown in the following screenshot:

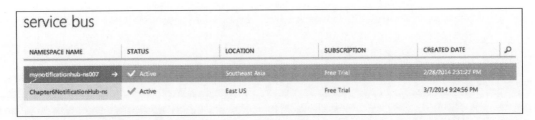

8. Click on the namespace name that you just created and click on **NOTIFICATION HUBS,** as shown in the following screenshot:

9. Click on the Notification Hub you just created, as shown in the following screenshot:

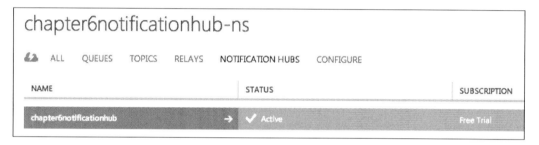

10. The **Dashboard** section for your Notification Hub will be displayed, as shown in the following screenshot:

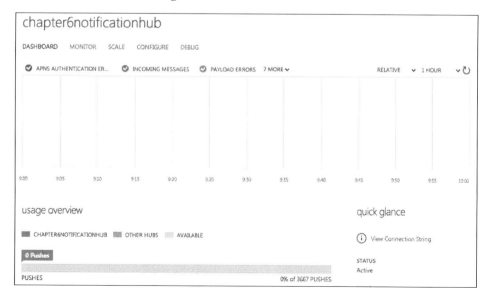

11. Click on **Configure**. Scroll down to the **google cloud messaging settings** section and enter the API key that you created in the *Configuring Google Cloud Messaging* section, as shown in the following screenshot:

12. Click on **Save**.
13. Select **Dashboard** and click on **View Connection String**. Make a note of the **DefaultListenSharedAccessSignature** connection string, as shown in the following screenshot:

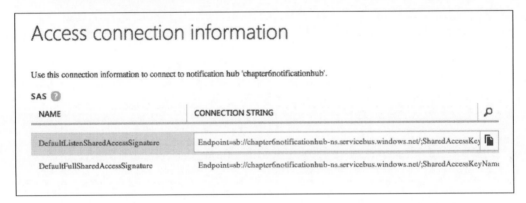

Your Notification Hub has now been configured for Google Cloud Messaging!

Getting the Azure Service Bus credentials

When we build the Force.com and Android components of the application, we will require the Azure Service Bus credentials to connect to and send messages through the Notification Hub. To get the required credentials, perform the following steps:

1. In the Azure Control Panel, select the **Service Bus** icon, as shown in the following screenshot:

2. In the **service bus** screen, select the Notification Hub namespace name you have created (by clicking on any cell but the first cell in a column), as shown in the following screenshot:

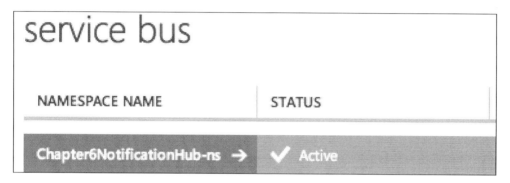

3. Click on **CONNECTION INFORMATION**, as shown in the following screenshot:

4. The connection information for the Notification Hub namespace will be displayed. Make a note of the endpoint (non-blurred string)in the **ACS CONNECTION STRING** window, as shown in the following screenshot:

5. Also make a note of the **DEFAULT ISSUER** and **DEFAULT KEY** values, as shown in the following screenshot:

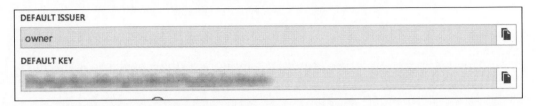

6. Click on the **Open ACS Management Portal** link.
7. Click on the **Application integration** link in the left-hand side menu.
8. In the list of **Endpoint Reference**, make a note of the **OAuth WRAP** and **Management Portal** endpoints, as shown in the following screenshot:

Downloading the Azure Android SDK

We will also need to download the Azure Android SDK. This will simplify development in our Android application when we need to interface with our Notification Hub.

To download the Azure Android SDK, perform the following steps:

1. Navigate to `http://www.windowsazure.com/en-us/`.
2. Select the **Downloads** link.
3. In the list of SDKs, select **Android Install** from the **Mobile** list.
4. The SDK will be downloaded as a compressed ZIP archive.
5. Expand the contents of the SDK in a working folder and make a note of the location of the `notification-hubs-0.1.jar` file in the `notificationhubs` subfolder of where you unzipped the SDK.

The version of the Azure Android SDK may have changed by the time you are reading this book.

Building an Android mobile application

We will now use the Salesforce Android Native Mobile SDK that we have downloaded earlier to build an application that will receive push notification messages from our Azure Notification Hub.

 To run the Android application and receive push notifications, you will need to create an **Android Virtual Device** (**AVD**) or Android device running the Google APIs, and sign in to it using a Google account. Refer to the *Installing the Android SDK* section of this chapter for more details.

Creating the Salesforce Android Mobile SDK application

To create an Android native application, perform the following steps:

1. Open a terminal window.
2. Navigate to a working folder.
3. Issue the following command to create a Force.com Android project:

```
$ forcedroid create --apptype="native" --appname="forceNotify"
--targetdir="forceNotifyApp"
--packagename="com.packt.forcenotify"
```

4. Press *Enter* to accept the default setting of not using SmartStore.

5. The following screenshot shows a sample session of creating the project:

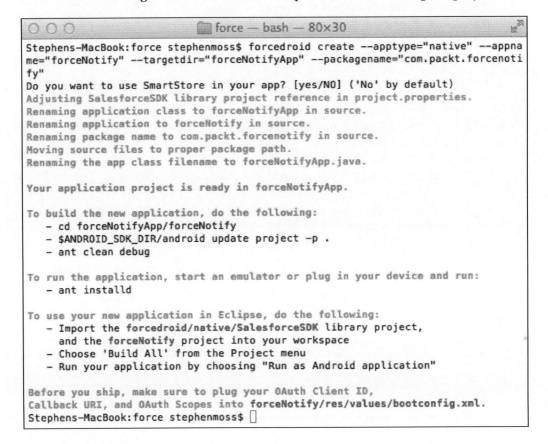

Configuring an application using ADT

We will be using ADT that we have downloaded earlier to build the rest of the Android application.

Importing the Salesforce Mobile SDK and Salesforce Android application

The first step in building the rest of the application is to import the Salesforce Mobile SDK and `forceNotify` projects into the ADT environment. To import the projects, perform the following steps:

1. Start ADT.
2. Navigate to **File | Import...**.

3. In the first step of the import wizard, select **Existing Android Code Into Workspace**, as shown in the following screenshot:

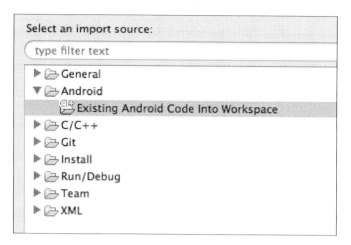

4. Click on **Next**.

5. Click on **Browse...** and navigate to the folder where you created the `forceNotify` application.

6. Select the `forcedroid/native/SalesforceSDK` folder, as shown in the following screenshot:

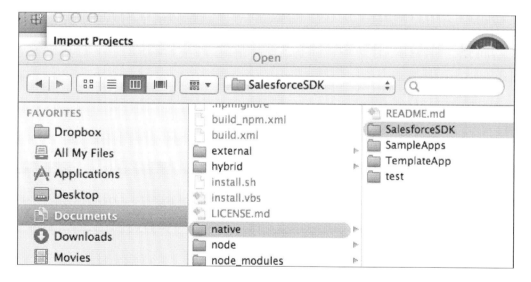

7. Click on **Open**. The wizard window will now be populated with the code that is to be imported, as shown in the following screenshot:

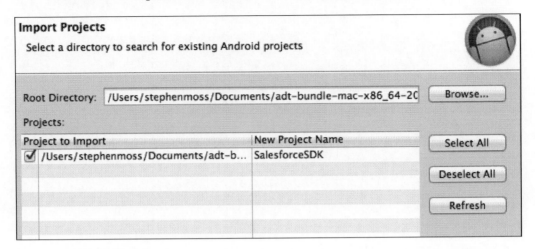

8. Click on **Finish**.

9. Perform the same steps to import the `forceNotify` project from the folder where you created the application.

10. Right-click on the `forceNotifyApp` project and select **Properties**.

11. Select **Android** in the list of property groups.

12. Select the latest version of the Google APIs for the **Project Build Target** option. At the time of writing, this was **Google APIs Platform 4.4.2 Level 19**.

13. Click on **OK**.

Updating the Android manifest file

The Android manifest file contains essential configuration information required for an Android application to run.

> For a full explanation of the Android manifest file and its components, refer to http://developer.android.com/guide/topics/manifest/manifest-intro.html.

To update the Android manifest file for the `forceNotifyApp` project, perform the following steps:

1. In the ADT, expand the `forceNotifyApp` project and open `AndroidManifest.xml`, as shown in the following screenshot:

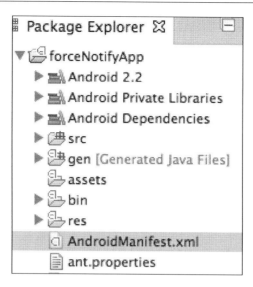

2. Open the source code view for the manifest file and update the <uses-sdk>
   tag to the following (your targetSdkVersion may differ if a higher level
   version is available) version:

```
<uses-sdk android:minSdkVersion="9"
    android:targetSdkVersion="19" />
```

3. At the top of the file, before the <application> tag, add the following
   application permissions:

```
<uses-permission
    android:name="android.permission.INTERNET"/>
<uses-permission
    android:name="android.permission.GET_ACCOUNTS"/>
<uses-permission
    android:name="android.permission.WAKE_LOCK"/>
<uses-permission
    android:name="com.google.android.c2dm.permission.RECEIVE"/>
```

4. Inside the <application> tag, add the following <receiver> tag:

```
<receiver
    android:name=".MyBroadcastReceiver"
    android:permission="com.google.android.c2dm.permission.SEND">
    <intent-filter>
        <action android:name="com.google.android.c2dm.intent.
RECEIVE" />
        <category android:name="com.packt.forcenotify" />
    </intent-filter>
</receiver>
```

Updating the bootconfig.xml file

We need to update the `bootconfig.xml` file with the consumer key from our Salesforce-connected application. To do this, perform the following steps:

1. In the `forceNotifyApp` project, open the `bootconfig.xml` file from the `res/values` folder.

2. Add the consumer key from your Salesforce-connected application to the `<string name="remoteAccessConsumerKey">` tag, using the following format:

   ```
   <string name="remoteAccessConsumerKey">[Your Consumer Key]</string>
   ```

Adding the Azure SDK and Android support libraries

We also need to add the Azure Notifications Hub SDK and Android v4 support libraries to the application. To do this, perform the following steps:

1. Add a new `lib` folder to the `forceNotifyApp` project by highlighting it and navigating to **File | New | Folder**.

2. Enter `libs` for the **Folder name:** field and click on **Finish**.

3. Open a folder explorer window in your operating system, and navigate to the folder where you installed the ADT. For example, on my system, I have installed the ADT in the `/Users/stephenmoss/Documents/adt-bundle-mac-x86_64-20130729` folder.

4. From the Android Developer Tools folder, navigate to the `sdk/extras/android/support/v4` folder.

5. Drag-and-drop the `android-support-v4.jar` file to the `libs` folder in ADT for the `forceNotifyApp` project.

6. Select **Copy Files** and click on **OK**.

7. Navigate to the folder where you installed the Azure Android SDK.

8. From the `notificationhubs` subfolder, drag-and-drop the `notification-hubs-0.1.jar` file to the `libs` folder in the `forceNotifyApp` project.

9. Select **Copy Files** and click on **OK**.

10. Your `forceNotifyApp` project should now resemble the following screenshot:

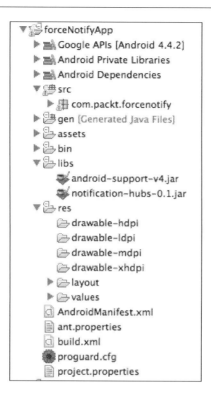

Importing the Google Play Services Library

To work with Google Cloud Messaging in our Android application, we require the Google Play Services Library. The Google Play Services Library adds extra Google features to an application such as Maps and Google+. To import Google Play Services and reference it from inside our `forceNotify` project, perform the following steps:

1. Navigate to **File | Import**.

2. Select to import using **Existing Android Code into workspace**. Click on **Next**.

3. Click on **Browse...** and navigate to the folder where you installed the ADT.

4. From the `Android Developer Tools` folder, navigate to the `sdk/extras/google/google_play_services/libproject/google-play-services_lib` folder and click on **Open**.

5. Click on **Finish** to import the Google Play Services Library project.

6. Right-click on the `forceNotifyApp` project and select **Properties**.

7. In the **Library** section of the **Android** properties group, click on **Add...** and select the **google-play-services_lib** library in the **Project Selection** window, as shown in the following screenshot:

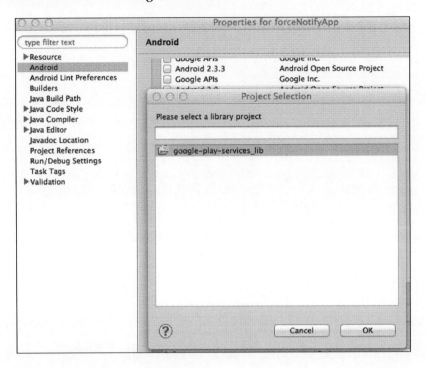

8. Click on **OK** and then on **Apply**.

9. Click on **OK** to close the **Project Properties** window.

Enhancing the Android Mobile SDK application code

Now we are ready to make the required code enhancements to the Android application. This will enable it to receive and process push notifications from the Azure Notification Hub. Fortunately, the Salesforce SDK creates an application with a lot of default functionalities that we will be taking advantage of the following parameters:

*   Salesforce login and authentication

*   Fetching and listing contacts from your Salesforce organization

*   Fetching and listing accounts from your Salesforce organization

In this chapter, I will only be covering the specific modifications to the generated Mobile SDK application required to process the Notification Hub messages. I encourage that you further explore the default code generated by the SDK to see how to leverage it in your own mobile applications.

Enhancing the MainActivity class

The first file that we will be enhancing is `MainActivity.java`. This is the default activity for the Android application and is displayed when a user successfully logs in. To enhance the `MainActivity` class, perform the following steps.

 The `MainActivity` class that we are modifying is a descendent of `SalesforceActivity`, which provides the methods we are modifying in this chapter. For more information, refer to the reference page at http://forcedotcom.github.io/SalesforceMobileSDK-Android/index.html.

1. Add the following imports to `MainActivity.java`:

```
import android.util.Log;
import android.os.AsyncTask;
import com.salesforce.androidsdk.rest.RestClient.ClientInfo;
import com.google.android.gms.gcm.*;
import com.microsoft.windowsazure.messaging.*;
```

2. Add the following class members to the `MainActivity` class:

```
private String SENDER_ID = "[Your Google API Project #]";
private GoogleCloudMessaging gcm;
private NotificationHub hub;
private String TAG = "MainActivity.java";
private String sfUserId = null;
```

 The SENDER_ID string is the Google API project number from the *Configuring Google Cloud Messaging* section.

3. Add the following highlighted code to the end of the `onCreate` method:

```
// Setup view
setContentView(R.layout.main);

// Set up Notification Hub
Log.d(TAG, "***Initializing Notification Hub...");
```

```
gcm = GoogleCloudMessaging.getInstance(this);
String connectionString = "[Your Hub Connection String]";
hub = new NotificationHub("[Your Hub Name]", connectionString,
this);
```

The Hub Connection String is the
DefaultListenSharedAccessSignature connection you noted
down earlier when creating the Azure Notification Hub. The
hub name is the name of the hub and not the namespace the
hub is created in. For example, if you have created the hub
using the naming in the screenshots for this chapter, your hub
name will be chapter6notificationhub.

For example, the Hub Connection String will look as
follows:

```
String connectionString = "Endpoint=sb://
chapter6notificationhub-ns.servicebus.windows.
net/;SharedAccessKeyName=DefaultListenSharedAcc
essSignature;SharedAccessKey=DCTgXeBODcq6mwB1Do
7Q0yuEenBXDJLBoasK5frdpic=";
```

```
hub = new NotificationHub("chapter6notification
hub", connectionString, this);
```

4. Add the registerNotificationHubs method to MainActivity.java,
   using the following code:

```
@SuppressWarnings("unchecked")
private void registerNotificationHubs() {
    // register device with Notification Hub
    new AsyncTask() {
        @Override
        protected Object doInBackground(Object... params) {
            try {
                Log.d(TAG, "***Executing Asynchronous Hub
Registration...");
                String regid = gcm.register(SENDER_ID);
                NativeRegistration hubRegistration = hub.register(regid,
sfUserId);
                Log.d(TAG, "***Asynchronous Hub Registration
Completed...");
            } catch (Exception e) {
                return e;
            }
            return null;
        }
```

```
    }.execute(null, null, null);

  }
```

5. Finally, add the following highlighted code to the `onResume(RestClient client)` method:

```
// Show everything
findViewById(R.id.root).setVisibility(View.VISIBLE);

Log.d(TAG, "***Getting Logged In User...");
ClientInfo ci = client.getClientInfo();
sfUserId = ci.userId.toString();
String username = ci.username.toString();
Log.d(TAG, "***Registering Notification Hub...");
registerNotificationHubs();
```

 Make sure that you modify the correct overloaded `onResume` method in `MainActivity.java`.

How the MainActivity class works

We start by importing the libraries we require, and adding some class members to `MainActivity`. We then proceed to add the code required to initialize Google Cloud Messaging and connect to the Azure Notification Hub in the `onCreate` method, using the following code:

```
gcm = GoogleCloudMessaging.getInstance(this);
String connectionString = "[Your Hub Connection String]";
hub = new NotificationHub("[Your Hub Name]", connectionString,
  this);
```

We also add the following code to the overloaded version of the `onResume` method to get the details of the logged in Salesforce user. We place the code here because this method is called after a user has logged in:

```
ClientInfo ci = client.getClientInfo();
sfUserId = ci.userId.toString();
String username = ci.username.toString();
```

Then we call the `registerNotificationHubs` method, using the following code:

```
registerNotificationHubs();
```

The `registerNotificationHubs` method runs asynchronously. It first registers the application with Google Cloud Messaging with the following line of code:

```
String regid = gcm.register(SENDER_ID);
```

It then registers the Android application with the Azure Notification Hub, by using the following code, passing in the identifier received from Google Cloud Messaging and the Salesforce user ID as a registration tag. We will see how we use the registration tag to target a specific user with a message when we build the Force.com application.

```
NativeRegistration hubRegistration = hub.register(regid, sfUserId);
```

Creating the Broadcast Receiver class

We will now create the `MyBroadcastReceiver` class. This class will be responsible for receiving and processing push notifications received from the Azure Notification Hub.

To create the class, perform the following steps:

1. Select the `com.packt.forcenotify` package in the `src` folder.
2. Navigate to **File | New | Class**.
3. In the **New Java Class** window, enter `MyBroadcastReceiver` in the **Name** field of the class.
4. Enter `android.content.BroadcastReceiver` for the **Superclass** field.
5. Your window should now resemble the following screenshot:

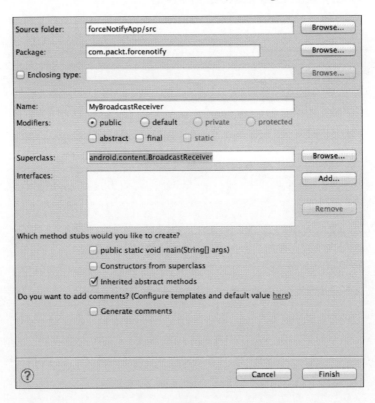

6. Click on **Finish**.

7. Add the following import statements to the MyBroadcastReceiver class:

```
import com.google.android.gms.gcm.GoogleCloudMessaging;
import android.app.Activity;
import android.app.NotificationManager;
import android.app.PendingIntent;
import android.support.v4.app.NotificationCompat;
import android.util.Log;
```

8. Add the following members to the MyBroadcastReceiver class:

```
public static final int NOTIFICATION_ID = 1;
private NotificationManager mNotificationManager;
NotificationCompat.Builder builder;
Context ctx;

private String TAG = "MyBroadcastReceiver.java";
```

9. Add the following code to the onReceive method:

```
// Set up Application Class to receive notification
// from Azure Notification Hub
GoogleCloudMessaging gcm =
                    GoogleCloudMessaging.getInstance(context);
ctx = context;
String messageType = gcm.getMessageType(intent);
if (GoogleCloudMessaging.MESSAGE_TYPE_SEND_ERROR.
equals(messageType)) {
  sendNotification("***Send error: " +
                            intent.getExtras().toString());
} else if (GoogleCloudMessaging.MESSAGE_TYPE_DELETED.
equals(messageType)) {
   sendNotification("***Deleted messages on server: "
                         + intent.getExtras().toString());
} else {
  sendNotification("Received: " +
                    intent.getExtras().getString("message"));
}
setResultCode(Activity.RESULT_OK);
```

10. Finally, add the sendNotification method, using the following code:

```
private void sendNotification(String msg) {

  Log.d(TAG, "***Processing Notification from Hub...");
```

```
        // Display Notification on Android Device
        mNotificationManager = (NotificationManager)ctx.
    getSystemService(Context.NOTIFICATION_SERVICE);
        PendingIntent contentIntent = PendingIntent.getActivity(ctx, 0,
    new Intent(ctx, MainActivity.class), 0);
        NotificationCompat.Builder mBuilder =
            new NotificationCompat.Builder(ctx)
              .setSmallIcon(R.drawable.sf__icon)
              .setContentTitle("ForceNotify")
              .setStyle(new
                        NotificationCompat.BigTextStyle().bigText(msg))
              .setContentInfo(msg);
        mBuilder.setContentIntent(contentIntent);
        mNotificationManager.notify(NOTIFICATION_ID, mBuilder.build());
        Log.d(TAG, "***Successfully Processed Notification from
    Hub...");


    }
```

How the Broadcast Receiver class works

We begin by importing the required libraries for the class and setting up the required class members.

The key code in the `onReceive` method is the `if` statement, which checks the type of notifications we receive. We first check for an error or a deleted message on the server, and route them to the `sendNotification` method with a suitable message. Finally, we route a valid push notification to the `sendNotification` method and extract the message received using the `else` statement, as follows:

```
    else {
      sendNotification("Received: " +
                            intent.getExtras().getString("message"));

    }
```

The `sendNotification` method commences by getting a reference to the notification service on the Android device and setting up a pending intent to allow us to return control to `MainActivity` when we have finished processing the notification. This is done with the following code:

```
    mNotificationManager =
      (NotificationManager)ctx.getSystemService(Context.NOTIFICATION_
    SERVICE);
    PendingIntent contentIntent =
      PendingIntent.getActivity(ctx, 0, new Intent(ctx, MainActivity.
    class), 0);
```

We then use a notification builder to build the message we wish to display in the Android device notification area, using the following code:

```
NotificationCompat.Builder mBuilder =
   new NotificationCompat.Builder(ctx)
     .setSmallIcon(R.drawable.sf__icon)
     .setContentTitle("ForceNotify")
     .setStyle(new NotificationCompat.BigTextStyle().bigText(msg))
     .setContentInfo(msg);
```

 We are using the `NotificationCompat.Builder` class to enable our code to work on older Android devices.

Finally, we pass the control back to `MainActivity` by calling the `mBuilder.setContentIntent` method and posting the notification to the Android device, using the following code:

```
mBuilder.setContentIntent(contentIntent);
mNotificationManager.notify(NOTIFICATION_ID, mBuilder.build());
```

Congratulations! The Android application is now complete.

Creating the Force.com broadcast application

With the Azure Notification Hub and Android Application now in place, it is time to build the Force.com application. This will consist of an Apex class, which acts as the interface between Force.com and Azure, a Visualforce page to provide an interface to the user, and a custom controller class for the Visualforce page.

Configuring the remote site settings

First, we need to add a Salesforce remote site for the Notification Hub authentication REST endpoint. This is done by performing the following steps:

1. Navigate to **Setup | Security Controls | Remote Site Settings**.
2. Click on the **New Remote Site** button.
3. Enter `AzureServiceBusAuthenticate` for the **Remote Site Name** field.
4. Enter `https://[Your Service Bus Management Portal]` for the **Remote Site URL** field.

5. Ensure that the **Active** checkbox is checked.

6. Click on **Save**.

 The Azure Service Bus management portal is the management portal endpoint from the *Getting the Azure Service Bus credentials* section.

For example, `https://chapter6notificationhub-ns-sb.accesscontrol.windows.net`.

Finally, we need to add a Salesforce remote site for the Notification Hub REST endpoint. This can be done by performing the following steps:

1. Navigate to **Setup | Security Controls | Remote Site Settings**.

2. Click on the **New Remote Site** button.

3. Enter `AzureServiceBusREST` in the **Remote Site Name** field.

4. Enter `https://[Your Notification Hub Namespace Endpoint]` in the **Remote Site URL** field.

5. Ensure that the **Active** checkbox is checked.

6. Click on **Save**.

 The Azure Service Notification Hub namespace endpoint is the endpoint contained in the ACS connection string from the *Getting the Azure Service Bus credentials* section. For example, `https://chapter6notificationhub-ns.servicebus.windows.net`.

Creating the Notification Hub Interface class

To create the Notification Hub Interface class, perform the following steps:

1. Navigate to **Setup | Develop | Apex Classes**.

2. All of the Apex classes for your organization will be displayed. Click on **New**.

3. In the code download for the chapter, locate the `azureNotificationHubInterface.cls` file in the `force_com` folder.

4. Copy and paste the contents of `azureNotificationHubInterface.cls` into the Apex code editor in your Force.com window.

5. Click on **Save**.

How the Notification Hub Interface class works

The Notification Hub Interface class consists of the following three methods:

Method	Description
getAzureAccessToken	This method obtains a security access token for Azure
getHubRegistrations	This method gets a list of registrations for a Notification Hub
sendHubMessage	This method sends a message through a Notification Hub

The getAzureAccessToken method commences by declaring Http and HttpRequest objects, using the following code:

```
Http h = new Http();
HttpRequest req = new HttpRequest();
```

We then declare the objects we will need to use when authenticating against Azure by using the following code:

```
string Url = '[Your OAuth WRAP Endpoint]';
string encodedLogin = EncodingUtil.urlEncode('[Your Default Issuer]',
'UTF-8');
string encodedPW = EncodingUtil.urlEncode('[Your Default Key]', 'UTF-
8');
```

The Azure endpoint and Service Bus credentials required are the **OAuth WRAP** endpoint, **DEFAULT ISSUER**, **DEFAULT KEY**, and the endpoint contained in the ACS connection string from the *Getting the Azure Service Bus credentials* section.

For example, the Azure endpoint and Service Bus credentials will look as follows:

```
string Url = 'https://chapter6notificationhub-
ns-sb.accesscontrol.windows.net/WRAPv0.9';

string encodedLogin = EncodingUtil.
urlEncode('owner', 'UTF-8');

string encodedPW = EncodingUtil.urlEncode('tM
reEBj2nMOwlgDA0HkkPcJ/CK8n5s2Ext12KtLFsI4=',
'UTF-8');
```

Next, we set up the `Http` request using the following code:

```
req.setEndpoint(Url);
req.setMethod('POST');
req.setBody('wrap_name=' + encodedLogin + '&wrap_password=' +
encodedPW +
'&wrap_scope=[Your Notification Hub Namespace Endpoint]');
req.setHeader('Content-Type', 'application/x-www-form-urlencoded');
```

> The Notification Hub namespace endpoint is the endpoint contained in the ACS connection string from the *Getting the Azure Service Bus credentials* section. For example, `https://chapter6notificationhub-ns.servicebus.windows.net`.

We set the request endpoint to the **OAuth WRAP** endpoint obtained when we configured Azure, and also embed the **DEFAULT ISSUER**, **DEFAULT KEY**, and Hub Namespace endpoints in the request body. We also set the request method to `POST`, and set the `Http` header content type.

We then send the `Http` request to Azure and obtain the `Http` response in the `result` variable with the following code:

```
HttpResponse res = h.send(req);
string result = res.getBody();
```

Finally, we use some Apex string methods to manipulate the result to build a valid Azure security token and return it to the caller by using the following code:

```
// process result to create properly formatted token
string suffixRemoved = result.split('&')[0];
string prefixRemoved = suffixRemoved.split('=')[1];
string decodedToken = EncodingUtil.urlDecode(prefixRemoved, 'UTF-8');
string finalToken = 'WRAP access_token=\"' + decodedToken + '\"';

return finalToken;
```

The `getHubRegistrations` method takes a string argument containing an Azure security access token, and returns a list of strings containing the registration tags (in our case, the Salesforce user IDs) for registered mobile device users, using the following code:

```
public List<string> getHubRegistrations(String token)
```

The method commences by declaring the endpoint for the Azure REST API request, as follows:

```
string readUrl = 'https://[Your Notification Hub Namespace
   Endpoint]/[Your Notification Hub Name]/registrations/?api-
version=2013-08';
```

> The Notification Hub namespace endpoint is the endpoint contained in the **ACS Connection String** connection from the *Getting the Azure Service Bus credentials* section. For example, `https://chapter6notificationhub-ns.servicebus.windows.net`. The Notification Hub name in this instance is `chapter6notificationhub`.
>
> For example, the Notification Hub namespace endpoint will look as follows:
>
> ```
> string readUrl = 'https://chapter6notificationhub-
> ns.servicebus.windows.net/chapter6notificationhub/
> registrations/?api-version=2013-08';
> ```

We then set up the `Http` request, REST endpoint, and `Http` headers with the following code:

```
Http h = new Http();
HttpRequest readRequest = new HttpRequest();
readRequest.setEndpoint(readUrl);
readRequest.setMethod('GET');
readRequest.setHeader('Authorization', token);
readRequest.setHeader('x-ms-version', '2013-08');
```

The highlighted line of code shows where we are passing the Azure security token in the authorization `Http` header.

We then issue the request against Azure and capture the response in the `readResult` variable with the following code:

```
HttpResponse readRes = h.send(readRequest);
string readResult = readRes.getBody();
```

The response from Azure gives us all of the XML data elements for an Azure registration. We are only interested in extracting the `<Tags>` element where it exists for each registration. To achieve this, we use an `XmlStreamReader` object to parse the XML and extract the contents of each `<Tags>` element using the following code:

```
// parse XML and extract registration tags
XmlStreamReader reader = readRes.getXmlStreamReader();
```

```
List<String> registrationTags = new List<String>();

// use XmlStreamReader to parse response and extract registration tags
boolean isSafeToGetNextXmlElement = true;
while (isSafeToGetNextXmlElement) {
  if (reader.getEventType() == XmlTag.START_ELEMENT) {
    if (reader.getLocalName() == 'Tags') {
      reader.next();
      registrationTags.add(reader.getText());
    }
  }
  // check if another node
  if (reader.hasNext()) {
    reader.next();
  } else {
    isSafeToGetNextXmlElement = false;
    break;
  }
}

}
```

Finally, we return the list of registration tags to the caller with the following code:

```
return registrationTags;
```

The final method in the following code is `sendHubMessage`, which triggers push notifications to be sent from the Azure Notification Hub:

```
public string sendHubMessage(String token, String message,
                                              String userTag)
```

The `sendHubMessage` method accepts parameters for the Azure security token, the message to be sent, and a user registration tag if we are sending a message to an individual user.

Similar to the `getHubRegistrations` method, we declare the endpoint for the Azure REST API request and some standard `Http` header information with the following code:

```
string messageUrl = 'https://[Your Notification Hub Namespace
Endpoint]/[Your Notification Hub Name]/messages/?api-version=2013-08';
Http h = new Http();
HttpRequest messageRequest = new HttpRequest();
messageRequest.setEndpoint(messageUrl);
messageRequest.setMethod('POST');
messageRequest.setHeader('Authorization', token);
messageRequest.setHeader('Content-Type', 'application/
json;charset=utf-8');
```

The Notification Hub namespace endpoint is the endpoint contained in the **ACS Connection String** connection from the *Getting the Azure Service Bus credentials* section. For example, `https://chapter6notificationhub-ns.servicebus.windows.net`. The Notification Hub name in this instance is `chapter6notificationhub`.

For example, the Notification Hub namespace endpoint will look as follows:

```
string readUrl = 'https://
chapter6notificationhub-ns.servicebus.windows.
net/chapter6notificationhub/messages/?api-
version=2013-08';
```

We then proceed to set up the specific `Http` header information and request the body to send a push notification through Azure using the following code:

```
messageRequest.setHeader('ServiceBusNotification-Format', 'gcm');
if (userTag != null) {
  messageRequest.setHeader('ServiceBusNotification-Tags',
                                                userTag);
}
messageRequest.setBody('{ "collapse_key": "test_message",
  "time_to_live": 108, "delay_while_idle": true, "data":
    { "message": "' + message + '"}}');
```

Finally, we send the `Http` request and pass the Azure response back to the caller with the following code:

```
HttpResponse messageRes = h.send(messageRequest);
string messageResult = messageRes.getBody() + ' ' + messageRes.
getStatus() + ' ' + messageRes.getStatusCode();
return messageResult;
```

Creating the broadcast application custom controller

To create the broadcast application custom controller, perform the following steps:

1. Navigate to **Setup | Develop | Apex Classes**.

2. All of the Apex classes for your organization will be displayed. Click on **New**.

3. In the code download for the chapter, locate the `forceNotifyController.cls` file in the `force_com` folder.

4. Copy and paste the contents of `forceNotifyController.cls` into the Apex code editor in your Force.com window.

5. Click on **Save**.

How the broadcast application custom controller works

We begin by declaring the controller properties we will be using, with the following code:

```
// Azure Interface Properties
private String azureSecurityToken { get; set; }
private azureNotificationHubInterface notificationHub = new
azureNotificationHubInterface();

// User picklist values
public List<selectOption> registeredDeviceUsers {get; set;}

// selected value in picklist
public string selectedUser {get; set;}

// Azure Notification Hub Registration Tags
List<String> registrationTags = new List<String>();

// message to send
public string messageToSend {get; set;}
```

Next, the constructor is defined. The first task is to get an Azure security token, which we can use for future requests, with the following code:

```
azureSecurityToken = notificationHub.getAzureAccessToken();
```

We then start to build the data source for the user's drop-down list on the Visualforce page with the following code:

```
// build dropdown list of users registered with Azure
registeredDeviceUsers = new List<selectOption>();
registeredDeviceUsers.add(new selectOption('All','All'));
registrationTags =
        notificationHub.getHubRegistrations(azureSecurityToken);
List<User> registeredUsers = [SELECT id, Name FROM User WHERE id
  IN :registrationTags ORDER BY Name];
```

We initialize the `registeredDeviceUsers` controller property and add a default item to represent all mobile device users. We then call the `notificationhub.getHubRegistrations` method to get a list of registered mobile device users (recall from the Android application that the registration tags in the Notification Hub are Salesforce user IDs). We then use this list as the criteria for an SOQL query to extract the Salesforce user IDs and usernames for those registered users.

Because it is possible for a user to register for more than one device (for example, a Smartphone and a tablet), we need to remove any duplicate user records. This is done with the following code:

```
List<User> finalDeviceUserList = new List<User>();
Set<string> idSet = new Set<String>();
for (User u : registeredUsers) {
  if (idSet.contains(u.id) == false) {
    idSet.add(u.id);
    finalDeviceUserList.add(u);
  }
}
```

After we have removed the duplicates from the list, we populate the data source for the list and set the initial selected value, using the following code:

```
for (User finalUser : finalDeviceUserList) {
  registeredDeviceUsers.add(new selectOption(finalUser.id,
                                             finalUser.Name));
}

// set initial value for selected User to 'All'
selectedUser = 'All';
```

The final method in the controller handles the button click event to broadcast a message through the Notification Hub, using the following code:

```
public PageReference sendNotificationHubMessage() {

  //check message not blank and < 255 characters
  if ((messageToSend.length() == 0) || (messageToSend.length() > 255))
  {
    ApexPages.addMessage(new
               ApexPages.Message(ApexPages.Severity.ERROR,
               'Message must not be blank or greater than 255
               characters'));
    return null;
  }
```

```
    // broadcast message to all users
    if (selectedUser == 'All') {

        string sendResult = notificationHub.sendHubMessage(
                                azureSecurityToken,
                                messageToSend, null);

        ApexPages.addMessage(new ApexPages.Message(
                        ApexPages.Severity.INFO,
                        'Message Send Result - ' + sendResult));
    } else {
        // broadcast to selected user only
        string sendResult = notificationHub.sendHubMessage(
                        azureSecurityToken,
                        messageToSend, selectedUser);

        ApexPages.addMessage(new ApexPages.Message(
                        ApexPages.Severity.INFO,
                        'Message Send Result - ' + sendResult));
    }

    return null;
}
```

We first check if the message is between 1 and 255 characters. If the message fails this validation, we issue an error message and exit the method.

If the message is valid, we check if we are broadcasting it to all users. If so, we call the notificationHub.sendHubMessage method and set the user tag to null to indicate that we are broadcasting the message to all users. We then display the result of the Azure send request. If we are not broadcasting it to all users, we pass in the ID of the selected user.

Creating the broadcast application Visualforce page

The broadcast application Visualforce page will present an interface to allow us to send a push notification message to one or all users in our Salesforce organization who have a registered Android device.

To create a broadcast application Visualforce page, perform the following steps:

1. Navigate to **Setup | Develop | Pages**.
2. All of the Visualforce pages for your organization will be displayed. Click on **New**.
3. In the **Page Information** section, enter `ForceNotify` in the **Label** field.
4. Enter `ForceNotify` in the **Name** field.
5. In the code download for the chapter, locate the `ForceNotify.page` file in the `force_com` folder.
6. Accept the default markup in the Visualforce page editor.
7. Click on **Save**.

How the broadcast application Visualforce page works

The following is the code for the Visualforce page and is fairly simple:

```
<apex:page controller="forceNotifyController" >
<apex:form >
  <apex:pageBlock title="Force Notify">
  <apex:pageBlockSection title="Notification Message" columns="1">
    <apex:pageMessages id="messages" ></apex:pageMessages>
    <apex:selectList label="Device Users" value="{!selectedUser}"
size="1">
      <apex:selectOptions value="{!registeredDeviceUsers}">
      </apex:selectOptions>
    </apex:selectList>
    <apex:inputTextarea label="Message" value="{!messageToSend}"
rows="3"/>
  </apex:pageBlockSection>
  <apex:pageBlockButtons location="bottom">
    <apex:commandButton value="Send Message"
      action="{!sendNotificationHubMessage}" />
  </apex:pageBlockButtons>
  </apex:pageBlock>
</apex:form>
</apex:page>
```

The highlighted blocks of code show where we are linking the drop-down list to the controller properties, thus providing an input text control to enter a broadcast message and the command button to the event handler in the controller.

Congratulations! The application is now complete.

Running the application

The first step in running the application is to start an Android emulator (or use your Android device) and run the forceNotify application. After you have logged into Salesforce, the main application screen will be displayed (I have selected **Fetch Contacts**), as shown in the following screenshot:

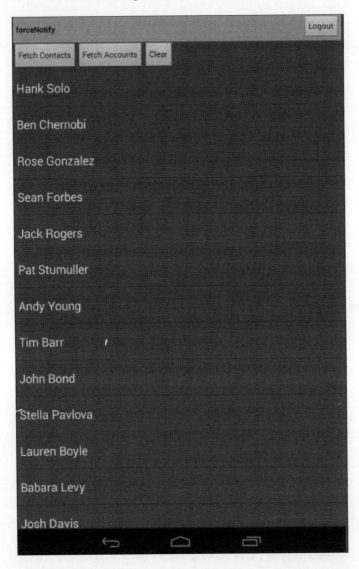

When the Android application starts, access the Visualforce page in Salesforce, as shown in the following screenshot:

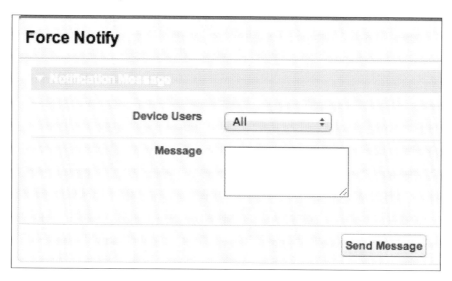

Type in a message and click on **Send Message**, as shown in the following screenshot:

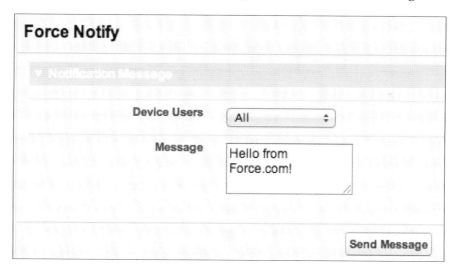

The message will be sent to the Azure Notification Hub and the result will displayed on the Visualforce page, as shown in the following screenshot:

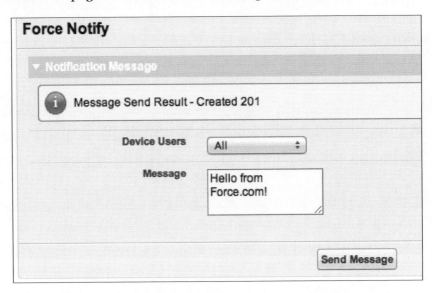

In the Android application, access the notifications area. The notification sent from Force.com will appear, as shown in the following screenshot:

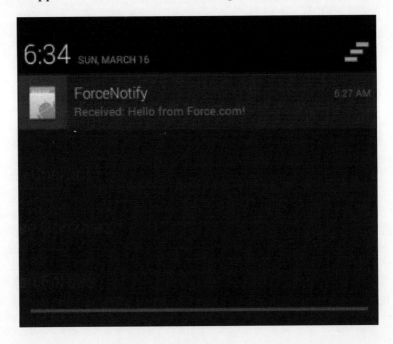

Debugging the Azure Notification Hub

The code download for the chapter contains extensive debug statements in the Force.com and Android applications to help you with debugging and tracking application execution. An additional debugging facility exists in Azure to help you isolate the problem if push notifications aren't being received by your Android application, as shown in the following screenshot:

The preceding screen allows you to send push notifications directly from Azure to registered mobile devices. If your device is receiving notifications from this screen, and not Force.com, it is likely that there is an issue in your Force.com application. Conversely, if your device isn't receiving notifications from this screen, there is likely an issue with your Android application.

Summary

In this chapter, we have successfully combined multiple techniques used throughout the entire book to build a cloud-connected Force.com application. We have seen that Force.com, the Azure Cloud, and Android can all be combined to build a compelling mobile application for your Force.com users.

A key learning from this chapter should be that as we move toward a more cloud-oriented computing paradigm, the configuration capabilities and metadata from working with cloud services goes hand-in-hand with traditional coding tools and SDKs. It is important to know the capabilities of both, and how to combine them into a working application.

As always, there are some improvements you can make to the application, as follows:

- Try sending messages through Azure to other mobile platforms (iOS and Windows). Even though we are only targeting Android devices in this chapter, it is extremely simple to configure a Notification Hub for other platforms. Refer to the Windows Azure documentation for more details. Microsoft has also developed a range of SDKs that simplify developing for Notification Hubs on each platform.

- You can implement a multiselect picklist instead of a drop-down list for user selection to target multiple users.

- You can add a dash of Ajax functionality to the Visualforce page to provide a more dynamic user interface.

Finally, if you have got this far and successfully built all of the example applications in the book, please accept my heartfelt congratulations and gratitude. I sincerely hope that you have learnt some new Force.com development techniques, and perhaps brushed up on a few existing ones. Ultimately, I hope that you can now use these techniques in your own Force.com applications, speed up your development cycles, and delight your customers!

A
Importing Data with the Apex Data Loader

You can load the sample data onto your development organization by using the LexiLoader (Apex Data Loader) in OS X by performing the following steps. Alternatively, for *Chapter 2, The E-Commerce Framework*, you can load the data as mentioned in the *Importing with the Custom Object Import Wizard* section. The steps to load the sample data onto your development organization for the Windows Apex Data Loader are identical to LexiLoader:

1. Start the Apex Data Loader on your computer.
2. Select **Insert** from the main window.
3. Enter your Salesforce **Username** and **Password**. Note that your password must be appended with your security token. Click on **Log in**.
4. When you have logged in successfully, click on **Next**.

5. In step 2 of the import wizard, select the **Order Line Item (Order_Line_Item_c)** option and the **Order Line Item.csv** file. Click on **Next**, as shown in the following screenshot:

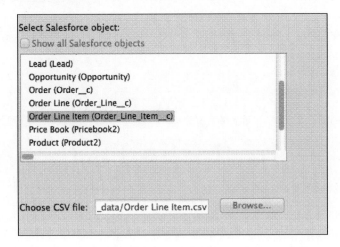

6. Click on **OK** in the dialog when the initialization is successful.

7. In step 3 of the import wizard, click on **Create or Edit a Map**.

8. In the **Mapping Dialog** window, click on **Auto-Match Fields to Columns**. The **Mapping Dialog** window on your screen should resemble the following screenshot. Click on **OK**:

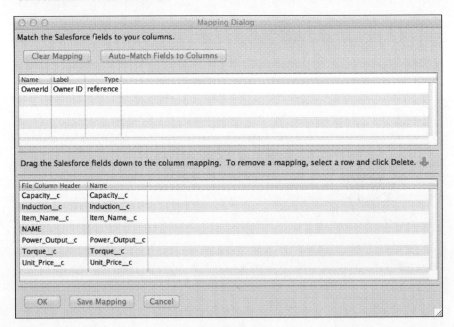

9. Upon doing this, you are returned to step 3 of the import wizard. Here, you need to click on **Next**.

10. In step 4 of the import wizard, select a folder for the success and error files and click on **Finish**.

11. Click on **Yes** in the dialog warning you have chosen to insert records.

12. The import process will begin importing records. When the import has completed, the **Operation Finished** dialog will be displayed, as shown in the following screenshot:

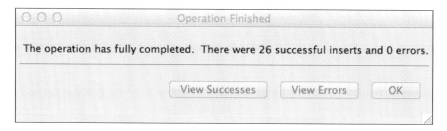

13. From this dialog, you can also view the audit reports for the import successes and failures by clicking on the **View Successes** or **View Errors** button.

14. Click on **OK** to complete the import.

15. Verify whether the import was successful by checking your development organization's order line items object.

16. Close the Data Loader.

Congratulations! You have now finished building the base application.

B
Installing Ruby on Rails on Ubuntu

I am assuming that you have a clean install of Ubuntu Desktop version 14.04 LTS, which was the version at the time of writing. You also need superuser (root) access to the system.

There are three main steps to install Ruby on Rails on Ubuntu:

- Install Ruby Version Manager (RVM)
- Install Ruby 2.0.0
- Install Rails 4.0.0

Installing Ruby on Rails

To install Ruby on Rails on your system, perform the following steps:

1. Open a terminal window in Ubuntu (I recommend **Terminal**):

2. Install cURL (a tool to transfer data to and from servers) by issuing the following command:

```
$ sudo apt-get install curl
```

3. Install RVM by issuing the following command:

```
$ curl -sSL https://get.rvm.io | bash -s stable
```

```
stephen@stephen-VirtualBox:~$ curl -sSL https://get.rvm.io | bash -s stable
Downloading https://github.com/wayneeseguin/rvm/archive/stable.tar.gz

Installing RVM to /home/stephen/.rvm/
    Adding rvm PATH line to /home/stephen/.profile /home/stephen/.bashrc /home/s
tephen/.zshrc.
    Adding rvm loading line to /home/stephen/.bash_profile /home/stephen/.zlogin
.
Installation of RVM in /home/stephen/.rvm/ is almost complete:

  * To start using RVM you need to run `source /home/stephen/.rvm/scripts/rvm`
    in all your open shell windows, in rare cases you need to reopen all shell w
indows.

# stephen,
#
#    Thank you for using RVM!
#    We sincerely hope that RVM helps to make your life easier and more enjoyable
!!!
#
# ~Wayne, Michal & team.

In case of problems: http://rvm.io/help and https://twitter.com/rvm_io
stephen@stephen-VirtualBox:~$ 
```

4. Add rvm to your Ubuntu environment:

```
$ source ~/.rvm/scripts/rvm
```

5. Instruct rvm to install and update the prerequisite Ubuntu modules required for it to run Ruby:

```
$ rvm requirements
```

```
* To start using RVM you need to run `source /home/stephen/.rvm/scripts/rvm`
  in all your open shell windows, in rare cases you need to reopen all shell w
indows.

# stephen,
#
#   Thank you for using RVM!
#   We sincerely hope that RVM helps to make your life easier and more enjoyable
!!!
#
# ~Wayne, Michal & team.

In case of problems: http://rvm.io/help and https://twitter.com/rvm_io
stephen@stephen-VirtualBox:~$ source ~/.rvm/scripts/rvm
stephen@stephen-VirtualBox:~$ rvm requirements
Checking requirements for ubuntu.
Installing requirements for ubuntu.
Updating system...........
Installing required packages: gawk, g++, libreadline6-dev, zlib1g-dev, libssl-de
v, libyaml-dev, libsqlite3-dev, sqlite3, autoconf, libgdbm-dev, libncurses5-dev,
 automake, libtool, bison, libffi-dev..................
Requirements installation successful.
stephen@stephen-VirtualBox:~$ []
```

6. Install Ruby 2.0.0 by issuing the following command:

```
$ rvm install 2.0.0 --with-openssl-dir=~/.rvm/usr
```

```
Requirements installation successful.
stephen@stephen-VirtualBox:~$ rvm install 2.0.0 --with-openssl-dir=~/.rvm/usr
Checking requirements for ubuntu.
Requirements installation successful.
Installing Ruby from source to: /home/stephen/.rvm/rubies/ruby-2.0.0-p451, this
may take a while depending on your cpu(s)...
ruby-2.0.0-p451 - #downloading ruby-2.0.0-p451, this may take a while depending
on your connection...
  % Total    % Received % Xferd  Average Speed   Time    Time     Time  Current
                                 Dload  Upload   Total   Spent    Left  Speed
100 10.2M  100 10.2M    0     0  2757k      0  0:00:03  0:00:03 --:--:-- 2758k
ruby-2.0.0-p451 - #extracting ruby-2.0.0-p451 to /home/stephen/.rvm/src/ruby-2.0
.0-p451...
ruby-2.0.0-p451 - #applying patch /home/stephen/.rvm/patches/ruby/changeset_r452
25.diff.
ruby-2.0.0-p451 - #applying patch /home/stephen/.rvm/patches/ruby/changeset_r452
40.diff.
ruby-2.0.0-p451 - #configuring.....................................
ruby-2.0.0-p451 - #post-configuration.
ruby-2.0.0-p451 - #compiling...............................
.................
ruby-2.0.0-p451 - #installing.........................
ruby-2.0.0-p451 - #making binaries executable..
ruby-2.0.0-p451 - #downloading rubygems-2.2.2
```

7. When Ruby has been installed, your terminal should look similar to the following screenshot:

```
⊙ ⊙ ⊙  stephen@stephen-VirtualBox: ~
 % Total     % Received % Xferd  Average Speed   Time    Time     Time  Current
                                 Dload  Upload   Total   Spent    Left  Speed
100  404k  100  404k    0     0   190k      0  0:00:02  0:00:02 --:--:--   190k
No checksum for downloaded archive, recording checksum in user configuration.
ruby-2.0.0-p451 - #extracting rubygems-2.2.2...
ruby-2.0.0-p451 - #removing old rubygems.........
ruby-2.0.0-p451 - #installing rubygems-2.2.2..............
ruby-2.0.0-p451 - #gemset created /home/stephen/.rvm/gems/ruby-2.0.0-p451@global
ruby-2.0.0-p451 - #importing gemset /home/stephen/.rvm/gemsets/global.gems......
.........................
ruby-2.0.0-p451 - #generating global wrappers.........
ruby-2.0.0-p451 - #gemset created /home/stephen/.rvm/gems/ruby-2.0.0-p451
ruby-2.0.0-p451 - #importing gemsetfile /home/stephen/.rvm/gemsets/default.gems
evaluated to empty gem list
ruby-2.0.0-p451 - #generating default wrappers.........
ruby-2.0.0-p451 - #adjusting #shebangs for (gem irb erb ri rdoc testrb rake).
Install of ruby-2.0.0-p451 - #complete
```

8. Once Ruby has been installed, you can install Rails 4.0.0 with the following command:

```
$ gem install rails --version 4.0.0
```

```
⊗ ⊙ ⊙  stephen@stephen-VirtualBox: ~
Ruby was built without documentation, to build it run: rvm docs generate-ri
stephen@stephen-VirtualBox:~$ gem install rails --version 4.0.0
Fetching: i18n-0.6.9.gem (100%)
Successfully installed i18n-0.6.9
Fetching: multi_json-1.9.3.gem (100%)
Successfully installed multi_json-1.9.3
Fetching: tzinfo-0.3.39.gem (100%)
Successfully installed tzinfo-0.3.39
Fetching: thread_safe-0.3.3.gem (100%)
Successfully installed thread_safe-0.3.3
Fetching: activesupport-4.0.0.gem (100%)
Successfully installed activesupport-4.0.0
Fetching: builder-3.1.4.gem (100%)
Successfully installed builder-3.1.4
Fetching: rack-1.5.2.gem (100%)
Successfully installed rack-1.5.2
Fetching: rack-test-0.6.2.gem (100%)
Successfully installed rack-test-0.6.2
Fetching: erubis-2.7.0.gem (100%)
Successfully installed erubis-2.7.0
Fetching: actionpack-4.0.0.gem (100%)
Successfully installed actionpack-4.0.0
Fetching: activemodel-4.0.0.gem (100%)
Successfully installed activemodel-4.0.0
```

9. The installation of Rails will take some time. When it has been installed, your terminal should look similar to the following screenshot:

```
ellow.gif, skipping
unable to convert "\x89" from ASCII-8BIT to UTF-8 for guides/assets/images/tab_y
ellow.png, skipping
unable to convert "\xFF" from ASCII-8BIT to UTF-8 for guides/assets/images/vijay
dev.jpg, skipping
Installing ri documentation for rails-4.0.0
Parsing documentation for railties-4.0.0
Installing ri documentation for railties-4.0.0
Parsing documentation for sprockets-2.12.1
Installing ri documentation for sprockets-2.12.1
Parsing documentation for sprockets-rails-2.0.1
Installing ri documentation for sprockets-rails-2.0.1
Parsing documentation for thor-0.19.1
Installing ri documentation for thor-0.19.1
Parsing documentation for thread_safe-0.3.3
Installing ri documentation for thread_safe-0.3.3
Parsing documentation for tilt-1.4.1
Installing ri documentation for tilt-1.4.1
Parsing documentation for treetop-1.4.15
Installing ri documentation for treetop-1.4.15
Parsing documentation for tzinfo-0.3.39
Installing ri documentation for tzinfo-0.3.39
26 gems installed
stephen@stephen-VirtualBox:~$
```

10. To support the running of the e-commerce application locally in *Chapter 2, The E-Commerce Framework*, we need to install a few Ubuntu modules with the following command (don't worry if the command reports that the latest versions of some of the modules are already installed):

```
$ sudo apt-get install libxslt-dev libxml2-dev libsqlite3-dev
```

```
stephen@stephen-VirtualBox:~$ sudo apt-get install libxslt-dev libxml2-dev libsq
lite3-dev
[sudo] password for stephen:
Reading package lists... Done
Building dependency tree
Reading state information... Done
Note, selecting 'libxslt1-dev' instead of 'libxslt-dev'
libsqlite3-dev is already the newest version.
The following NEW packages will be installed:
  libxml2-dev libxslt1-dev
0 to upgrade, 2 to newly install, 0 to remove and 23 not to upgrade.
Need to get 1,036 kB of archives.
After this operation, 5,377 kB of additional disk space will be used.
Do you want to continue? [Y/n] y
Get:1 http://au.archive.ubuntu.com/ubuntu/ trusty/main libxml2-dev amd64 2.9.1+d
fsg1-3ubuntu4 [628 kB]
Get:2 http://au.archive.ubuntu.com/ubuntu/ trusty/main libxslt1-dev amd64 1.1.28
-2build1 [407 kB]
Fetched 1,036 kB in 6s (171 kB/s)
Selecting previously unselected package libxml2-dev:amd64.
(Reading database ... 165228 files and directories currently installed.)
Preparing to unpack .../libxml2-dev_2.9.1+dfsg1-3ubuntu4_amd64.deb ...
Unpacking libxml2-dev:amd64 (2.9.1+dfsg1-3ubuntu4) ...
Selecting previously unselected package libxslt1-dev:amd64.
```

11. Finally, the e-commerce application requires a JavaScript runtime, so we will install **Node.js** with the following command:

```
$ sudo apt-get install nodejs
```

12. Congratulations! Ruby on Rails is now installed.

Index

Software Development Kit (SDK) **264**
static site page
  creating 41
  text, adding to 42, 43
student admissions system
  about 121
  building 124
  business requirements, analyzing 122
  Chatter, enabling 143
  Course Application routing logic 168
  custom object tabs, defining 147
  custom settings, creating 166, 167
  data objects, defining 124
  data requirements 123
  Force.com application, creating 149
  functional requirements, analyzing 122, 123
  Organization-Wide Defaults,
    configuring 136, 137
  publisher action 172
  queues, creating 157
  role hierarchy, configuring 137, 138
  security requirements, analyzing 123
  user interface, customizing 149
  user profile, configuring 133
styles
  adding, to Site.com 39-41

T

text
  adding, to static site page 42, 43
Twitter Bootstrap
  downloading 220, 221
  URL, for downloading 220

U

Ubuntu
  URL, for installation 79
user interface, student admissions system
  Applicant 149, 150
  Applicants tab 154, 155
  Course Application page layout 152, 153
  Course Applications tab 156
  Courses 151, 152
  Courses tab 155
  customizing 149

user profile, student admissions system
  Admissions Office profile, creating 134, 135
  configuring 133
  Course Administration profile, creating 133
  Selection Officer profile, creating 135, 136
users
  creating, for Volunteer Community 53

V

VirtualBox
  URL 79
Visualforce 7, 30
Volunteer Community
  Account and VolunteerEvent objects,
    connecting 15-17
  Account object, customizing 12
  authenticated user profile, creating 20, 21
  branding element 29, 30
  Chatter, configuring 23
  creating 11
  custom objects, configuring 12
  Force volunteers user profile,
    configuring 22, 23
  members, adding 27-29
  progress check 26
  public user profile, configuring 18, 19
  publishing, on Salesforce 54, 55
  Site.com, designing for 30-31
  user profile, configuring 12
  users, creating 53
  volunteering event custom field,
    creating 14
  volunteering event custom object,
    creating 13
  volunteers page, securing 51-53
VolunteerEvent custom object tab
  creating 24
volunteering event custom field
  creating 14
  Description 14
  End Date/Time 14
  Location 14
  Special Skills 14
volunteering event custom object
  and Account object, connecting 15-17
  creating 13

W

Thank you for buying
Force.com Development Blueprints

About Packt Publishing

Packt, pronounced 'packed', published its first book "Mastering phpMyAdmin for Effective MySQL Management" in April 2004 and subsequently continued to specialize in publishing highly focused books on specific technologies and solutions.

Our books and publications share the experiences of your fellow IT professionals in adapting and customizing today's systems, applications, and frameworks. Our solution based books give you the knowledge and power to customize the software and technologies you're using to get the job done. Packt books are more specific and less general than the IT books you have seen in the past. Our unique business model allows us to bring you more focused information, giving you more of what you need to know, and less of what you don't.

Packt is a modern, yet unique publishing company, which focuses on producing quality, cutting-edge books for communities of developers, administrators, and newbies alike. For more information, please visit our website: www.packtpub.com.

About Packt Enterprise

In 2010, Packt launched two new brands, Packt Enterprise and Packt Open Source, in order to continue its focus on specialization. This book is part of the Packt Enterprise brand, home to books published on enterprise software – software created by major vendors, including (but not limited to) IBM, Microsoft and Oracle, often for use in other corporations. Its titles will offer information relevant to a range of users of this software, including administrators, developers, architects, and end users.

Writing for Packt

We welcome all inquiries from people who are interested in authoring. Book proposals should be sent to author@packtpub.com. If your book idea is still at an early stage and you would like to discuss it first before writing a formal book proposal, contact us; one of our commissioning editors will get in touch with you.

We're not just looking for published authors; if you have strong technical skills but no writing experience, our experienced editors can help you develop a writing career, or simply get some additional reward for your expertise.

Salesforce CRM: The Definitive Admin Handbook

ISBN: 978-1-84968-306-7   Paperback: 376 pages

A comprehensive, power-packed guide for all Salesforce Administrators covering everything from setup and configuration, to the customization of Salesforce CRM

1. Get to grips with tips, tricks, best-practice administration principles, and critical design considerations for setting up and customizing Salesforce CRM with this book and e-book.

2. Master the mechanisms for controlling access to, and the quality of, data and information sharing.

3. Take advantage of the only guide with real-world business scenarios for Salesforce CRM.

Force.com Developer Certification Handbook (DEV401)

ISBN: 978-1-84968-348-7   Paperback: 280 pages

A comprehensive handbook to guide Force.com developers through important fundamentals and prepare them for the DEV401 exam

1. Simple and to-the-point examples that can be tried out in your developer org.

2. A practical book for professionals who want to take the DEV401 Certification exam.

3. Sample questions for every topic in an exam pattern to help you prepare better, and tips to get things started.

Force.com Tips and Tricks

ISBN: 978-1-84968-474-3   Paperback: 224 pages

A quick reference guide for administrators and developers to get more productive with Force.com

1. Tips and tricks for topics ranging from point-and-click administration, to fine development techniques with Apex and Visualforce.

2. Avoids technical jargon, and expresses concepts in a clear and simple manner.

3. A pocket guide for experienced Force.com developers.

Salesforce CRM Admin Cookbook

ISBN: 978-1-84968-424-8   Paperback: 266 pages

Over 40 recipes to make effective use of Salesforce CRM with the use of hidden features, advanced user interface techniques, and real-world solutions

1. Implement advanced user interface techniques to improve the look and feel of Salesforce CRM.

2. Discover hidden features and hacks that extend standard configuration to provide enhanced functionality and customization.

3. Build real-world process automation, using the detailed recipes to harness the full power of Salesforce CRM.

Please check **www.PacktPub.com** for information on our titles